# PEOPLE OF THE AMERICAN FRONTIER

# PEOPLE OF THE AMERICAN FRONTIER

## The Coming of the American Revolution

Walter S. Dunn Jr.

PRAEGER

Westport, Connecticut
London

**Library of Congress Cataloging-in-Publication Data**

Dunn, Walter S. (Walter Scott), 1928–
    People of the American frontier : the coming of the American revolution /
    Walter S. Dunn, Jr.
        p. cm.
    Includes bibliographical references and index.
    ISBN 0-275-98181-9 (alk. paper)
1. Frontier and pioneer life—United States. 2. United States—History—
    Colonial period, ca. 1600–1775. 3. United States—Social conditions—To 1865.
    4. United States—Ethnic relations. 5. United States—History—Revolution,
    1775–1783—Causes. I. Title.
E179.5.D95 2005
973.2—dc22          2004022486

British Library Cataloguing in Publication Data is available.

Library of Congress Catalog Card Number: 2004022486
ISBN: 0-275-98181-9

First published in 2005

Praeger Publishers, 88 Post Road West, Westport, CT 06881
An imprint of Greenwood Publishing Group, Inc.
www.praeger.com

Printed in the United States of America

The paper used in this book complies with the
Permanent Paper Standard issued by the National
Information Standards Organization (Z39.48-1984).

10  9  8  7  6  5  4  3  2  1

Dedicated to John G. M. Barth and his descendants

# Contents

# Preface

Fifty years ago my first article on an Indian war party raiding Kentucky in the 1770s was published in the *Detroit Historical Society Bulletin*. At the time I wondered why there was so much data on that raid and very little on others. I assumed from the secondary sources (studies of the period that were done at a later time) that many raids had been conducted on the frontier settlements. The facts were quite different. Even during the Revolution few war parties attacked the settlers. War parties attacking settlers were comparatively rare in the previous twenty years as well. For the most part the Indians and the whites coexisted.

The notable examples of friction were about money. The basic issue was contention over fur and land. The French and colonial traders competed for the wealth imbedded in the control of the fur trade. The land jobbers schemed to seize title to Indian lands.

When the colonists gained the upper hand in the fur trade from 1760 to 1763, the French encouraged the Indians to drive out the colonists and destroy the British army forts that provided havens for the colonial traders. In 1763 the Indians slaughtered British army garrisons and colonial traders while the French watched passively or helped the Indians. The natives stole the trader's goods, and whatever the Indians left the French confiscated.

When the land jobbers manipulated a few Indians to give land to the land companies in 1768, the British government intervened to the outrage of the powerful merchants, leading them to resist the British. In 1775 the British army paid the Indians to attack the colonial settlers. In both instances the motivation was not traditional hostility or vague concepts, but financial gain. On both occasions the Indians were well rewarded for their efforts.

Not only have secondary sources missed the basic issue but have created the illusion of widespread violence and death on the basis of contemporary documents written by individuals hundreds—if not thousands—of miles from the frontier. In the past fifty years I have meticulously created a file of more than twelve thousand names associated with frontier activity. The index is based on primary sources (original documents of the period). Missing from the huge index are the names of the Indians and the French and colonial farmers, few of whom could read or write and who therefore were seldom mentioned by name. Names of members of the other groups were found in widely scattered sources. Given that most names appeared repeatedly, I must assume that the file is fairly complete and provides a basis for generalizations; for example, that few traders were killed by the Indians. The file tells us that the French traders remained active for a decade or more, but the paddlers worked only two or three years.

Another source of statistical data is the large quantity of financial records from the period. The number of shirts, guns, and other merchandise carried west by the traders gives us a fairly accurate estimate of the number of Indians in contact with the French and the colonists. Data showing exports of fur compared to the quantities of fur in the financial records indicates the shifting control of the fur trade. The lack of significant quantities of goods needed by the frontier farmers tells us that there were far fewer settlers than the secondary sources imply.

Although social life is not often mentioned in the documents, here and there a snippet appears. The lives of women and children were almost completely ignored. Gathering and meshing the notes together provided a basis for much of the lifestyle described in this book.

Firsthand experience has been helpful in writing the book. My family were dairy farmers for more than a hundred years in Wisconsin, from 1881 to 1983. My wife's great-grandfather, John G. M. Barth (1834–1917), was born in Germany and married Frederika Kurdt (1841–1929) in 1864. After being discharged from the German cavalry after the Franco-Prussian War in 1870, the family with six children emigrated from Bremen, Germany, in 1881 to seek a better life in the United States and, with a son of draft age, to escape the many conflicts in Europe fought to unite Germany into one empire.

Barth soon had his own farm in Wisconsin. After joining the family in 1959 and helping with chores from time to time, I learned firsthand the backbreaking labor of farming. My older relatives were a gold mine of information concerning crop yields, planting, and other agricultural activities.

Until the 1930s farming had not changed significantly from the methods described in the eighteenth-century documents. The horses still needed loving care and were otherwise prone to sickness. Corn was planted in rows in cultivated fields rather than in rows of small hillocks as the Indians had planted it centuries before. Nature determined the most productive methods. The plows were still pulled by horses. Hunting still provided a source of meat. Cattle and pigs were raised and butchered on the farm for beef and pork. The major change in agriculture was the railroad, which opened new markets and made dairying a profitable business.

As a museum curator and director for more than forty years I had the opportunity to work with every weapon and implement mentioned in the text. At museum meetings, entertaining Indian ceremonies matched the descriptions in the documents. With local tribes I developed displays, and I even attended a meeting of the Iroquois tribes in New York under the name "Doccadun" (Dr. Dunn).

As part of my undergraduate education, I lived in England for three years and learned about rigid class distinctions. My university friends lived a completely different lifestyle from my relatives in Sunderland. The aristocratic attitude, difficult to describe, was alive and well in the 1950s and helped me comprehend the positions taken by the British government in the eighteenth century.

All of these life experiences helped me understand everyday life on the eighteenth-century American frontier. A few words in a reference evoked an immediate response. For example, rather than finding myself faced with endless research to describe a duffle coat, I remembered that I had worn one for three years!

Heather Staines of Greenwood Press has been helpful in suggesting the theme of this book and seeing it through publication. I especially thank George, William, and Robert Wendeberg for spending time explaining to me many details about farming and hunting. The book never would have been completed without the assistance of my wife, Jean.

# Introduction

Before 1760 the thirteen American colonies were closely tied to the seaboard. Although a few traders from Albany dealt with the Indians south of Lake Ontario, the primary exports to Europe from America were tobacco from Virginia; flour, provisions, and lumber from Philadelphia; naval stores (material used in ship building) from New England; and deerskin from the South. None of these exports involved a very complex business organization. In Pennsylvania the farmers took their wheat to the miller, where it was ground into flour and sold to the merchants in Philadelphia for export. In Virginia ships from England came directly to docks on rivers bordering the plantations to pick up loads of tobacco. Credits earned by the exports to England, the West Indies, and southern Europe were used to purchase English manufactured goods.

All of this exchange of commodities shifted in the decade of the 1760s. Great Britain decisively defeated its protagonist France after a bitter war that acquired the name "The Great War," until that name was superseded by the conflict of 1914–18. The French and Indian War, or the Seven Years' War as it is now called, created an economic upheaval throughout the world. An incredible expansion of British manufacturing was spurred on by the demands of the war, creating the Industrial Revolution. The demand for weapons, uniforms, rations, and subsidies for European armies nurtured the Industrial Revolution in Britain, based on new technology, just as World War II would later foster a similar revolution in the U.S. economy. The

Seven Years' War transformed Britain into the dominant world power of that era, just as the United States became the dominant power in 1945.

The spoils of the war included the undisputed acquisition by Britain of Canada, along with the American Midwest, which became one of the most productive regions in the world. The West, previously blocked by the French, was then open for exploitation. The westward movement began in the middle of the eighteenth century when a few colonial fur traders crossed the Appalachian Mountains to compete with French traders in the Ohio Valley. The defeat of the French opened the way for colonial merchants and land speculators to begin westward expansion on a grand scale.

The golden opportunity for gaining wealth from the natural resources of the region was obvious to the colonial merchants of the eighteenth century. Immediately after the war a flood of adventurers went west to make their fortunes trading low-cost British guns, cloth, kettles, and other products to the Indians for furs to supply the rapidly growing number of English hatmakers. British and colonial merchants also flocked to Montreal, Quebec, Albany, Fort Pitt, Detroit, Michilimackinac, and Illinois when the restraining hand of the French government was removed in 1760. Multimillion-dollar investments were made in merchandise and the means to deliver it to consumers.

The downside was that the Seven Years' War had left Britain with an enormous debt that the wealthy British landowners were reluctant to pay. The British tax structure placed the heaviest burden on the landowners, whereas few taxes were paid by the beneficiaries of the Industrial Revolution in the new imperial economy—the manufacturers. Faced with opposition from landowners in the British Parliament to the continued high taxes, the British government looked for additional sources to help finance control of the western land. Prior to its acquisition of Canada and the West, Britain had spent very little money in the American colonies. Expenditures changed radically during the war and continued after 1760. To London, the seat of the British government, the obvious source for funds to pay the cost was the American colonies themselves, for they would reap the greatest rewards from westward expansion. However, American merchants were as reluctant to pay as the British landowners, especially as the proposed taxes were to be paid in British currency referred to as "sterling" and sent back to London. The unfortunate result was that the sterling received by American merchants from lavish expenditures on the British army in America, which had financed an enormous boom in the colonies, would be sent back to London to pay the taxes rather than to purchase British goods. Without the sterling from army purchases in America, merchants would be hard pressed to pay for imports from England. The dispute regarding who was to pay for western expansion led to the dissolution of the empire.

In the mid-eighteenth century the everyday lives of the people on the American frontier were scarcely mentioned in documents, letters, or newspapers. However, 10,000 people in contact with the Indians on the frontier north of the Ohio River played a major role in determining the future of America. More than a century ago Frederick Jackson Turner declared that the frontier was the dynamic force that shaped the United States. The continual drive westward created an open society that lasted until most of the desirable land was occupied by the end of the nineteenth century.

For centuries the various Indian tribes east of the Mississippi River maintained a village life with limited trade with other tribes and annual moves from summer villages to winter hunting grounds. This relatively uneventful existence ended when Indians were contacted by the French after their exploration and occupation of the Great Lakes. The Indians were fascinated by exposure to new and sturdier utensils compared with their clay pots, for example, and were very much attracted to the guns used by the French. As their medium of exchange they offered to trade their furs for these guns. Even though the tribes added such niceties to their lifestyle, as well as the guns for convenience in hunting, their way of life did not change. They still hunted and trapped in the winter near their villages and farmed at their summer villages in the spring. The women and young girls continued to work the fields while the men hunted, and the young warriors trained with their bows and arrows in anticipation of hunting and tribal warfare.

Contact between the Europeans and the tribes did bring about some changes in Indian society. For over a century French traders had been supplying the tribes with guns, cloth, hardware, tobacco, and brandy at comparatively high prices. The traders' goods improved the life of the Indians. Wool trousers replaced the buckskins, which turned hard and scratchy once they got wet and dried. Kettles for boiling tough venison, needles for sewing clothes, and blankets for warmth were all products that improved Indian life. Because beaver, deer, and other fur-bearing animals were plentiful, the Indians had little trouble meeting the French demands.

The Indians could not be characterized as drunken brawlers because their only opportunity for unlimited access to that pleasure was at or near the trading posts during trades. Although the French limited liquor sales and gifts, the less compassionate colonial traders from New York and Pennsylvania used excessive gifts and sales of liquor in an attempt to wrest the trade from the French. A little liquor goes a long way when the imbiber is not used to alcohol. When drunk, the natives were known not only to sell their furs cheap but also to sell even the clothes off their backs. Stealing was a natural characteristic of anyone involved in the trade. The traders more or less stole the furs from the Indians, and the natives stole from the stores, but usually only small items placed conspicuously to entice theft and encourage them to do business at a particular store. On occasion, however, Indians would rob a trader of his entire stock.

The French Canadian lifestyle revolved around the fur trade. The most sought-after commodity in the colder climates was the furs. The cold winters of Canada, New York, and the Ohio Valley produced animals with heavy, fine fur. Deerskin was the product of the warmer southern areas such as Illinois. Each spring about a hundred canoes left Montreal for the West, paddled by about six hundred experienced traders and raw farm boys making a trip to obtain cash for their farm families. In the fall the canoes headed back to Montreal laden with furs, but some of the French traders remained behind in the Indian villages to continue supplying the Indians during the winter with ammunition, brandy, and other needs. The close association of the Indians and the French made it very difficult for the colonial traders to compete, even though they offered goods at lower prices.

The French were comfortably situated in North America in 1754 and getting along well with the natives, but their lives were suddenly disrupted by the Seven Years' War between France and England. The French territory in America became one of the spoils of the war. However, the British occupation of its new colony was not without its thorny issues, such as the French resistance to surrender the lucrative fur trade.

The French farmers, who were not as interested in expanding their agricultural economy as the colonial farmers, were a good market for manufactured goods from Europe in exchange for their produce. Although all farmers brought their farming methods from Europe, they were very much influenced by and adopted some Indian ways. Corn introduced by the Indians became a staple in the newcomers' diets, and they also used their planting, harvesting, and food preparation techniques.

When the French army left America in 1760, the French traders stayed. Indian affairs became troubled when the French used the tribes as a weapon against the British merchants from Montreal and the colonists from New York and Pennsylvania in order to maintain a stranglehold on the fur trade. After many years of friendly coexistence with the French, the Indians were inclined to trust them and believed their lies that the British and the colonists were the natives' enemies.

The French influence on the Indians was furthered by a cultural intermingling with the tribes over the years. The winterers often had Indian common-law wives and raised children who became traders and the wives of traders. The métis, the children of these marriages, played a major role in the fur trade. Because of their tribal heritage, their Indian relatives protected them during the winter and made it safe for them to trade without fear of being robbed by roving bands.

The French had not seriously infringed on Indian territory in more than a century, but the colonial traders were the forerunners of permanent occupation by settlers. They came from Albany, New York, and Pennsylvania. Because of the French opposition the colonials did most of their business at posts including Detroit, Michilimackinac, Oswego, Fort Niagara, and Fort Pitt. However, some ventured into the Indian villages in the early 1760s, and many were killed during an Indian uprising in 1763.

The traders for the most part can be characterized as surly and bold, obviously necessary attitudes to lead a dangerous life in the wilderness. In New York the Albany traders were less adventurous and were satisfied to trade at Oswego and Fort Niagara. The Pennsylvania traders often ventured into the Indian villages west of Fort Pitt. Most of them traded in the forts rather than risk their lives in the Indian villages.

Close behind the traders were settlers eager to acquire land of their own for farming. Much of the good land east of the mountains had been occupied by 1760. The West beckoned those who looked for economic security in owning and cultivating their own land. Younger sons, indentured servants who had served their terms, and discharged soldiers all wanted land.

When soldiers were discharged many decided to remain in America as farmers and traders. Many Germans had been enlisted in the four battalions of the Royal American Regiment, and Scots had formed three regiments to fight against the French in America. In 1775 Germans made up 10 percent of the colonial population. The discharged soldiers made up the ranks of the traders who were provided with goods by seaboard merchants and then made their way into the wilderness to trade with the Indians. Many of them were eager to obtain land and begin farming. The former soldiers and indentured servants obtained farms and raised families, a way of life that was very difficult to attain in Europe, where they worked for small wages or gave most of their harvest to landlords.

The soldiers still in uniform lived a comparably good life as long as the Indians were peaceful. Garrison duty on the frontier was far more relaxed than the harsh life in barracks in Europe. Food and drink were plentiful and few demands were made on their time. Many did some trading on the side with the Indians, using part of their rum ration to obtain favors.

Greed was the major cause of disturbance that in the end brought the entire fabric of frontier society crashing. The French in Canada and along the Mississippi River did their best to maintain control of the fur trade. The colonial merchants who wanted an ever-increasing share of the furs saw half of the fur going down the Mississippi River to New Orleans for shipment to France and most of the rest going to Montreal to Scottish merchants who sent the fur to England. The British army made no attempt to prevent the wealth's escaping from the colonists, yet the British government insisted unfairly that the colonists pay to maintain the army.

Over and above the competition for fur, America became a very large market for British goods, especially from the British industries developed for the production of war materials. The Indians, the farmers, and the merchants were excellent customers for this high productive capacity. At the same time the British army became a very good customer for colonial provisions.

Britain sent regiments to America supposedly to replace the French army in the new colony in order to keep the peace and to protect the natives from overzealous traders and colonists. In reality, America was a good holding ground and an excellent excuse for King George III, who became king in 1760, to maintain a larger peacetime army than Parliament would have agreed to finance at home. Royal politics even led him to discharge potentially troublesome Scottish officers in America rather than have them return to England, where they could possibly threaten the throne again.

The merchants were the middlemen between the frontier and the manufacturers in England. As the wholesalers with warehouses who imported in bulk, they made and lost fortunes. More than any other group in America, the colonial merchants suffered from British regulations and lack of support in colonial struggles with the French. The largest and most overextended Pennsylvania merchant company, Baynton and Wharton, finally lost its shirt in Illinois in a last-ditch attempt to seek a larger slice of the trade, only to be thwarted again by the French. Its last grandstand attempt left Baynton and Wharton with a fortune of unsaleable merchandise that it sold at a loss to other traders and the French.

To the colonists, the army played a lesser role in protection and more of a role as a substantial market for provisions, an avenue readily exploited by the merchants. After losing the struggle for the fur trade to the French, the merchants rebounded to a certain extent by supplying the army in return for sterling bills of exchange that could be used to pay off their debts in England to balance their trade. However, when George III economized by moving the army from the frontier to the East Coast, that market also disappeared. After a wholehearted attempt to take control of the trade from the French, by 1768 the colonial merchants had failed and faced bankruptcy.

Again, not all was lost. In a final attempt to succeed in America these same merchants became land "jobbers," or speculators, hoping to sell land to the colonial farmers in their thirst to move westward across the boundary of the Appalachian Mountains. One last time the colonists were thwarted when Britain discouraged westward expansion fearing unrest and resistance from the Indians who held the land.

In addition to furs and land, another commodity for sale in the colonies was slaves bought in Africa from tribal kings who had captured them from other tribes during warfare. The slaves were used particularly as workers in the Virginia tobacco fields, the sugarcane fields in the West Indies, rice plantations around New Orleans, and cornfields in Illinois. They also worked as servants and, sometimes, concubines in wealthy homes in colonial cities.

The various groups and individuals in America had set the stage for a healthy economy not only to supply furs for beaver hats in aristocratic Europe, but as a haven for adventurous newcomers either fleeing from oppression or just enticed by the magic of a new life in a land that promised to fulfill their dreams.

The eighteenth-century frontier was in a continual upheaval as the various cultures interacted and competed. Any change in economic conditions created friction as some groups gained and others lost. In the early 1760s the Indians, the newly arrived British merchants in Canada, and the colonial merchants were gaining, whereas the French lost their monopoly of the fur trade. The pioneer settlers were rapidly absorbing land east of the Appala-chians and anticipated taking Indian land west of the mountains. But the settlers' hopes were quickly dashed by the Proclamation of 1763, which limited development to the area east of the mountains.

Even though France lost the Seven Years' War, the French traders persis-tently resisted colonial efforts to trade with the Indians, often using them to violently oppose the colonists. Indian tempers flared and led to Pontiac's Uprising in 1763. After that fracas, in an attempt to protect both the Indians and the traders, the British leaders ordered the restriction of trading to the army posts, where the army could regulate trade, control the flow of liquor, and protect the traders. This restriction worked to the advantage of the French, who did not intend to abide by any rules.

The attempt of the colonial merchants to profit by using rum and British goods to compete with the French for the fur trade in Canada was rebuffed by Pontiac's Uprising, which was directed at the colonial traders and instigated by the persistent French. The rules promulgated by the British government to maintain peace on the frontier in reality returned the fur trade to the French, who were assisted by new British entrepreneurs in Montreal and Quebec, many of them former army officers. Eventually the American mer-chants were shut out completely by the French and British merchants in Canada. The potential profits from the British acquisition of Canada were closed to the colonists while newly arrived British merchants made alliances with the French in Quebec and Montreal. The refusal of the French in

Illinois to sell their furs to American merchants left the colonists with only the army as their primary market. When the army left Illinois in 1768, that market vanished as well.

The colonial market of consumers, on the other hand, was expanding. After the Seven Years' War manufactured goods, cloth, guns, hardware, leather goods, china, and more were available at low cost as British merchants vigorously entered the North American market. The American colonies became the largest market for British goods. The merchandise was purchased with money from British expenditures on the regiments in America and the colonies' exports to Europe and the West Indies.

The Middle Colonies and the frontier offered a limitless opportunity for the sale of British goods. Ninety percent of the colonists were farmers. In both New England and the middle colonies, most were subsistence farmers cultivating ten acres and raising cattle and hogs. Their small surpluses paid for the purchase of luxury items. The small size of the farms was restricted by the ability of an overburdened farm family to plow, plant, and harvest the crops while caring for the animals that formed a necessary part of farm life. Nevertheless, the combination of the small quantities of surplus wheat from thousands of farms did provide grist for flour mills that found a ready market in the British West Indies and southern Europe.

The domestic market was fueled by the explosive growth in population. The thirteen colonies grew rapidly in the mid-eighteenth century fed by a steady stream of immigration and a high birthrate. In 1760 there were 1.6 million people living in the thirteen colonies and 76,000 in Canada. In that same year, the population of the British Isles was less than 10 million, and so the Americans represented a substantial portion of the total population of the British Empire. By 1775 one-third of Americans had been born abroad or were children of immigrants. Blacks made up 17 percent of the population. In 1756 there were 13,500 blacks in New York and 85,000 whites. There were 10,000 blacks out of 180,000 people in Pennsylvania.

The population of New York in 1760 was 117,000 and of Pennsylvania, 217,000. The largest cities in 1763 were Philadelphia, with over 22,000 people; New York, with 18,000; Boston, with 22,000; and Charleston, with 10,000. Philadelphia was the fifth-largest city in the British Empire. In the same period there were 50,000 Iroquois in New York, 75,000 other Indians north of the Ohio River, and over 90,000 Indians south of the Ohio River, for a total of 215,000 Indians. In 1766 in Canada there were 69,000 French, 7,400 Indians, and a few British immigrants and colonists.

All of the people on the colonial frontier were dependent on one another. If the Indians were displeased by colonial traders who used cheap rum to take their fur, the Indians reacted against the traders and settlers. Pontiac's

Uprising in 1763 forced the English to stop the trade with the Indians temporarily. If the traders were robbed, the merchants in the ports lost enormous amounts of money and went bankrupt. The presence of the army to maintain peace on the frontier placed a heavy burden on the British taxpayer.

To the best interest of all was maintaining a peaceful climate on the frontier. Everyone benefited. The Indians obtained goods that made their lives far more pleasant. The traders and merchants made fortunes to enable them to live well when they returned to the coast, and the settlers could farm in safety.

With England favoring the fate of the Indians and protecting tribal land while French competition limited their profits in the fur trade, the colonists became even more disgruntled, and many merchants were instrumental in the coming revolution. Although the media was far simpler in the eighteenth century, still it played a role in shaping colonial actions. The news that people read in their local newspapers and inflammatory information on handbills posted in public places as well as flamboyant speeches at gatherings determined their attitudes. The colonial media in the eighteenth century was controlled by merchants in New York, Philadelphia, Boston, and other large cities. During the 1760s the merchants began a campaign to reduce— if not end—the power of Parliament on American affairs. The motives of this campaign were to prevent sterling being returned to England in the form of colonial taxes and to end British efforts to block the exploitation of the West.

Rather than using the more intellectual argument of the loss of sterling, the colonial media concentrated on abstract issues; for example, taxation without representation. Revenue taxes had been collected in America for over a century without protest because the money remained in the colonies. Rather than a reaction against increased taxation, the Boston Tea Party was in fact staged to protest the reduction of British taxes on Indian tea, threatening the profitable illegal tea trade with Holland. All but ignored in the press and in speeches was the second issue, London's interference with western expansion.

When opposition to the Indians intensified in the 1770s in the drive for expansion, the Indians allied themselves with the British and the French Canadians who were attacking the frontier settlements. For that reason military resources had to be diverted, from time to time, from the coast to the frontier, a measure General George Washington could ill afford. Taking advantage of the situation, the French government, always eager to embarrass Britain, supplied the colonial army with weapons and other goods. French assistance proved invaluable to the Americans in the Revolution.

The interpretation in this book varies somewhat from the consensus of opinion among current authors. My emphasis on the economic causes of the Revolution contrasts to the emphasis on the political and philosophical reasons others have forwarded. On the frontier the issues were land and trade. As long as the British army paid its bills with sterling, few frontier merchants objected.

Others may question my view of the Indians. Despite their growing dependence on the fur traders for the enrichment to their lives in adding metal pots, trousers, and guns, the Indians could have survived without these luxuries. The use of the bow and arrow continued into the nineteenth century. Trade among the tribes took place as characterized here before the coming of the fur traders.

Another issue is why so many Scottish troops were sent to America and disbanded there, while English regiments were sent back to England on a rotation scheme. There is little if any documentation on this issue, but the Scots may have been expressing their loyalty to King George II by volunteering and, once in America, saw economic opportunities.

Perhaps the main disagreement is my contention that the frontier was a unique environment. Life and ideas in the Philadelphia, New York, and Boston areas may have been similar to those on farms in western Pennsylvania. I am sure that we all agree on the heroism of the people on the frontier who fostered the foundation of today's United States of America.

# 1

# The Indians

In the mid-eighteenth century Indian life and culture in the area north of the Ohio River and surrounding the Great Lakes was based on agriculture. Hunting and fishing were used to supplement what was basically a vegetarian diet. The Indians did not hunt on a major scale because they had no way to preserve meat other than smoking it. They did not become full-time hunters but hunted in the fall and winter because that was when the animal coats were at their prime.

The arrival of the white man did not change the Indians' life a great deal. The trade goods, though adding convenience, did not alter basic patterns. Hoes made of bone were replaced by metal tools, but the process of cultivating corn remained the same. American farmers today still plant corn just as the Indians did except that they use machines instead of deer antlers to dig and sow crops. Sweet corn planting was staggered so that part of the crop ripened at biweekly intervals. Nature still determines successful farming and sets the rules of life. If corn rows are planted too close together, the yield will be less. The main difference is that the Indian women did most of the field work, while men did most of work in colonial families. However, colonial farm wives often worked in the fields as well.

Even the availability of liquor did not make a major change in their life because they drank very little compared to the Europeans. Tales of drunken Indians were exaggerated because most white men saw Indians only when they visited the trading posts, an event similar to a modern convention.

As game in the vicinity of their permanent summer villages was soon exhausted, the tribes were forced to travel to hunting grounds each fall. The hunting ground changed as the supply of game was reduced. They made minimal use of furs and deerskins for clothing. The Indian cycle of farming during the summer and hunting in the fall was the same as the twenty-first-century American farmers'. The hunting tradition was not common in Europe because hunting preserves were reserved for the aristocracy, but the colonists on the American frontier soon adopted the Indian tradition.

Neither was violence a way of life. Taking white captives or captives from other tribes was intended not to harm people but to introduce new blood lines to a village. The tradition in most cultures has long been that marrying close relatives breeds defective children. The war parties were an opportunity for the young braves to prove their manhood while adding to the gene pool.

The war parties consisted of twenty to forty young men. The tribes north of the Ohio River and east of the Mississippi River attacked the Cherokee in the south and the Pawnee in the west. The southern Indians relied on deerskin for clothing and venison for food. The tribes in the west used buffalo for meat and clothing.

Before the Seven Years' War disrupted life in the Great Lakes area by transferring the territory from France to Britain, the Indians had lived at peace with the French and the colonists. The long years of a good tribal relationship with the French would have continued with the colonists were it not for the competition for the fur trade. The French would not give up the profitable fur trade even though France had lost the war and its land in America. In order to retain control of the fur trade in America, the French encouraged the Indians to conduct a type of guerilla warfare by subsidizing the Indians to fight the colonists. The relationship between the Iroquois and the New York colonists is a peaceful example because the French could not interfere. From the time of its first encounter with the "noble savage," the British government was protective and treated the Indians with respect.

Because of the continuing French-British conflict regarding the fur trade, the intuitive Indians saw an opportunity to play one nation against the other and became amateur entrepreneurs in finding the best deals for their fur and skins. European trade goods were an enticement as metal pots made life easier compared with fragile clay utensils. Liquor became a factor only when the colonists tried desperately to upstage the French traders by bribing the Indians with this new pleasure to get their furs. The Indian trust in the French was imbedded in their long amicable experience.

The insatiable European demand for fine beaver hats, which shed the rain just as the beaver fur had for the animal, was the burning ember that maintained the French-colonial-Indian conflict in America. As the embittered colonists lost out, the Indians still enjoyed their native ways only somewhat enhanced by the stimulating European trade goods.

The contemporary European attitude toward the American Indians was influenced by the French philosopher and writer Jean-Jacques Rousseau and his concept of the noble savage. Regarding the Indians as innocents, British politicians sought to protect them from the rapacious colonial traders and land jobbers. The attitude of the British government was that the innocent Indians threatened violence only as a ruse to obtain more gifts. Moreover, London did not believe that the Indians were fooled by the French lies that the French would join the Indians in fighting the English. The Indians resented the British in America because they were not as friendly as the French and did not give presents or respect Indian culture. As suspected, the opportunistic Indians did use the threat of violence to obtain presents from the British.

The French had more than a century of experience with the Indians and respected them as valued customers. The alliance of the Algonquin and Huron Indians and the French was formed in the early seventeenth century. The French assisted them in attacks on their traditional enemies, the Iroquois, who found support from the British and colonists. The Iroquois threatened the trade route via the upper St. Lawrence River and Lake Ontario to reach the upper Great Lakes. Because of the Iroquois the French more often used the Ottawa River route to Lake Nipissing, the French River, Georgian Bay, Lake Huron, and the upper lakes.

Well-worn paths led to hunting grounds and to neighboring tribes. Trading among tribes for special items was common. For fur and corn the Western Indians traded obsidian, a glasslike mineral from the Rocky Mountains used for knife blades.

Europeans became the prime source of desirable goods that were exchanged for furs in the mid-eighteenth century. The Indians were at the end of a long chain of people in western commerce, beginning with the manufacturers in Europe. The middlemen were importers and wholesalers in the ports of New York City, Philadelphia, and Quebec and in frontier commercial centers in Montreal, Albany and Schenectady in New York, and Lancaster and Carlisle in Pennsylvania. Hundreds of petty traders operated in the western posts and forests. In the American colonies the traders employed 1,500 men as canoe men, wagon drivers, carpenters, shipwrights, coopers, and blacksmiths. More than a thousand Frenchmen were employed in Canada. The merchants and their employees were French, Scottish, English,

New Yorkers, Pennsylvanians, and Jews from all the colonies, who formed a closely knit commercial network as a result of prejudice and religious ties.

The French and the colonists competed to obtain fur and deerskin from the Indians. The restriction of trade to forts imposed by the Indian Department favored the colonial merchants and forced the Indians to carry their fur to the posts. The French and some colonial traders ignored the restriction and took merchandise to the villages and the hunting grounds in the winter. Consequently, the Indians often traded their furs and deerskin to the winterers rather than to colonial merchants in the posts.

The Indians' simple culture was modified from one of self-sufficient villages to dependence on the convenience of European goods. This dependence altered the Indian way of life and encouraged them to hunt for saleable pelts and deerskin rather than hunting only to satisfy their personal need for skins and meat. The colonists and the French used alcohol to stimulate the Indians to bring in ever-greater numbers of furs and deerskins. Instead of going directly to their hunting ground in the fall, the hunters stopped at the nearest trading post to exchange their pelts for merchandise and liquor. The long-term effect of Indian desire for alcohol and European goods was demoralizing at a time when the tribes needed to cope with changing conditions. Nevertheless, the Indians could not resist the metal utensils, tools, and firearms that made life easier, and the alcohol provided a new pleasure.

A typical Ojibwa family in a summer village northwest of Lake Superior lived in a shelter made of boughs of wood covered with sheets of bark stitched together and placed under a huge pine tree. In the center of the shelter was a fire, and its smoke passed through a hole above. The smoke also cured venison hung from the frame.

Hanging on the tree were a pair of snowshoes, a blanket, a bow, and a quiver of arrows. On the ground were metal pots, pairs of moccasins, a gun, and a cradle with a small child. Near the shelter were pieces of deerskin, firewood, an axe, and a dog. The presence of the bow and the gun indicated that the Indians continued to use both.

Inside the shelter were piled rabbit skins and a few packs of other furs. An old woman plucked a duck, saving the feathers. She was dressed in a garment made of rabbit skins and a pair of blue cloth leggings. A young woman dressed the same way mended a net. A young man wrapped in a blanket sat on a buffalo robe smoking a pipe. There were several young boys. In the summer the men wore only a breechclout, a loincloth that was draped between a man's legs and held in place by a cord around his waist. The men painted their bodies with bright red vermillion in combination with black, brown, blue, and other colors. Black denoted anger. Vermillion was the war paint. At times the Indians wore a shirt in addition to the breechclout.

In the summer camp the men fished for sturgeon and whitefish in the rapids of the Namakan River using seines, or hand nets, thrown over the water and catching foot-long whitefish. In a half hour one Indian might catch six fish. They also speared the sturgeon. The women and children tended the crops in nearby gardens.

The tribes in the Detroit area were the Ottawas in the northern part of the Lower Peninsula of Michigan; the Pottawatomis from along the Lake Michigan shore; the Hurons, or Wyandots, from Michilimackinac; and the Chippewas, or Ojibwas, from Sault Ste. Marie. Each of these tribes built a village near Detroit. During the winter when the tribes hunted, the entire village moved, taking with them the grass mats that made up their summer lodges.

The Pottawatomis had a village in the Detroit area in 1718. Men were well clothed and spent time hunting. The women did all the work in the gardens. In winter the men wore richly painted buffalo robes. In summer they wore red or white breechclouts and moccasins and used vermillion paint on their bodies. For recreation the men often played lacrosse in the summer with teams from other tribes.

The Hurons had three villages on Bois Blanc, an island in the Detroit River. They cultivated 200 arpents of corn fields (slightly less than 200 acres), north of Detroit. The French took a census during the winter of 1747 and found that the three villages on Bois Blanc had thirty-three cabins or lodges in all. While most of the tribe went to the winter hunting ground, the few inhabitants left behind to guard the village were several old women, two drunkards, and other elders. The French considered the Hurons knaves and drunkards, but very proud. In 1747 during the summer, there were 534 Hurons plus children in the cabins on Bois Blanc.

The Hurons were very industrious, seldom danced, and worked very hard. While the men hunted, the women worked in the fields. The corn grew to twelve feet and was well cultivated with no weeds. They raised a great deal of Indian corn, peas, beans, and some wheat. Their cabins, divided into sleeping compartments, were built of bark, strong, solid, high, and long. Their village was surrounded by a protective picket fence. The men were well dressed; some wore close-fitting coats.

The Wyandot town in Detroit had 230 warriors including 70 boys aged ten to seventeen. At the summer village the tribe had large cornfields. The Wyandots had a winter camp at Sandusky with eleven cabins and a stockade to defend against the Cherokee. The stockade had decayed by 1760. The village was used as the winter residence for hunting on the Scioto River while the summer village at Detroit was almost deserted except for a few poor women left to care for the town. From the end of October to mid-April the men hunted for deer and trapped beaver.

The Ottawas lived in cabins like the Hurons and used the grass-mat shelters during the hunting season. They were well dressed and they hunted and farmed.

A typical Indian family might consist of a mature male, a young male, two elders, two women, and four children. Other families might include an adult male, his wife, and two children. Assuming an eight-person family as the average, 12,500 Indian families north of the Ohio River purchased or received as gifts £182,000 pounds sterling's worth (or $36,400,000) of French, British, and colonial goods annually, an average of 14 pounds, 10 shillings sterling ($2,900) per family. (There were 20 shillings in a pound, so 10 shillings was worth half a pound. One pound sterling was worth approximately $200 in 2004 U.S. dollars. The symbols for pounds, shillings, and pence are £, s., and d.) Some of the goods were traded to tribes farther west for furs that were subsequently exchanged for European goods. The Indians in contact with the Europeans and the colonists lived well because they received gifts and traded for a considerable amount of merchandise. They had more disposable income—money for uses other than food and shelter—than most families in England.

The number of Indians in the area north of the Ohio River fluctuated in the eighteenth century. Disease, starvation from interrupted food supplies, and killing could have reduced the number of Indians. However, despite a series of epidemics in the first half of the eighteenth century, the number of Indians on the American frontier east of the Mississippi River was somewhat stable in the period from 1765 to 1775, at more than 15,000 adult males and 75,000 women and children. The Indian tribes constituted a major market for European goods. Sir William Johnson, superintendent of the Northern Department for Indian Affairs, estimated their number at 10,000 hunters in his Northern Department. Thomas Hutchins's estimate was more than 4,000 warriors in twenty tribes excluding the Iroquois, the Sioux, and western Canadian Indians.

In the 1760s the large area north of the Ohio River and east of the Rocky Mountains there were about 100,000 Indians. In New York there were approximately 12,000 Iroquois: 2,000 adult males and 10,000 elders, women, and children. In the Michigan peninsula, there were 24,000 Wyandots, Pottawatomis, Ottawas, Chippewas, and Saulters; in the Wisconsin area, 6,000 Sacs, Foxes, Menominies, and Puans; in Illinois, 4,000 Menominies, Kickapoos, Vermillions, Piankashaws, and Mascutens. Between the Ohio River and the Great Lakes there were 7,500 Shawnees, Sciotos, Delawares, Muskingums, and Miamis. In the Missouri Valley there were 17,500 Little Osages, Missouris, and Sioux. North of Lake Superior the French Canadians were trading with at least another 15,000. West of the Mississippi

River were at least 14,000 Sioux and other tribes with some contact with traders.

With the gradual encroachment of the white settlers after 1750, some tribes began to migrate westward, driving the previous occupants farther west. Some of the Iroquois in New York moved to western New York and northwestern Pennsylvania. The Delawares moved from eastern to western Pennsylvania. The Shawnees were pushed by the Delawares farther west to the area north of the Ohio River. The Miamis were moved from the Illinois area northeast.

The Indian population had recovered by the second half of the eighteenth century. The change in the population was related to the weakening of Indian culture. Three elements attacked the Indian culture: disease weakened their faith in traditions; Christianity challenged the old beliefs; and the fur trade provided a motive for unrestricted hunting and ended their peaceful coexistence with nature.

The impact of disease had a devastating effect. Diseases contracted from the Europeans caused the deaths of thousands of Indians. Beginning in the sixteenth century, smallpox, typhus, and other epidemics killed from 20 percent to more than half of the tribes with each onslaught, although some of the losses were recouped within a few generations.

The major killer was smallpox. Epidemics of this disease could strike tribes and cause the death of nearly an entire village. Horrible descriptions were recorded by people who visited villages where no living souls remained and the lodges were filled with corpses. Lacking any knowledge to cure the sick, the healthy Indians left them to starve, knowing that to remain would expose them to the same horror. A tribe could lose half of its members in one year to smallpox contracted from traders. When smallpox took the only male from a family, the women joined another family. Because of the catastrophic loss of hunters, women and children often died of starvation.

The epidemics struck certain areas and moved on as infected individuals fled to neighboring areas. In this way disease often preceded direct contact with the Europeans. In 1734 a smallpox epidemic struck the lower Mississippi River valley and extended as far north as the French villages in southern Illinois. Other smallpox epidemics struck in 1738 and 1752. A smallpox epidemic in the area northwest of Lake Superior in the 1730s reduced the Indian population severely. Venereal disease introduced by the British soldiers was passed on to Indian women and subsequently to other British soldiers. In 1773 venereal disease was so prevalent among the troops at Detroit that the commander requested a doctor to treat the men.

Disease broke traditional Indian customs and beliefs. Prior to contact with the Europeans and their insatiable demand for fur, the natural bond between the Indians and the animals prohibited excessive killing. Because the old traditions could not cope with the devastation of disease, Indian conduct lost its spiritual control. If the old ways could not cure the sick, why should the hunters be prevented from killing as many animals as they wished?

Epidemics had an impact on the fur trade when fewer hunters meant a rapid increase in the number of animals. Although the number of hunters was increasing by 1760, for several decades there had been fewer hunters. Smallpox killed proportionally more men than women and children, reducing the number of hunters and allowing the number of beaver to increase in the late 1750s compared to the previous several decades. With a healthy new generation of hunters and a plentiful supply of beaver, the fur trade peaked in the late 1750s and continued strong through the early 1760s until the numbers of animals were once again diminished by increased hunting.

Related to the epidemics was the Indian desire for rum. The fear of the unknown created stress that disturbed Indian culture, and rum provided a palliative—a means to escape from fear. On the other hand, the rum made the Indians even less able to cope with their problems.

The impact of disease and alcohol on the fur trade is difficult to quantify in trade statistics of the period because of other trade-disrupting factors, including the cutting of the French trade route by the Royal Navy during the Seven Years' War, which left a large quantity of fur in the Great Lakes area in 1760. Pontiac's Uprising severely disrupted the fur trade in 1763 and 1764, and after that illegal trading diverted a sizable portion of furs to Illinois and elsewhere.

The Indians were rather aggressive hunters even before white contact because fur was used as a medium of exchange with other tribes. The Indians in the eighteenth century could survive by hunting, fishing, and trapping for about twenty-eight hours a week. Travel took an average of fifteen hours per week. The Indians had the technology to kill more animals before the availability of European goods but chose not to because of a wise limit on what they could consume, preserve for later use, and carry. Rather than having a wretched life, the Indians were happy to live off the abundance of the land. The tools of the white man were merely improvements on their existing handmade tools.

Restrictions on hunting soon disappeared in the face of European demand for pelts as well as the new tools to make hunting easier. The luxuries provided in exchange for the furs were an incentive for more hunting. Native American culture was sacrificed as the Indians' desire grew for European weapons; clothing, household goods, tobacco, and alcohol encouraged them to hunt far more aggressively. Many animal species east of the Mississippi River were near extinction. Previously, the French Canadians' healthier policy of restricting the amount of alcohol and sparing the extinction of the animals limited Indian incentive. Under the British, on the other hand, the unlimited supply of alcohol encouraged unrestrained hunting, and the Europeans provided an unlimited market for the fur. With comparative ease, an Indian hunter could kill enough beavers and other fur-bearing animals to purchase from the traders whatever he needed for the year.

When disease and warfare reduced the number of hunters in the twenty years before 1760, the number of animals increased sharply. In the 1760s the hunters found ample numbers of deer, beaver, and other game. In May 1760 King Beaver, a Delaware chief, had forty horse-loads (at least 7,200 pounds of fur and deerskin worth at least $216,000) to pay off his debt and to buy additional goods.

From 1760 to 1764 an unusually large supply of beaver pelts and deerskins was traded north of the Ohio River when the Indian hunters reduced the overabundance of animals. Between 1764, after Pontiac's Uprising, and the beginning of the Revolution, most of the Indians between the Ohio River and the Great Lakes enjoyed a decade of prosperity, although a smallpox epidemic in 1765 decimated the Delawares and Shawnees in Ohio. Substantial quantities of fur arrived at Fort Pitt in 1766. However, the surplus of animals was soon eliminated, and by the late eighteenth century the Iroquois and the Algonquins had almost exhausted the beaver in their areas.

The increasing availability of horses to the Indians between the Great Lakes and the Ohio River by the mid-eighteenth century made further changes in Indian life. Although the canoe was the preferred means of travel, an increasing number of horses were obtained from tribes west of the Mississippi, either by trade or through capture by war parties. Horses were a major trade item with the Plains Indians. Stealing from the colonists and the British army was another source. At Fort Pitt horse theft was a very serious problem. On July 10, 1761, Colonel Henry Bouquet, a British officer, cut off all trade with the Shawnees until they promised to stop stealing horses and returned the white prisoners being held. In later years Johnson complained that the Indians were stealing horses from both the British government and the traders.

Horses were used by war parties and made it easier to move from villages to hunting grounds in the winter. They were also used by messengers. Communication between Detroit and Fort Pitt was very tenuous during the winter months. Indians were hired to travel by horse overland. On January 31, 1762, James Sterling, a merchant in Detroit, sent a letter with an Indian carrier to George Croghan, the Indian agent at Fort Pitt, regarding the rental of a house. After losing the letter the Indian returned to Detroit. On February 12 Sterling had to send a duplicate letter by the same means.

Canoes were the preferred mode of transportation. All of the tribes made bark canoes. Making a canoe was a considerable job. First the women sewed pieces of bark together with sinew, a strong cord made from tendons taken from deer. Then the men made curved wooden ribs to form the sides and put in wooden floors. The women applied gum to the seams.

On the upper Missouri River the Indians lived in earth lodges in villages located near a river for good soil and a woodland for firewood. Soil by a river was soft and easy to work compared with the hard, dry prairie soil. In New York the Indians lived in wooden longhouses, which were communal residences. In Wisconsin they lived in bark-covered shelters.

While farming provided most of the Indians' food, hunting supplied both meat and pelts for clothing. The fur was also a means of purchasing goods from the traders and other tribes. The traders were dependent on the Indians, for without them there would be no one to hunt the animals. The Indians were the ultimate source of most of the peltry, or raw furs. More Indians meant more hunters and more fur. Too few Indian hunters meant fewer furs but also led to a rapid expansion in the animal population, followed by a greater abundance of furs a few years later. Given a sharp reduction in hunting and several mild winters, a deer herd doubled in number. But then again, overgrazing would reduce the herd during the first severe winter. Therefore the number of Indians determined the availability of fur and the market for goods.

Although the colonists offered the most products in exchange for fur and deerskin, the French were friendlier toward the tribes. The French had been dealing with the Indians since the seventeenth century and in many instances had formed ties dating back several generations. The goal of the French traders from Illinois and Montreal was obtaining the maximum number of furs for the minimum amount of merchandise, so they limited the amount of brandy and rum for the Indians. The major cause of friction between the Indians and the colonists was the French competition from both Illinois and Montreal.

The colonial traders had ready access to British manufactures and colonial rum and were eager to sell their merchandise at lower prices to compete with the French. A new, different focus emerging among colonial traders from New York and Pennsylvania was on a high volume of sales at a reasonable price rather than obtaining the maximum number of furs. In 1761 the colonial merchants in Detroit were able to sell their merchandise at double the wholesale cost they paid in New York and Pennsylvania and still charge lower prices than the French in Detroit. James Sterling sold a stroud, a blanket made of two yards of a heavy woolen cloth also called stroud, for three or four beavers; a blanket or match coat for two beavers; and a large shirt for two beavers. He sold rum from a low of 18 shillings and 10 pence New York per gallon to as high as 30s. 17d. per gallon ($30 to $45 per quart) based on the amount purchased and the promised date of payment.

With the end of the fighting in 1760 the Indians no longer received generous gifts to maintain their allegiance to either the British or the French. Instead they had to hunt for furs to purchase goods from the flood of colonial traders who arrived on the frontier. In 1761 the Indians complained that the colonial traders were charging more than the established prices. Hoping to alleviate Indian complaints, in 1762 Johnson restricted trading to the posts at set prices. This action was of little help to the Indians who were paying the French traders even higher prices. Because both colonial and French traders ignored Johnson's restriction to the posts, the Indians continued to complain of the exorbitant prices.

Johnson believed that Indian behavior improved in Pennsylvania in 1761 and that with good management they would become friends rather than enemies. Instead, at a meeting with the Senecas, Onondagas, and Mohawks at Fort Johnson, the Indians complained that the British had failed to open the trade freely and that goods were sold at a very high price at the posts. Furthermore, because the reluctance of the British to provide them with ammunition limited their hunting, the Indians had fewer skins and furs to trade.

The Indians were not totally dependent on European technology. Most Indians visited a trading post only once a year, although additional goods were provided by the traders who spent the winter in Indian villages. The transition was slow from handmade implements to the metal tools of the Europeans; some tribes continued to use stone implements into the early nineteenth century. Handmade traps and snares were also used after 1800. Nevertheless, the Indians' customs and habits changed by their desire for European merchandise. When sober, the Indians were often skilled traders. A Delaware could mentally calculate a parcel of beaver worth £100 Pennsylvania and bargain with a trader. Some of the Indians were accomplished thieves, crowding a store, attempting to get behind the counter, or pretending to delay a decision to distract the trader while others stole small items, all familiar techniques of any shoplifter. Traders took advantage of this by placing needles and other small items in easy-to-steal locations to encourage the Indians to return to their stores.

More often, however, the Indians were cheated by unscrupulous traders. Traders would use inaccurate steelyards (a type of balance scale) to weigh the skins or would accuse others of doing so to win the Indians' trust. The dishonest trader would take an inaccurate steelyard along with a prospective Indian seller and compare it with his competitors' steelyards.

The comparison naturally would favor the underhanded trader to whom the Indian would then sell his pelts. In August 1761 James Kenny, the agent for the Indian Commission at Fort Pitt, reported that while he was trading with an Indian, another trader, John Ormsby, came in with an Indian who accused Kenny of using light steelyards. When Kenny and Ormsby's steelyards were compared, there was a difference of one pound per hundredweight. Kenny expected that Ormsby had two keys, or weights, for his steelyard—one accurate and the other designed to discredit other traders.

On another occasion, a Seneca chief came in to trade seven buckskins, while many Indians were crowding the store stealing. The warrior was not pleased with the trade, so Kenny gave him a loaf of bread. Another Indian hesitated in choosing some brass wire in exchange for a very small skin to divert Kenny's attention while other Indians stole. The Indians tried to get behind the counter, but Kenny turned them back. One of the Indians took a keg that was behind the door so Kenny turned them all out, giving one a handful of salt for which he begged. Some buckskins were traded for powder. These anecdotes reveal the often-shady conduct of trade on the part of both sellers and customers.

The dishonest colonial traders were a continual source of friction. The extremely risky action of entering Indian country with little protection attracted men who sought to make enormous gain by any means. In July 1766 at a conference in Oswego, New York, attended by the Ottawas, Pottawatomis, Hurons, and Chippewas, Pontiac informed Johnson that the Indians were threatening war because of dishonest business practices by colonial traders who were cheating on weights and using rum to buy the Indians' fur.

Although some Indians paid for their merchandise immediately with their furs, most trade was conducted on credit, from the time merchandise was purchased in England to its delivery to the Indians. Merchants in Montreal, Albany, Philadelphia, and Illinois would order merchandise in Europe and engage traders to deliver it to the Indians. If the traders knew an Indian in distress, they would supply him with ammunition and other goods for the winter and the following summer would receive payment in furs and skins. The pelts were then sent to the merchants on the coast and used to pay for the merchandise from England.

In severe winters the Indians lacked enough fur to balance their accounts but needed additional credit to hunt the next winter. Starvation faced them if they did not receive guns, ammunition, and clothing. Opinion was divided on their degree of honesty at this point. In 1749 Thomas Lee, a frontier merchant, believed that the Indians seldom failed to pay their debts because they needed good credit for the coming year. A missionary named David

Zeisberger, on the other hand, believed that regardless of any previous debts they owed, the Indians would return to the posts in the spring with pelts and bargain with various traders for the best price. However, the traders at the posts were less likely to grant credit. Traders in the villages, where there was no competition, were more willing.

With such a huge influx of European goods to exchange for a valuable commodity, fur, the relations between colonial and Indian society were economically beneficial to both. Despite all other problems, their contact remained peaceful for the most part. Otherwise the relationship would have collapsed, with a more serious impact on the Indians.

In January 1768 Robert McCulley was sent to the Shawnee Towns on the Scioto River with a stock of merchandise belonging to Baynton and Wharton and sold all of the goods. He sent twelve horse-loads of deerskin from the Shawnee Towns in the next few months (valued at £360 sterling, or $72,000). In July Joseph Spear, a close associate and former partner of Baynton and Wharton, sent six wagonloads of deerskin (at least six tons, worth £1,800 sterling, or $360,000) from Carlisle to Philadelphia. These amounts are significant compared with the total annual legal export of fur and deerskin from Philadelphia of only £4,000 sterling.

An analysis of the types of goods carried to the frontier reveals the nature of a slowly developing economic network that reached a stage of considerable complexity in the 1760s. The arrival of the Europeans disrupted an existing Indian economy. Having been practically self-sufficient, the changed Indian society could not resist and became dependent on the European merchandise to improve its standard of living. Copper kettles that replaced fragile clay pots were easily used to boil tough venison into a palatable stew. Given the lack of dental care, tender meat was a delightful improvement. A kettle was an inexpensive purchase from the traders, who included a nest of kettles of graduated sizes in every trading inventory. By 1770 comfortable woolen trousers had replaced the harsh buckskins, which became stiff when soaked and dried. East of the Mississippi River the "Indian gun," a small-caliber, smoothbore, and lightweight fowler that fired either round bullets or bird shot, replaced the bow and arrow. Given a few hours of trapping and hunting each day, an Indian family had an ample supply of fur and deerskin to purchase a wide variety of products.

A wide array of merchandise was sent to the frontier for the Indians, the French inhabitants, the frontier farmers, and the army, including guns, knives, tomahawks, cloth, tools and other metal objects, liquor, and tobacco. Except for rum, tobacco, and some metal products, most of these items came from Europe. Johnson estimated the annual needs of the Indians north of the Ohio River at £179,594 sterling ($35,918,800). This sum would provide each of 10,000 families two blankets, three strouds, four shirts, four pairs of stockings, two knives, a razor, six awls, five gallons of rum, eight pounds of gunpowder, sixteen pounds of lead, an axe, a kettle, a looking glass, silver trinkets, and wampum, and a beaver trap for every other family and a gun for every third family. The value of these goods equaled about $3,600 per family.

Various estimates were made for the amount of goods that the Indian Department at Fort Chartres should present to each Indian. In 1768 the list included a ruffled shirt (24s.), a stroud (32s.), a pair of leggings (12s.), a breechclout (12s.), three pounds of gunpowder (24s.), eight pounds of lead (each 18 d.), a pound of paint (32s.), three pounds of tobacco (4s.), and a quart of rum (6s.). Favored Indians also received a knife (2s.), a shirt (16s.), a match coat (a heavy winter overcoat, 20s.), a hundred flints (16s.), wampum (8s.), and a fusil (40s.). The standard allotment cost £7 7s. 6d. Pennsylvania ($848) and the addition for the favored Indians, £5 2s. Pennsylvania ($586), less than half the amount estimated by Johnson.

When preparing for the expedition to Illinois, Baynton and Wharton prepared 5,000 outfits to sell to the Indian Department or exchange for fur. If half were sold to the Indian Department, the cost would have been £18,375 ($2,113,125!), an average of less than $450. About five hundred fusils were also included in Baynton and Wharton's estimate, which indicates that about five hundred favored Indians would have received the additional package.

The amount of goods per Indian was similar to the amount given to Indians at Fort Pitt though the Fort Pitt cost was less. Each Indian would receive from the Indian Department a blanket (20s.), a stroud (22s. 6d.), a shirt (10s.), a pair of leggings (7s. 6d.), a breechclout (7s. 6d.), a pound of gunpowder (7s. 6d.), two and a half pounds of lead (2s. 6d.), a knife (2s.), and a half pound of paint (20s.) for a total of £4.19 ($570). Special packages for chiefs and others added five pounds of tobacco (10s.), a match coat (20s.), a rifle (150s.), a kettle (75s.), and fifteen flints (1s. 3d.), for a total of £10 16s. Pennsylvania ($1,472). Presenting the standard package to a thousand Indians in the Fort Pitt area cost over a half-million dollars, and a hundred of the special packages were an additional $147,000.

A canoe-load of Indian goods leaving from Montreal carried one hundred blankets, twenty-four gallons of liquor, two bales of kettles, a barrel of knives, two barrels of gunpowder, eleven bags of lead shot and ball, six bales of tobacco, plus other items with a total value of £180 15s. Quebec ($25,340). This canoe-load would supply approximately forty families. The proportion of liquor carried by the Canadians was far lower than that carried by the colonial traders—less than a gallon per family, compared with the five gallons estimated by Johnson. The cost per family was less than $650 but did not include replacement guns and included only twenty-four gallons of liquor. About one hundred canoes served the northwest fur trade in the late 1760s that would have supplied four thousand families.

At Fort Pitt in 1765 Croghan, the Indian agent, purchased trade goods valued at £2,037 11s. 10d. Pennsylvania ($234,370) to be given to the Indians as presents. This merchandise would have supplied as many as 190 families. The fact that the relative quantity of blankets and strouds was only a third of Johnson's estimate may have reflected the warmer climate in the Ohio Valley. The order for gifts from the Indian Department was based on the assumption that the Indians would bring in fur to purchase additional merchandise.

In Detroit in June 1762 Sterling ordered twenty-four one-gallon kettles, checked linen, corned gunpowder (gunpowder with a preservative to resist dampness for use by the Indians, rather than the usual glazed gunpowder), four hundred to five hundred French blankets, ten pieces of stroud material, and nearly six hundred scalping knives. Nine days later Sterling ordered an additional three thousand pounds of gunpowder for the Indians.

On June 7, 1761, Johnson wrote to Jeffrey Amherst, governor-general of British North America, concerning a proposed tour of the lakes and presented his estimate of £1,845 for presents, including four hundred shirts, blankets, stockings, vermillion, looking glasses, knives, hats, pipes, and kettles, but no guns or ammunition.

The knife, axe, and tomahawk were important tools of the Indians as well as the frontiersmen. Many were made by colonists and Canadians, and others came from European suppliers. The ironworks at Three Rivers on the St. Lawrence River and in Pennsylvania produced large quantities of iron that could be made into useful tools.

Next to his gun, the most essential tool to the Indian man was a knife to assist in hunting, clearing land, cooking, and eating. Frequent replacement was necessary because harsh wear and continual sharpening gradually weakened blades. The knives resembled a modern butcher knife. Joseph Dobson, a merchant in Carlisle, Pennsylvania, described a shipment of knives in 1768 with sloping blades and sharp points. These so-called scalping knives were obviously used for more general purposes. Another reference mentions both 147 "cutteaus" and 47 dozen butcher knives. In 1766 an outfit for an Indian included two knives, a fusil, a shirt, two handkerchiefs, a match coat, a large piece of stroud material, eighteen gunflints, four pounds of powder, and four pounds of lead.

The tomahawk, often called an axe in eighteenth-century documents, is usually regarded as a weapon, but from the frequency of orders was probably used on a daily basis as a hatchet. The tomahawks were probably made by local blacksmiths as well as being imported from England. In 1766 Johnson purchased eighty Indian axes from John B. Van Eps made by Myndert Wempel, A. Bradsteet, and T. Van Petten. Van Eps purchased axes from local blacksmiths and sold them in bulk to Johnson and to Indian traders. In 1766 Johnson was billed by Van Eps for eighty Indian axes made by local blacksmiths in the Albany area.

Brass kettles were a necessity for the Indians to boil their corn and meat. The Indians moved twice each year, and clay pots shattered easily so breakage was common. Even the kettles were damaged at times, and one of the duties of the gunsmiths assigned to the posts was to repair kettles as well as axes, knives, and guns. Kettles from Flanders were shipped first to England and then to America in nests of graduated sizes stored one inside the other for convenient shipment. The wire for the kettle handles was shipped separately. Smaller nests containing from 25 to 30 kettles weighing a total of 100 pounds were carried to the point of exchange with the tribes. The kettles weighed from 3 to 49 pounds each, and some were even heavier. One consignment of goods to Johnson included 150 brass Indian kettles packed in two casks, weighing a total of 1,137 pounds and priced at 16d. per pound.

Beaver traps were manufactured in the colonies. Dobson shipped a box of forty-five traps to Fort Pitt in spring 1768 along with 158 kegs of rum and a hogshead of kettles filled with flaxseed.

After metal objects, cloth was the item most in demand. Both wool and linen were sold throughout the West and in Canada. For the most part, cloth was imported to the commercial centers of Philadelphia, New York, Quebec, and Montreal to be made into garments such as linen shirts, duffle coats, and match coats trimmed with brightly colored cloth. These articles were then sent to the frontier along with uncut cloth.

Shirts were made by seamstresses in Philadelphia. They cost from 6d. to 83d. In January 1765 Baynton and Wharton paid £220 Pennsylvania for about 5,700 shirts. Considering that there were fewer then 10,000 Indian adult males in the territory north of the Ohio River and east of the Mississippi River, the partners expected a major share of the trade.

An example of a mixed shipment of Indian goods sent west was Croghan's account with Simon, Levy & Co. for 1765 that listed strouds and "half-thicks," another kind of blanket material by the piece, French match coats, English match coats, black-striped blankets, scarlet cloth by the yard, embossed serge by the yard, calico shirts, plain white shirts, worsted caps, scarlet gartering, and linen by the yard. All of the shipment was for the Indians at Fort Pitt. Sterling described French blankets as having a blue stripe not more than one and a quarter inches wide with a row of capital letters near one of the stripes. Sterling's agents were cautioned never to send blankets with black stripes or English blankets with red stripes because the Indians preferred the French style with blue stripes.

Silver in the form of brooches and other ornaments was popular. Shipments by the Pennsylvania Indian Commission to Fort Pitt in April 1762 had a value of more than £414 Pennsylvania of which £200 was in silver work by Joseph Hollingshead and J. Richardson.

Rum was part of every cargo delivered to the Indians and constituted 50 percent of the total value of the trade goods. The demand was limited only by the Indians' ability to pay for it with fur. The Indian Department used a gift of rum as part of all negotiations with the Indians. However, rum created serious problems because some Indians became uncontrollable when they were drunk.

Rum was already a problem at Fort Pitt in 1760 when Croghan reported that there was too much rum around and that drunken Indians were killing the soldiers. Although Croghan encouraged General Robert Monckton to prohibit the sale of rum in the fall of 1760, by March 1761 Colonel Bouquet informed Monckton that preventing the movement of rum to Fort Pitt was impossible. In a fight resulting from drunkenness, three Indians had been killed.

In Detroit the British army prohibited bringing in rum in 1761. Prior to 1760 the colonists sold unlimited quantities to the Indians at Oswego. Little danger was involved because rather than drinking it there, the Indians carried the rum away with them. However, in 1761 the tribes at Detroit who had villages in the area remained near the fort to trade and became unruly.

Regardless of the rules, large quantities of rum came via Niagara to Detroit. By May 1761 many traders (including Robert Callender, Fred Hambuck, and John Baird, a former Pennsylvania militia officer) were ignoring the rule, and brought rum from Fort Pitt. The Detroit commandant, Captain Daniel Campbell, tried to prevent rum sales to the Indians in Detroit, but they could buy rum from the Albany traders at Fort Niagara and take it back to Detroit. The ready flow of rum made the Indians troublesome and difficult to manage.

Transporting the rum was always risky. Detroit trader Sterling received forty-one barrels of rum in four canoes manned by twelve men in August 1761. The barrels had been damaged by the soldiers when they were carried around the falls at Niagara, and a great deal of rum was lost. Sterling hoped to sell the rum to the Detroit garrison and the French. He believed that rum was the worst thing to sell to the Indians because the local people in Detroit suffered when the Indians were drunk, but he did discreetly sell them an occasional keg for a large profit.

In September 1761 Sterling reported that another forty barrels of rum were on the way to Detroit but that he still had some on hand because Campbell had prohibited the open sale of rum to the Indians. This limitation apparently was successful because in October 1761 Sterling requested that no more rum be sent to him. His goal was to have a vintner make wine from local fruit in Detroit that would sell at a greater profit than rum.

Although the Indians found no presents of rum and powder awaiting them in Detroit in spring 1762, they did find traders with gunpowder to sell, a few gifts, and a gunsmith. The prohibition of rum had no noticeable effect in Detroit by June. Although the Indians grumbled about it and threatened the English at first, they resigned themselves to hunting and raising their corn, causing less trouble than the previous year.

The Indian consumption of rum was far less per person than others in America. The colonists, the British army, Canadians, and Indians consumed more than 7 million gallons annually. The colonies produced at least 4.8 million gallons and imported 3.8 million gallons annually, of which more than 1 million gallons was exported. Most of the remaining rum was consumed by the adult male colonists. There were 1.6 million people in thirteen colonies, with an average of five people per family, or 320,000 adult males consuming 6.4 million gallons—twenty gallons of rum a year each.

The British army consumed 230,000 gallons, 23 gallons per soldier a year, and the Canadians consumed 300,000 gallons. The Indians, in contrast, consumed only 150,000 gallons annually, about 10 gallons each for 15,000 warriors. However, while the others drank frequently, the Indians drank heavily but only while they were at the trading posts.

The British army issued a gill of rum (one fourth of a pint, or four fluid ounces, enough to make a man drunk) daily to each soldier (11.5 gallons per year), and 10,000 soldiers would consume 115,000 gallons per year. The soldiers bought additional rum equal to their ration from the local traders, for a total of 230,000 gallons.

About 250,000 gallons of rum were exported to Canada for 65,000 Canadians (including 15,000 adult males) and the fur traders. Baynton and Wharton sent 167 hogsheads (10,521 gallons) of rum and other spirits to Canada on the brig *Lark* on April 13, 1764. Included in the cost of the shipment was £99 paid to Joseph Coleman for 521 twenty-gallon kegs and the charge for filling them. The rum for the Indians was usually carried by canoe in such twenty-gallon kegs, which weighed 160 pounds. Therefore, this shipment was intended for the Indians rather than the French inhabitants of Quebec. The cargo was valued at £2,150 Pennsylvania (nearly $250,000) including expenses. Baynton and Wharton and its partners were in a large-scale liquor business intended for the Indians despite the British army's prohibition.

Despite the 1761 orders concerning the sale of rum to Indians traders and settlers were both giving and selling them rum in order to attract business. An unscrupulous trader would give an Indian some rum to encourage him to buy goods and more rum. Once the Indians had sold all their furs to purchase rum, they would sell their clothing and weapons for more. On August 3, 1761, one Indian family obtained rum in Fort Pitt, for example, by pawning their clothes, wampum, and everything else they had. The results of heavy drinking at Fort Pitt were tragic. One Mohawk Indian killed another during a drunken spree.

In 1761 Albany-based traders at Oswego and Niagara traded mostly rum. The Indians received few other goods. In November 1761 the Seneca chiefs came to Niagara and asked for ammunition, clothing, and provisions. The army provided some and advised the chiefs to use the few skins they had left to buy more supplies from the traders.

Outside the military posts the traders lived at high risk because the Indians might kill them and take their rum. So the traders in the villages limited the supply of rum. The traders survived because some Indians would protect them to ensure their return the next year with a new load of merchandise and rum.

The British army tried to enforce the ban on rum. At Fort Bedford, halfway from Carlisle to Fort Pitt, the army seized a shipment of 100 kegs of liquor (at least 800 gallons if the kegs were the small, 8-gallon size used on packhorses). The Indians learned of the seizure and attempted to steal it. During the robbery the Indians shot several drunken laborers, and the army arrested the traders for illegal trading. In June 1761, when the army seized more liquor, they had trouble removing the Indians from the surrounding area.

Rum continued to be a problem in 1762. The New York traders stated that they should have the same right as the Canadians to trade rum, but Amherst insisted on continuing the ban on its sale. The Indians supported the limitation of rum according to a petition signed by twelve Niagara traders. They realized that too much rum would destroy the trade and therefore asked that the quantity of rum carried by a trader be limited to a reasonable amount compared with his other goods. The traders' attitude was based on the conviction that the tribes would not come to Niagara if there were no rum, and the traders would be bankrupted.

The petition suggested that a reasonable amount would be two gallons for each Indian who came a long distance, and the post commander would supervise the distribution. But the policy was not changed. In April 1762 the British army took all of the rum in Fort Niagara, a total of 2,600 gallons held by ten traders, to its storage area. The average French trading canoe carried only 120 gallons, so the total seized was equal to the amount normally carried by about twenty canoes. Johnson agreed with Amherst that only total prohibition would be effective because eager Indians would travel any distance and pay any price for liquor. The traders who offered rum would get all the furs, and those without rum would get none. In June 1762 traders from Canada with passes from General Thomas Gage were selling rum at Toronto and drawing the Indians away from Niagara. New York merchants favored the restriction of all trade including rum to Fort Pitt, Niagara, Detroit, and some minor posts, believing that most profits could be made at the posts that made free use of rum. Regardless of official attempts, the Indians continued to find supplies of rum.

Next to rum the Indians placed a high priority on guns and ammunition. The guns were used primarily for hunting but also in warfare with other tribes and occasional attacks on the colonists. The traders' best interest was served by providing the tribes with dependable arms for hunting. The most favored design was the lightweight Indian gun, which was easy to carry compared with the heavy military musket. The Indian guns, or fusils, had a characteristic dragon plate on the left side of the stock opposite the lock mechanism that fired the piece. The plate was an anchor for the screws that attached the lock to the gunstock. This ornate device was simplified into a plain strap on most guns used by Europeans during the eighteenth century, but the Indians preferred the more decorative dragon.

The guns evolved from the fowling pieces first carried into the Hudson Valley in the seventeenth century by the Dutch and varied in size and quality. In 1764 Johnson requested that the army provide him with two hundred good, light, short guns for the Indians. Gage promised to provide the guns from army arsenals, including 111 French guns and various additional light guns.

The cost of fusils was estimated at 30s. sterling ($300) each by Sir William Johnson in 1764. In 1766 three fusils were sold to John Jennings, an agent for Baynton and Wharton in Illinois, for 30s. each. In 1770 Johnson placed an order for varying grades of fusils: 400 at 16s. each, 150 at 20s. each, and 50 at 30s. each. The most expensive ones were ornamental pieces for presentation to chiefs. The cheaper guns were made in Liège, in Europe, and were as sturdy as the products from Birmingham, England.

Guns were the most essential trade item in the 1760s. Two or three generations of Indian hunters had been using firearms, and although some retained bows and arrows, their effective range was less than the gun's. A functioning gun was essential to the Indians both for hunting and for warring on neighboring tribes. Having a gunsmith at the nearest fort was crucial to keeping the weapons in repair. The Indian Department provided free gun repairs to the Indians, and the presence of a gunsmith at a trading post was often demanded by the Indians at conferences. At Fort Niagara in 1761 Seneca chiefs asked for ammunition, clothing, and provisions and also requested a gunsmith to repair their guns. In 1762 the Indians at Green Bay requested that a smith be sent to repair their guns. In 1768 Dobson was given two horse-loads of fur for blacksmith work at the Shawnee Towns repairing guns and traps. In 1770 Johnson paid Michael Klyne £38 New York ($4,788) for miscellaneous gun repairs from April 5 to November 4. Croghan's payroll for six men at Fort Pitt and Detroit included Richard Butler and Theophilus, gunsmiths; St. Martin and La Bute, interpreters; and Thomas McKee and Alexander Potts, agents.

The Indians used the fusils in warfare with other tribes. As the Indians east of the Mississippi obtained more guns, they gained ascendancy over the tribes farther west and therefore created a strong demand for guns from the western tribes. The eastern tribes cleverly traded their damaged and worn guns to the western tribes at high prices and obtained new guns from the traders. The tribes west of the Mississippi were good customers for Baynton and Wharton in Illinois. In 1768 James and Drinker sold Baynton and Wharton three hundred French guns fitted with neat blue and gilt barrels for 32s. Pennsylvania each ($202). The guns were shipped thirty in a case. George Morgan of Illinois expected the guns in November and planned to sell them for six Spanish dollars each ($240). He sold all three hundred guns and ordered four hundred more with shorter barrels and a larger caliber, two features preferred by the Indians. In addition, he wanted fifty fusils with barrels four inches longer and with silver thumb pieces, which cost 4s. Pennsylvania more than the common fusils. Morgan supplied many of the tribes west of the Mississippi.

In 1768 Baynton and Wharton purchased forty-eight fusils for 155 livres ($39) at a sale of goods stolen by Indians from a wrecked boat and recovered by James Rumsey and William Storer. (The French livres in Illinois were worth 25 cents.) Baynton and Wharton expected guns to be resold for 1,000 livres ($250). The price of a fusil was 32s. Pennsylvania in Philadelphia and at least £2 Pennsylvania ($230) in Illinois.

Most of the fusils for the Indians were ordered from England and manufactured in Birmingham. In 1770 John Blackburn sent a merchant to Birmingham to arrange the manufacture of guns that Sir William Johnson had ordered in September. In 1762 Simon and Henry of Lancaster advertised imported English guns for sale. In 1767 Baynton and Wharton purchased 105 fusils from Henry White of New York. The fusils arrived from England on the sloop *Endeavor*. Thirty of them were from James McEver and the rest were from Ellis Debrofies. The cost was 30s. New York ($189) for 67 of them and 27s. for the remainder. Including a 5 percent commission to

White and the fee for cartage, the total cost of the guns was £149 9s. Pennsylvania ($17,192).

In 1770 John Blackburn sent Johnson 400 fusils with blue barrels at 16s. sterling ($160) each, 150 fusils with glazed barrels for 20s. each, and 50 neat fowling pieces with blue barrels at 30s. each, for a total of £545 plus £20 for the cases in which they were packed ($133,000). The whole order including other Indian goods cost £1,040 ($200,080). In 1769 Phyn and Ellice ordered from Benjamin Booth, its agent in New York, 60 fusils at 16s. made by Wilson & Company, a Birmingham gun maker, along with ammunition and 1,050 French blankets.

The Indian Department gave guns as gifts to the Indians. Decorative guns were used as special presents to impress the chiefs. To show special favoritism to chiefs and other honored Indians, guns with added ornamentation and additional barrel length were made in a variety of grades. The gun makers of Birmingham made these to order for the merchants supplying the American market, who then shipped the guns to Quebec, New York, and Philadelphia.

The gunsmiths of Liège and Holland also made lightweight fowlers, but few were sent to America during the 1760s. Baynton and Wharton bought nine fowling pieces from William Pusey in 1766 for 12s. 6d. Pennsylvania ($72), far less than the price of an Indian gun. Some unscrupulous traders sold cheap guns made in Liège that, though appealing to the eye, endangered the user because of the poor quality of the barrel. A British traveler in the West described the guns as fitted up in a very neat manner to attract the notice of the Indians. Once one had been fired five or six times, the gun would burst and the unfortunate user would either be killed or lose a hand or arm. No evidence has been found in other documents to indicate that such accidents were frequent compared with the many accidents later on in the American Civil War, when soldiers placed more than one charge in a barrel. Accidents could have resulted from carelessness by the Indian in measuring powder and not making certain that the barrel was clear. Misuse rather than poor gun quality was more likely the cause of most accidents.

Knowing the inexperience of the Indians, the Birmingham gun makers provided a strong barrel. The trader's best interest was to provide Indians with the most dependable arms at the lowest cost so that they would have furs to trade. Without his gun, the warrior could not hunt and gather furs.

Rifles were much more expensive than Indian guns. Because the rifled barrel gave greater velocity to the bullet, less gunpowder was needed, a fact that appealed to the Ohio Valley and Great Lakes warriors who eagerly sought rifles. Heavy rifles were less desirable in the far Northwest, where weapons were carried for long distances. Far heavier than fusil barrels, rifle barrels were drilled from solid octagonal steel bars, rather than welded from spirals of thin straps. In 1767 Alexander McKee at Fort Pitt ordered twenty smoothbore guns and twelve rifles as well as a long list of other items to be given to the Indians in the area as presents.

A rifle was sometimes given to a chief as a special favor. The rifle was also preferred by the white settlers, who appreciated the advantages of accuracy and economy of ammunition as compensation for the added weight. The rifle was seldom used by the British army because it took more time to load. Colonel John Bradstreet, commander of a punitive expedition in 1764, suggested limiting the sale of rifles to Indians because they needed less powder and were more effective than the musket.

Pennsylvania was a center for rifle manufacturing in the eighteenth century. The famous Pennsylvania rifle maker John Henry, of the Simons and Henry partnership, purchased parts to be assembled into rifles in 1765 including 281 hammers, 292 sear springs, jaws for holding the flint, and other items for a total of £72 Pennsylvania ($8,280). Within twelve months all of these parts were to be assembled into nearly 300 rifles (worth over $500 each retail, or $150,000 in all). Henry himself drilled the barrels, the most difficult task, and he hired carpenters to shape the wooden stocks. Henry was duplicating the practice of the British government, which bought gun parts from various manufacturers and then assembled the weapons in the royal armories. Henry purchased his parts from the same manufacturers.

In June 1762 Henry sent a shipment of rifles for the Pennsylvania Indian Commission valued at more than £576 Pennsylvania, and that September the commission purchased eighteen rifles for £4 10s. Pennsylvania ($517) from Henry at Lancaster. In 1766 Baynton and Wharton ordered two lots of six rifles at £4 10s. each from Simons and Henry. In September 1766 Baynton and Wharton paid £95 Pennsylvania ($10,925) for twenty rifles sent to Fort Pitt. Henry used the bill of exchange to pay Hugh and George Roberts for service. In August 1767 a bill from Simon and Milligan included delivery of two rifles, both for £17 Pennsylvania, to John Irwin for the use of the Indian Department as a gift. And in October 1767 George Morgan at Fort Pitt ordered thirty-two rifles and fifty fusils for the Indian Department, along with ammunition, cloth for 280 shirts, 100 pairs of shoes, and 600 gallons of rum. Henry sold Rinkin & Edgar in Detroit fourteen rifles and repaired thirteen rifles and fusils in 1773.

Others were making rifles during this period as well. In 1767 Balser Goehr made twenty strong rifles for Baynton and Wharton at a cost of £3 10s., £1 less than Henry. Goehr was a blacksmith and made a hundred beaver traps for the partners as well. Pistols were seldom mentioned in documents of the period. In 1766 Edmund Moran, an Indian trader active in Carlisle and Green Bay, purchased pistols from James Gorrell, the British commander at Green Bay, and other firearms from Joseph Coxe.

Because of the inaccuracy of the smoothbore gun, the Indian favored a small-caliber gun that required less gunpowder and lead. Ammunition was a major item in any batch of goods for sale to the Indians, as they did not conserve their ammunition. According to Sir William Johnson, each Indian hunter carelessly used about 8 pounds of powder and 20 pounds of lead during the two hunting seasons each year. In 1761 Gorrell gave the Indians 100 pounds of powder and 80 pounds of bar lead in October. The next May he presented a group of Indians with 150 pounds of lead and 200 pounds of powder along with three shirts and four strouds. Another Indian received 30 pounds of powder and 30 pounds of lead along with 2 yards of stroud, a shirt, and 2 pounds of vermillion. In May 1762 some Ottawas received 200 pounds of powder, 100 pounds of lead, 6 yards of stroud, and 2 pounds of vermillion. Large quantities of ammunition were given to small groups of Indians, indicating that they were stockpiling in anticipation of the uprising to come in 1763.

According to Johnson, 200 pounds of powder would have been sufficient for twenty-five Indians, but only three shirts were included in Gorrell's May 1762 gift. More lead than powder was usually given. In 1768 Phyn and Ellice ordered 46 pounds of fusil balls, 26 pounds of lead, and 16 pounds of gunpowder. In 1767 a flotilla of boats sent to Illinois from Fort Pitt included in its cargo 200 pounds of powder and 1,462 pounds of lead, most of which came from the British army stores in Fort Pitt. However, 400 pounds of the lead were purchased from Charles McClure, a trader at Fort Pitt, and 200 pounds were from Devereaux Smith, also a Fort Pitt trader. Purchasing lead from other traders would not have been profitable unless a great markup was expected in Illinois.

The Indians used a considerable quantity of powder. Amherst transferred 20 quarter-barrels of powder, 10 hundredweight of musket shot, and 2,000 flints to Johnson for use by the Indians in April 1761. On May 30, 1761, Amherst sent 300 hundredweights of powder to Johnson.

The price of powder was high. In 1760 John and Peter Chevalier sold Baynton and Wharton 400 pounds of powder for 5s. Pennsylvania per pound ($28.75, or $11,700 for the entire order). In 1769 Daniel Campbell was trying to fill an order for 300 pounds of gunpowder placed by Johnson but none was available in Schenectady or Albany, and there were only a few pounds at 4s. 6d. New York ($28.35), which Campbell considered too high. The 200 pounds of powder that Gorrell gave to a few Indians in 1762 was worth $5,750.

Bullets were sold in a variety of forms. Some rifles came with bullet molds, and the customer purchased bar lead that was then melted and poured into the mold to make the bullets. In 1768 Morgan purchased four brass bullet molds that made thirty bullets from James and Drinker for 55s. each for a total of £11 Pennsylvania ($1,265). Joseph Simons made the bullets for John Henry's rifles, purchasing bar lead worth £13 7s. ($1,535) from William West in 1770.

West also sold "dropped" shot made by dropping small quantities of lead from a tower into a vat of water. The fall created a perfectly round shot that was instantly cooled by the water. The result was perfect balls, in contrast to molded balls rounded with a file. Dropped shot was more accurate than molded shot and was most frequently used in rifles. West supplied many merchants with large quantities of powder and shot, including Silas Newcomb, John Hopson, George Graff, and George Mead, and quantities varying from £4 to £93 Pennsylvania ($10,695) to Robert Callender.

Guns were used both for hunting and warfare. The war party was an essential part of the Indian way of life. Taking part in a raid on a traditional enemy tribe was a symbol of a young man's becoming an adult. Before going on a raid the young men danced a war dance, struck posts, recounted their past victories, and painted their bodies with vermillion. War parties included from twenty to forty men, some boys, and a few women and older people to take care of the camp, usually located fifteen miles from the objective of the raid. Two war parties sent against colonists in the 1770s included twenty-five warriors in one and thirty-five warriors in the other.

The visits of the war parties to the frontier posts caused considerable difficulty as the Indians demanded ammunition and other supplies. The Shawnee visited the Illinois posts on their way to raid the Pawnees west of the Mississippi. The Iroquois stopped at Fort Pitt for weapons and provisions on their way to fight the Cherokees south of the Ohio. Presents to these war parties included rum, which created a good market for the merchants at Fort Pitt. In March 1762 Croghan reported that the winter had been very severe and few Indians had visited Fort Pitt other than some Senecas on their way to fight the Cherokees. The Senecas became angry when merchants refused to sell them ammunition, vermillion, knives, and other war supplies prohibited by Amherst's orders. Supporting the Indians, Colonel Bouquet and Croghan believed that the merchandise should have been given to them. Providing war parties with gifts of ammunition and other needs was essential to retain their friendship. In April 1762 eighty warriors of the Six Nations stopped at Fort Pitt on their return from the Cherokee expedition. Their request for supplies was also refused by Bouquet under Amherst's policy. Again they objected, so Croghan acquiesced and delivered the necessary provisions and supplies at his own expense.

One purpose of the raids was to capture men, women, and children, who were adopted into the attacking tribe to introduce new blood lines. In November 1756 Indians raided a settlement and captured a woman and four children but took nothing else other than a saddle and a white coat. The captives were adopted by Indian families. A captive named Smith was adopted by an Indian chief and he was made to look like an Indian. The Indians pulled the hair out of his head except for a small area four inches square on the Crown. The remaining hair was trimmed except for three locks that hung down. One lock was braided with silver brooches, and the other two locks were wrapped with strips of cloth with red feathers attached.

Smith was then stripped and given a breechclout to wear. The Indians painted his body with various colors. A large belt of wampum was placed around his neck and silver bands were put on his hands and right arm. They gave Smith a new ruffled shirt, a pair of leggings adorned with ribbons and beads, a pair of moccasins, garters with beads, porcupine quills, a pipe, a tomahawk, and a polecat-skin pouch filled with tobacco and dry leaves.

Many white women and children were captured during the Seven Years' War. In October 1761 the Delawares and the Shawnees released some of their captives in return for presents. During Pontiac's Uprising captives were taken too. At Fort Pitt in February 1765 Croghan conferred with the Shawnees, who promised to release white captives. He put off giving presents until the Indians had met the terms of the agreement, though. Croghan had £1,200 sterling's worth of presents and £2,000 in cash to purchase more.

Captives provided a necessary addition to the gene pool in small Indian villages. Some captives were even happy with their new lives and were reluctant to leave when the British ordered their return in 1764. A warrior would often have an Indian wife from his own tribe, and another wife captured from a different tribe. By the mid-eighteenth century there were many Indians with mixed French and Indian blood in the villages as well as those whose ancestors came from different tribes. Many of the French traders were of mixed lineage. Having family ties with the tribes assured them of protection through a winter of trading.

The comparatively serene and profitable business of trading with the Indians on the frontier came to an abrupt halt in May 1763 with the eruption of Pontiac's Uprising. Encouraged—if not instigated—by the French, the Indians attacked the colonists and British at Michilimackinac, Fort Niagara, Detroit, and other posts.

Chief Pontiac had an illustrious history as a mighty chief. He was born 1720 on the Ottawa River to an Ottawa father and an Ojibwa mother. He became the leader of the Ottawa tribe. In 1746 Pontiac aided the French at Detroit against northern tribes. He became chief in 1755 and may have led the Indians who defeated General Edward Braddock and his army in Pennsylvania. Pontiac later became leader of the council of three tribes—the Ottawa, the Pottawatomi, and the Ojibwa. In 1760 the British defeated the French and sent Major Robert Rogers to take over Detroit. Pontiac met with Rogers on the shore of Lake Erie and allowed him to proceed peacefully once Pontiac learned that the French had surrendered.

The British remained contemptuous of the Indians, and in 1762, preparing for the uprising, Pontiac enlisted the tribes east of the Mississippi to fight the English. At a conference near Detroit on April 27, 1763, he convinced the tribes that the British had come to take their hunting grounds and drive away the game. Eighteen tribes were supposed to attack British posts in their territory in May 1763. Pontiac intended to attack Detroit on May 7, 1763, but an Indian girl informed the British of the plan and the surprise failed. Pontiac then laid siege on Detroit to block supplies and reinforcements from arriving, but he was unsuccessful. Supplies and men came over the lakes from Fort Niagara.

The French in Detroit remained outwardly neutral. During the siege Indian parties raided the French farms for provisions, stealing horses, hogs, and chickens. Although unable to overcome the garrison, the Indians defeated a sortie on July 31, 1763, killing or wounding fifty-nine British soldiers. The siege was abandoned on October 12, 1763, when the hunting season arrived and the Indian supply of ammunition ran short.

A total of twelve posts had been attacked, and eight of them were taken and destroyed: Michilimackinac, Fort Sandusky, Fort St. Joseph, Fort Miami, Fort Ouiatanon, Presque Isle, Fort LeBeouf, and Fort Venango. In May 1763 a large party of Mingos and Delawares from the Ohio area came to Fort Pitt and sold £300 worth of peltry for powder and ammunition. They then went down the Ohio River and began robbing traders at Bushy Run. Thomas Colhoun, who had been dealing along with fourteen other traders near Fort Pitt, reported that six men were killed.

Probably one hundred men from Pennsylvania were killed during Pontiac's Uprising, including horse drivers and other employees of the traders. Among those killed were two Jewish traders, associates of Franks & Company, and Colonel John Clapham, who was killed on his way to Detroit.

The Indians also went to Fort Niagara in May 1763 demanding rum but were refused by the commanding officer. They returned on June 2, 1763, and murdered a trader, John Wendell, and wounded his brother at a day's travel from Niagara. The Wendells had supplied the Indians with rum in Toronto in 1762, and when the Indians attacked them they were selling rum illegally outside of the fort. Henry Van Schaak and Peter Ryckman reported to Johnson that other traders had been killed. Despite Johnson's efforts to quiet the Indians in New York, the British army suffered a serious setback in September 1763. Seneca Indians from the Gennesseo Village killed sixty-four men from the 80th Regiment, the 55th Regiment, and the New York Provincial Regiment at Fort Niagara. Three hundred and ninety Indians were involved, and they claimed eighty scalps with only one Indian being wounded.

On October 30, 1763, a message from Illinois informed Pontiac that he would get no help from the French there. Two days later Pontiac sent a note to Major Henry Gladwin, the British commandant, that the war was over. He withdrew to the Maumee River in Ohio. After two punitive campaigns in 1764 to pacify the Indians, the British adopted a policy of providing presents.

In June 1765, with the help of the Shawnees, Croghan convinced Pontiac to permit the British army to take possession of Illinois in July. In July 1766 Pontiac formally made peace with Sir William Johnson at Oswego and at Fort Chartres in Illinois. On April 20, 1769, Pontiac was murdered by a Kaskaskia or Peoria Indian.

As soon as the uprising was crushed, the colonial merchants intended to resume trading with the Indians. Baynton and Wharton was planning in 1764 to expand its market to Illinois. The enthusiasm of the Philadelphia merchants to begin selling merchandise to the Indians was not shared by the people who lived on the frontier and had suffered from numerous attacks in 1764 as part of the uprising. Indian attacks on Pennsylvania traders continued in 1765. In June the Seneca Indians killed a trader near Fort Pitt. William Dice and another colonist were killed earlier by three Indians near Redstone.

In June 1765 Gage had urged Governor John Penn to open the Indian trade officially despite the objections of the fearful settlers on the frontier. The Indians had met all terms of the agreements negotiated by Croghan in February. If goods were not available at Fort Pitt, Gage said, the Indians would deal with the French in Illinois. By the end of June, Penn reopened trade, but in retaliation the frontiersmen were still threatening to attack the convoys of horses carrying Indian merchandise to Fort Pitt.

Johnson had promised the Delaware Indians that trade would be reopened as a condition of peace on the frontier, and he was also making the same promise to the Chippewas and the Shawnees. He was concerned that the unhappy frontiersmen would continue to obstruct the movement of merchandise unless the army provided an escort. Baynton and Wharton asked the British army to provide protection for its goods. When the first escorted convoys went forward, shots were exchanged between the soldiers and the settlers. The settlers were at odds with the Pennsylvania traders, and because the Indians did not trust the Pennsylvania merchants to supply them at Fort Pitt, they went to Detroit to trade their fur with the French and New York traders. Baynton and Wharton and the other traders at Fort Pitt were left with unsold merchandise.

The Indians in the Ohio Valley were still hostile. The Miami Indians robbed and captured John Fraser, a trader dealing on the Wabash. Fraser was taken to Illinois and released. He subsequently arrived in New Orleans on June 19, 1765. On June 8, 1765, a party of Kickapoo Indians robbed Croghan of all his goods and took him as a prisoner to Pontiac at Vincennes.

The French from Illinois who encouraged the Indians to oppose the colonists were always a problem. In December 1764 Captain John Howard reported that the Chippewa Indians had obtained ammunition from the French on the west side of Lake Michigan and that Indians were intercepting canoes on their way from Detroit to Michilimackinac. In May 1765 Howard sent Baptiste Cadot with a belt to show the Indians at Sault Ste. Marie that the Delawares and Shawnees had made peace with the British. However, in April 1765 the relentless French in Illinois had sent a false message to the Indians at Michilimackinac that the French army had retaken Quebec and driven the English up to Montreal. The message questioned how the Indians would survive after selling all their furs to the British for rum. In late 1765 the Indians were pacified, with the exception of one tribe.

After two years of comparative quiet, however, the Indians resumed their attacks on the Ohio River. In April 1767 Johnson warned General Gage of the Indian danger. Fearing the hostile Indians, colonial traders from Illinois could not trade in Vincennes or travel up the Illinois or Mississippi River in 1767. The French had complete control of the area outside the posts. George Morgan believed that unless the British army could control the French and the Indians, Illinois should be abandoned. Gage was alarmed and the pressure to take some action continued.

In September 1767 Gage blamed the trouble on William Petty, Earl of Shelburne, and on other British government ministers for refusing to permit settlement beyond the line established by the Proclamation of 1763. In a letter to Benjamin Franklin, Thomas Wharton again linked the prospect of an Indian uprising to the need to move the boundary. Countering any efforts to win over the Indians were the frontier farmers, who reacted violently to the Indian attacks.

Malevolent Indians had ample opportunity to attack the colonial traders, especially on the rivers. Further disaster befell Baynton and Wharton in July 1767 when the Chippewas attacked two boats on the Ohio River, murdered fourteen men, and stole merchandise worth £3,000 Pennsylvania ($345,000) owned by the trading company.

In another incident in 1767, Henry O'Brien, John Little Peter Brown, and seven others were killed on the Ohio River, and their two boats with merchandise worth £8,000 Pennsylvania ($920,000) were stolen. Some of the merchandise was later recovered and sold by Morgan in Illinois for £353 sterling ($70,000). Traders continued to die at the hands of the Indians. Thomas Mitchell was killed in a Shawnee village in the fall of 1767, and John McDonald was killed near Fort Pitt in December 1767.

Johnson told Shelburne that these actions were an indication of another uprising. These few losses occurred after two years of comparative tranquility. Previously, boats had moved regularly from Fort Pitt to Illinois supplying the army and taking merchandise to Baynton and Wharton's agent in Illinois to sell to the Indians and French farmers.

The summer of 1768 saw renewed violence against the colonial traders, motivated by the French who believed the attacks were the best method to maintain their control of the fur trade. In July 1768 a band of Indians returned to Vincennes in Illinois with nine British and colonial scalps and eight horse-loads of fur. They had attacked two groups of traders in the Ohio Valley near Fort Pitt. The British arrested the chiefs, demanding that they turn over the Indians who had committed the crimes. Later that year three colonial traders were killed and their merchandise stolen by the French.

In September a hunting party from Fort Chartres was attacked by Indians in the Wabash Valley. Nine people were killed and eight horse-loads of fur were taken to Vincennes. The Indians considered the hunting ground their own and believed that whites had no right to take game without permission. The hunters had permission from the Indians to hunt buffalo for meat for the garrison but were killed when they ignored the rule by also hunting deer, bear, and beaver. Gage noted that the Ohio River was becoming more dangerous in 1768 and told the commander in Illinois that he should not try to protect any hunters who broke the rules by hunting furs without permission.

The Indians were also troublesome at Niagara, partly because of the large amount of rum provided by the traders to encourage the Indians to trade their furs at low prices. In 1766 the Indians were prohibited from entering the fort after a sentry had threatened a Seneca chief with a bayonet, which infuriated the Indians. Adding to their displeasure, they were permitted to sell venison at the post market but could receive only bread in payment.

The conflict between the settlers and Indians could not be resolved because eventually the encroachment on Indian land would destroy the Indian culture. The Indians realized that the French fur traders improved their life, but the settlers would push them off their land. Later claims by land speculators that the Indians were willing to sell an enormous tract of their land to Croghan and his associates at Fort Stanwix in 1768 seem unlikely.

Concerning Indian opposition to the colonial fur traders, many traders worked in the Indian villages year after year. There were very few robberies or murders between 1764 and 1766. Fred Hambuck had traded with the Indians since 1761. He was captured in 1763, released in 1764, and was trading again in 1766. Hambuck was assassinated in 1768 by Pottawatomi Indians paid by Louis Chevallier, a French trader at St. Joseph, who owed Hambuck a large sum of money. His murder was mentioned by Gage in a report to the Earl of Hillsborough, the British minister responsible for the American colonies, an indication of how rare such an event was. In the author's biographical file of over ten thousand individuals involved in western commerce, such killings were very rare between 1764 and 1767.

Gage's mention of Hambuck's murder to Hillsborough coincided with an August 1768 report from Johnson to Hillsborough in which he opposed transfer of Indian affairs to the colonies. If the colonies mishandled the Indians, Johnson feared that the Indians would take revenge on the traders, who regardless of the risk would continue to enter into Indian country in their fanatical desire to make money. Killings of traders would cause trouble for all parties. The implication was that the traders were in great danger.

Regardless of the facts, Hillsborough was convinced by Johnson that the Indians were on the verge of open warfare because of the land issue and other complaints. Gage believed that whatever problems existed with the Indians were caused by the Pennsylvania and Virginia settlers on the frontier who abused them. Gage was more concerned that the Indians be compensated and the settlers be punished. He informed Johnson that he would provide as many soldiers as needed to enforce the laws and protect the Indians. Governor Penn of Pennsylvania promised Gage that he would ask the Pennsylvania Assembly to pass new laws to control the settlers who were taking over the land west of the boundary established in 1763; however, he would need British troops to enforce the laws.

Life on the frontier was dangerous, subject to Indian attacks at any time. The colonial traders could survive in the wilderness only with the consent of the tribes. The tribes allowed the traders on Indian land because of their keen desire for European goods. At a 1760 conference with Croghan at Fort Pitt, the Indians asked that traders be allowed to come to their villages. Croghan agreed based on a promise that the traders would not be harmed.

The British government wanted to protect the Indians from unscrupulous traders who used rum to corrupt them. The Indians preferred to deal with the French traders, many of whom were part Indian and understood the Indian ways. The Indian culture did not change greatly despite the new luxuries; it merely became easier to survive. Hunting and farming were easier with guns and new tools. When the Indians visited the trading posts, rum provided an enjoyable respite from the annual routine of summer farming and winter hunting.

Even before the Europeans arrived the Indian culture was quite complex. They had developed an economy based on agriculture and hunting and traded extensively among tribes. Indian life was determined by the need to move to hunting grounds every fall. Near the summer villages deer and other game were soon eradicated, and the tribes had to find new areas for hunting. While the summer villages were permanent and the land improved over the years to increase crop yields, the winter village locations changed frequently as the game was exhausted.

The colonists viewed the Indians as a valuable market for British manufactured goods and colonial rum. They also saw them as obstacles in the way of land settlement. The colonial settlers wanted the Indians to leave so that the colonists could farm the land.

The evidence shows that both French and colonial traders conducted business with little risk because the Indians welcomed the new luxuries they brought: firearms, cloth, kettles, steel traps, and other European products. Despite French intrigue and lies about the colonial traders, some Indians continued to trade with them because the colonists offered better prices for their furs and provided large quantities of rum.

The high value of the merchandise traded or given to the Indians established their dependence on the trade goods. Trading was no longer a luxury but a necessary function for survival. Had the French not continually stirred up trouble with the Indians, the trade might have been more peaceful and gratifying to everyone concerned. If the Indians chose to resist, a few thousand soldiers and a few hundred traders could not control the West.

# 2

# The French Farmers

The French in Illinois and Canada controlled the American frontier throughout the seventeenth century and until 1760, when the French surrendered to the British in Canada. Even though they had lost the Seven Years' War by 1763, the French regained control of the fur trade after that. The power of the British army and the colonials did not extend much farther than the gates to the forts. The British merchants supplanted the French as sources of goods in Canada, but the French merchants in New Orleans continued to link France and the Illinois traders.

The leaders of the French population in Canada in 1760 were 130 *seigneurs*, 100 gentlemen and bourgeoisie, 125 notable merchants, and 50 legal and medical professionals. The French seigneurs and the former British military officers established ties, and marriages were common between the officers and the Frenchwomen of this upper class. British and French merchants also established commercial links, becoming interdependent. British merchants had the capital and the contacts in London needed to obtain merchandise, and the French had the means of moving goods to the Indians in return for furs.

The French in Canada had little interest in expanding agricultural settlements beyond the St. Lawrence Valley except for farms on both sides of the Detroit River and a few at Michilimackinac to supply provisions to the fur traders. Their primary interest was fur, not land, and the traders feared that farmers would disturb the Indians and harm the fur trade.

The French traders and their colonial competitors had customers other than the Indians on the frontier. British army officers and French farmers were both good customers for fine-quality liquor to bolster their strength to face the rigors of the frontier. In June 1762 James Sterling sent two canoes from Detroit to Niagara to pick up six barrels of brandy, six barrels of shrub (a beverage made of fruit juice, sugar, and rum or brandy), and four kegs of cordials (aromatic, syrupy alcoholic beverages). Captain Donald Campbell, the commandant at Detroit, provided a special pass for the shipment, intended for the army and the French.

After 1760 the colonial merchants were the first to exploit the Canadian market. In February 1761 Bernard Gratz of Philadelphia had his agent, Preston Paine, in Quebec selling the garrison wine, leather breeches, and shoes. Daniel Clark of Philadelphia sent two cargoes to Quebec in March 1761 worth £600 Pennsylvania ($69,000), including calico, cotton, dishes, spoons, basins, tankards, mugs, teapots, buttons, buckles, "cutteau knives," pistol caps, knives, razors, scissors, iron, candles, and wine. Fishwick and Pentlington, also from Philadelphia, went to Quebec with several tons of merchandise in the spring of 1761.

The colonial merchants in Quebec and Montreal were involved in a variety of enterprises in Quebec early in 1763. Baynton and Wharton had plans for exporting wheat from Canada, but its agents, John Collins and William Govet, could not locate a vessel in Quebec. Therefore, a ship loaded with goods was sent from Philadelphia for the wheat in the spring. Even then, legal difficulties had to be surmounted. Collins cautioned Baynton and Wharton to claim that the ship from Philadelphia was bound for Salem, not Canada, because the lemons and claret wine on board were not legal exports to Canada. Baynton and Wharton were advised to ship the illegal products as prize goods (merchandise captured from the French). Meanwhile, in Quebec Collins and Govet were buying large quantities of wheat produced on the small family farms along the St. Lawrence River. Collins and Govet purchased eleven thousand bushels of wheat at 3s. 9d. and 4s. Quebec per bushel ($308,000) from Thomas Story, Joseph Horton Jr., John White, and others who had obtained it from French merchants.

Some wheat came from Detroit, the major agricultural settlement in the Great Lakes area. Detroit was founded in the spring of 1701 by Sieur de Lamothe Cadillac, who reached the area via the Ottawa River because of the danger from the Iroquois on Lake Ontario. The French measured off a square arpent (nearly an acre) and built a church, a warehouse, and homes surrounded by a twelve-foot-high stockade. The wives of Cadillac and Alphonse de Tonti, his deputy, arrived a few months later. The development was opposed by the Jesuits and the Montreal fur merchants, who feared that an agricultural colony at Detroit would interfere with the fur trade and with attempts to convert the Indians to Catholicism.

The houses at Detroit were small. In 1774 St. Andre sold a log house that measured sixteen by seventeen feet. The largest houses in sale documents measured twenty by twenty feet. Some were made of logs, and others were frame construction using white oak. The roofs were bark. Glass windowpanes were available after 1750.

The first crop of wheat was sown in October 1702 as winter wheat and harvested the following July. The farmers harvested the grain using hand scythes. Another crop of wheat sown in the spring of 1703 was not as good as the winter wheat. In the following years the wheat was sown on September 20. Indian corn that was sown in May grew to eight feet high and was harvested on August 20. Cadillac had 12 arpents cultivated for the government, and each soldier had a garden. The plan for 1702 was to sow 60 arpents with corn and plant a garden of 1 arpent with fruit trees and vines.

Detroit was considered a dangerous outpost, and even offers of free land in 1708 did not attract newcomers. By 1710 there were only sixty-three white men in Detroit in addition to the army. By 1716 the attempts to create a farming community had failed, and all of the land grants were revoked. The few settlers who had come began to leave Detroit, reducing it to a trading post.

Conditions improved in Detroit, however, as the Indians became more dependent on trade, and in 1730 settlement began again. Immigrants from Montreal and discharged soldiers received land grants. In the 1740s the Jesuit missionaries operated a farm, a forge, and a store near Detroit. They traded blankets, gunpowder, lead, iron, vermillion, cutlery, guns, cotton, wampum (beads), and trinkets to Indians, and lumber, iron, grain, brandy, and hides to the settlers.

In 1747 a proclamation offered every man who settled in Detroit a spade, an axe, a plow, two augers, and other tools on credit. In addition settlers received a cow to be returned after she had a calf, a sow under the same condition, and seed to be repaid in three years. Women and children would be provided with rations for one year, which was then extended to eighteen months in 1750. If the men entered the fur trade instead of farming, however, they had to forfeit all of the implements and the land.

Most of the settlers in 1749 were recruited in Quebec from good farming communities. Each new family of two or more people received a plow, two oxen, two cows, a horse, and a pig. The cattle came from Illinois. Each man received an axe, a hoe, a plane, an iron tool, an adze, a one-inch auger, a pit saw, a cross-cut saw, a stone-cutters saw, a kettle, two pairs of shoes, a gun, eight pounds of gunpowder, twenty-four pounds of lead, a tomahawk, a pair of leggings, and a four-point blanket. The tools were for use in building their homes, barns, and stables. Each person received rations for a year.

In 1749 twenty-two settlers were awarded land, but only ten came to Detroit and settled there. Each grant in 1749 was 120 arpents (about 100 acres) with 3-arpent frontage on the Detroit River. The farms were adjacent on a 2.5-mile stretch along the river and are still part of the legal description of land in downtown Detroit!

Many settlers came from Montreal, Quebec, and Three Rivers. Some, if not all, had previously visited Detroit as canoe men. Those granted 120 arpents in 1749 were Louis Gervais St. Louis, St. Etienne, Drouillard, Lafeuillade, Baptiste LeBeau, Bequette, Rení LeBeaux, Contois dit Coussin, François LeBeaux, Pillet, Des Lignes, St. Jacques, Jean Leduc, Pierre Descompes dit Labadie, Charles Campeault, Pataine, Lareine, St. Louis, and Lafleur. Most of these families came from Montreal.

In July 1749 Louis Plichon arrived in Detroit from Montreal with his wife and two children to occupy land granted to him. He was granted 120 square arpents along with tools and rations for a year. A brother who came to stay with them in 1750 received the meat from two deer, two pounds of flour, a hoe, an axe, a plow, a scythe, two augers, a sow, a cow, an ox, seven chickens, eighty roofing nails, four pounds of powder, and six pounds of lead. The brother also received seed to be repaid later, twenty bushels of wheat, and a bushel of corn.

The French farm families were productive. Louis Plichon's son, François, was baptized on November 26, 1749. In September 1750 the census lists Plichon as having three children under age fifteen. According to baptism records, an average of twenty children were born each year from 1760 to 1770 on the south shore of the Detroit River. During that period slightly more than twenty families were living there. A similar number of families lived on the north shore. Despite infant mortality, the average family consisted of a couple with four children.

Land records reveal the makeup of French farm families. Pierre Dinan, his wife, and six children received eight rations; Jean-Baptiste Drouillard, his wife, and eight children received ten rations; Jean-Baptiste Lebeau, who had lived in Detroit, sent for his wife to qualify for a land grant but received only three rations for his wife and two children because he was previously a resident. The wife of Pierre Becquet and her three children were granted land even though her husband was in Illinois. Because he died before returning, she lost the land but received four rations while awaiting his return. François Leduc dit Persil, who arrived from Montreal, received only one ration for himself plus land and tools. Louis Villers, a soldier married at Detroit, was granted land in 1749. Rení Lebeau, a bachelor, arrived from Montreal and received land and tools. In 1751 Lebeau went back to Montreal, married, and returned with his wife, who received an additional ration.

Forty-five marriages were recorded in the area in the 1770s. Most French girls married at age sixteen or seventeen. Some were only fourteen or fifteen because of the great demand for wives on the frontier. Men were usually twenty or older. Few of the men could read or write, and they signed marriage records with an X. The French seldom intermarried with the Indians. Of eighty-two marriages recorded from 1761 to 1781 on the south shore of Detroit, only two were with half-Indian women, and one was with a "pani"—a Pawnee captive—to legitimize the children. None was with pure-blooded Huron Indians. Under rules set by Cadillac, French soldiers and Canadians were permitted to marry Indian maidens after they had become Catholic and learned French. Indian girls lived with soldiers and settlers but they seldom married.

By 1750 the number of settlers around Detroit had increased to more than five hundred. More settlers arrived in 1750–51, and there were twenty-five farms on the south shore of the Detroit River, and the same number on the north shore. Twenty-three more grants were made in 1752, but few grants were made later because of a shortage of supplies.

The grants made to favored people were larger, with a 6- or 9-arpent frontage and the same 40-arpent depth. The former commandant of Detroit received a grant that measured 12 arpents by 40 arpents, four times the size of a normal farm.

Some settlers sold their farms after a short time. Alexis Delisle dit Bienvenue received a grant on November 24, 1751, and sold it to Charles Bouron in 1752. The Delisle family was in the fur trade later. Pierre Reaume received a grant of 120 square arpents in 1751, and the Reaume family became well established in Detroit within the next three decades. This farm later passed through Reaume's daughter, the wife of Jacques Duperon Baby, to the Baby family. After her husband died she continued to live on the farm and willed it to her son François, who built a house in 1811.

Some land went to merchants in Detroit who fulfilled the requirement of establishing a home by hiring a family to till the land. Few immigrants to Detroit came from France. Most were discharged soldiers or farmers from lower Canada and very poor. British army officers remarked that the French were destitute when the army arrived in 1760. Providing rations to the French army had left little for the farmers. In 1766 the French complained that more than half of them could not pay their taxes. The fault lay with the settlers themselves according to the pastor of the church in Detroit. He complained in 1768 that half the French householders had used their wheat to buy liquor and did not have enough to feed their families through the winter.

In 1760 Detroit had 300 houses and 2,500 inhabitants. There were 70 or 80 houses in the fort, laid out in regular streets. Outside the fort were farms stretching for ten miles on both sides of the river. The river at Detroit was nine hundred yards wide and very deep. Although the primary industry was the fur trade, agriculture was adequate in the Detroit area to feed the populace and helped provide food for the men trading in Michilimackinac and the other posts on the Great Lakes.

The fur trade also provided the farm families with a source of cash in the wages paid to the canoe men, the sons of farm families, who would take the seasonal job for one or two years in order to help their family. Nearly every Canadian family had at least one member in the fur trade. Planting and harvesting could be done before and after the summer's voyage. Farm families had little opportunity to sell produce, and employment in the fur trade was the only significant source of cash. The cash was used to buy luxuries such as sugar and coffee as well as metal tools and other essentials that could not be produced on the farm. In 1766 Montreal merchants complained that restraining trade with the Indians to the posts would result in forfeiture of more than £2,000 sterling by the "country people in this district who usually make the voyage between spring and harvest."

The wages of the canoe men varied with their experience. The men signed contracts, many of which have survived. Each contract carried the name of the lead man in the canoe, the *voyageur*, and the names of some of the paddlers. The farm boys were called *mangeurs de lard* ("fat eaters") because they were unaccustomed to the spartan diet of the voyageurs. The farm boys signed on to paddle the canoes for a few years. Experienced men, the *avant* (the man in front) and the *gouvernails* (the steersmen at the rear), who appeared on the licenses for three or more years were paid 200 or 300 livres ($2,000 to $3,000). The middlemen, the farm boys, received as little as 125 livres ($1,250). Payment was made at the end of the voyage. While a full crew was needed to paddle the heavily loaded canoes upstream, fewer men were needed for the return to Montreal. Therefore one or two men were left behind at Detroit to pursue their fortunes on the frontier. For a one-way trip a paddler named LeBeau was paid 150 livres, of which 100 livres was paid to his father and 50 livres to LeBeau himself. In 1768 a steersman received £8 7s. sterling ($1,670) for a round trip and a front man received the same. The total wages for one canoe were £66 ($13,200) plus provisions and a clothing allowance that included *métasses* (moccasins) and a loin cloth.

British officers accused the French farmers of not cultivating the soil, instead preferring fishing, hunting, and trading to make their living. The officers were accustomed to farmers who rented land in England and worked constantly to improve its fertility. In contrast many of the French settlers were former canoe men quite willing to leave their farms for a profitable voyage paddling a canoe for a trader. Others who had been soldiers and tradesmen at the fort also were unaccustomed to the hard labor of farming. Furthermore, much of the land given to the new settlers was poor quality, and those who wished to farm soon moved to other parcels.

The French farmers in Detroit began producing sizable surpluses that were available for sale to the British army and the fur traders. In 1750 a thousand acres cultivated in Detroit by sixty farmers produced 52 tons of wheat, at six bushels per acre. The amount of flour obtained from grinding wheat was nearly equal to the weight of the wheat. In 1766 twenty-seven French farmers (from nearly half of the sixty farms in the area) offered to provide rations to the British garrison including 279 hundredweight of flour (16 tons, or nearly a third of the harvest). Because each soldier needed a pound of flour per day, the quantity offered was enough to feed eighty-five troops for a year. The French price of £1 13s. 4d. New York ($170) per hundredweight was exorbitant compared with the price of less than 17s. Pennsylvania ($98) in Philadelphia in 1768. The French also engaged to supply 1,340 pounds of pork to vary the garrison diet of salt beef, a trifling amount but according to the French all that they could spare after their own needs. The average farmer provided a half ton of flour and a few bushels of peas. Because the market was limited, the farmers generally grew only enough for their personal use and did spend most of their time hunting and fishing.

In 1773 only 1,424 arpents were under cultivation on the south shore of the Detroit River. Most of the farmers cultivated only the 18 arpents near the shore, leaving untilled the remaining 102 arpents farther inland. However this was still more than the colonial settler in Pennsylvania cultivated during this period—10 acres of a 40-acre farm. The amount of land under cultivation was determined by the acreage that a single horse and plow could work, as well as by the needs of a family. The French families were often larger than the typical colonial frontier family, and they cultivated more land as their families grew.

The yearly rental of the land grants was a quarter bushel of wheat per arpent of river frontage and a quarter bushel of wheat for each square arpent. An average farm with a 3-arpent frontage and 40-arpent depth paid 10.75 bushels. These taxes were due on November 11 each year. When the British came the tax was two cords of wood for each arpent of frontage, still a relatively small amount. In 1765 the tax was changed to 10s. New York ($60) per arpent of river frontage but it could be paid in firewood valued at 8s. per cord. In 1768 taxes were reduced to three quarters of a cord (6s. New York) for 1 arpent of frontage and two cords for 3 arpents.

The land away from the river was often woods and swamps and was cleared later. The land near the river was usually meadow and easy to farm. Both oxen and horses were used to pull the plows. The farms included orchards of apples, pears, and cherries. In 1782 a thousand barrels of apple cider were produced. The grain was ground at gristmills powered by windmills thirty feet high and twenty feet in diameter. The land around Detroit was too flat to harness waterpower.

Neighbors often joined in bees to haul logs, thresh grain, or raise a building. Communal family baking was done in clay ovens located in the open. In 1751 an oven was large enough for twenty-four one-pound loaves, enough for as many as six families for a day. Houses were surrounded by high picket fences to protect children, cattle, hogs, and chickens from animals.

Farms were laid out as narrow strips 3 arpents wide because with no roads the river frontage was needed. When a settler had cleared all 40 arpents, he was sometimes given an additional 40 arpents behind the original grant. When these farms were divided among children, they became narrow ribbons because everyone wanted river frontage.

By 1763 the original farms had been divided. Usually five farms were carved from the original 120 arpents. There were sixty families on the south shore in 1768, almost equal to the number on the north shore. The British were reluctant to grant land around Detroit because they considered it Indian property. The Indians did give some land to the French in this period.

Some of the farms were cultivated by sharecroppers. Jean-Baptiste Goyau worked the farm owned by the Huron Mission, established by the Jesuits to convert the Indians to Christianity. The mission made a contract with Goyau to sharecrop their farm on Bois Blanc, an island located in the Detroit River south of Detroit. The term of six years could be terminated on a one-year notice. Goyau agreed to move his family to the farm in September 1743. The mission supplied Goyau with seed and they shared the produce of that seed equally; he was also expected to share any other crops he sowed, except for some corn for his personal use. Also, Goyau agreed to plow 2 arpents for the mission so that the missionaries could plant corn for their own use.

As part of the agreement to work the land, Goyau was provided with farm implements, a cart, and harness. All of these were to be returned in like condition at the end of the lease, as were the same number of animals that he began with plus one half of any newborn animals. Goyau received a new plow complete with wheels, a cart, a new sled, three oxen, three cows, a yearling heifer, and two mares. He later received three Illinois heifers to replace three cows that died or were killed. He agreed to maintain an enclosure and a pasture for the animals and was permitted to use them for carting and plowing for the Indians and other Frenchmen. The animals were to be loaned to the mission whenever they were needed for hauling and carting. Goyau agreed to haul forty cords of wood for the mission and its forge. He received 6.5 bushels of peas, 5 bushels of oats, and 14.5 bushels of wheat for seed. An equal amount of seed was to be returned at the end of the lease.

Madame Goyau, the sharecropper's wife, was to do laundry and the baking for the mission for 100 livres per year ($1,000, less than a paddler received for one trip). She received a shirt, three quarts of brandy, two pairs of *molleton* (flannel-type) leggings, 2 bushels of peas, six blankets, and one pair of other leggings.

When another farmer rented the farm in 1748 he received 30 bushels of wheat seed and 4 bushels of peas, an indication that the amount of land devoted to raising wheat had doubled. He was obliged to plow 3 rather than 2 arpents for the missionaries for planting corn. His wife was also paid 100 livres for laundry and baking.

In 1750 the farm produced 1,050 sheaves of wheat (150 bushels). Forty bushels were stored for seed for the next year, and the mission received 55 bushels as its share. The farm also produced 40 bushels of corn, 16 bushels of oats, and 2 bushels of peas.

When the British arrived in 1760 they found a prosperous farming community. The major issue in 1763 was how to control the Indians disaffected by the French. The British had already made an effort to win over the French in Detroit. In April 1760 the commandant, Captain William Turnbull, appointed Philippe Dejean to hold court and settle civil disputes. DeJean was one of four French traders who petitioned Jehu Hay in September 1767 concerning the competition from Illinois. The other petitioners included Jean-Baptiste Chapaton, Duperon Baby, and Pierre Fleurimont, leading traders in Detroit; Isaac Todd, described in the record as a Jew; Henry VanSchaack, a Dutchman from Albany; and four British merchants, Thomas Williams, William Edgar, Richard McNeal, and Samuel Tyms.

But France was still at war with England in 1762. A conspiracy began at a council between the Indians and the French in May or June 1762 to plan an attack on the British in 1763. Attending the conference were some of the principal French inhabitants of Detroit (Navarre, Augustin Sicotte, Currie, Baptiste Campeau, François and Baptist Meloshe, Sancho P. Obain, Domelte, Pero Barth, and Louisan Denter). The French themselves would not fight with the Indians because of the risk to their families and property, but they were happy to pass on the responsibility by telling Pontiac that they would supply ammunition and young Frenchmen disguised as Indians to fight with them.

Major Henry Gladwin, the British commandant, had a serious problem with the French in Detroit. In a letter to Governor-General Jeffrey Amherst he stated, "that one half of the settlement merit a gibbet and the other half ought to be decimated." On May 12, 1763, four days after the siege of Detroit began, Pontiac sent five Frenchmen, Minni Chesne, Jacques Godfroy, Charles Beaubien, Chauvin, and Labadie Jr., to arouse the Indians in Illinois to fight the English too, and to support Pontiac and the Indians in their uprising. On their way, at the mouth of the Miami River, the Frenchmen met John Welch, who had two canoes of fur. Aided by the Indians, they captured Welch and divided his goods. Welch was later murdered by the Ottawas, who double-crossed the French and seized their stolen fur. Four other colonial prisoners were taken by Chesne and Godfroy to Illinois. Later, Chesne, Godfroy, and the Indians attacked the garrisons at Miami and Ouiatanon.

Although the merchandise in Detroit was saved, traders coming into the post were caught unawares and captured or murdered by the Indians as they approached the town. On May 13, 1763, Benjamin Chapman, a Jewish merchant on his way from Niagara with five boatloads of trading goods, was taken prisoner just outside of Detroit. On May 20, 1763, Major Thomas Smallman (a trader from Pennsylvania and a cousin of George Croghan, the Indian agent at Fort Pitt), Gershon Levy, Levy Andrew Levy, and two British employees were also taken prisoner outside Detroit.

Help for Detroit was soon on the way. On June 30, 1763, a ship arrived in Detroit with reinforcements of fifty men under Captain Dalzell as well as 120 barrels of provisions and ammunition. In July a sortie resulted in soldiers being killed and wounded. Otherwise, the siege in Detroit did not go badly for the British. Despite the siege the soldiers at the fort remained in good health. Only one was killed and twelve wounded during the sixty-four day siege that ended July 12, 1763, whereas twenty Indians were killed and thirty wounded. Gladwin, however, was completely disgusted with the situation in Detroit. In a bitter letter to Sir William Johnson, Gladwin stated that he had gone to Detroit against his will, as he foresaw what would happen. Results were expected that he could not achieve. He was forced into a bad situation and then abandoned, and he blamed the French scoundrels living in Detroit.

Much of the malevolent French influence came from Illinois. In August 1767 French officers lied to the Indians in Illinois that the British had given them poisoned rum. The French also claimed that the British were infecting the Indians with smallpox. Convinced, the Shawnee Indians from Ohio planned to go to Illinois to get ammunition from the French in order to attack the British. However Pontiac opposed any action. Persisting in their intrigue, the French from Canada, Detroit, and Illinois followed the Indians to their hunting grounds and prevented colonial trading by deceiving the Indians. The Illinois French obtained some financial assistance from Paris and from the Spanish who nominally ruled Louisiana, the area west of the Mississippi River.

Tranquility returned to Detroit by 1768. The population was 530 people—100 men, 80 women, 200 boys, and 150 girls. There were also 33 slaves. By 1780 there were 100 families on the south shore with 600 people. A similar number lived on the north shore. When the Revolution broke out the British provided lavish gifts to the Indians to attack the colonial frontier.

By 1778 the British commander at Detroit complained that the farms around Detroit were small and the families large, and that the young men became canoe men and itinerant traders. He stated that the settlement at Detroit did not increase much from 1766 to 1776 and blamed their poor farming methods on the laziness of the backward French (compared with English farmers), who had every advantage of nature but were unable to see the opportunity. Wood was at hand, and within a few hours enough fish could be caught for several families, but no one had a seine for fishing. Hunting for birds and deer was easy for them. He wrote that the good soil needed little care, the climate was agreeable, and the water was clear. Because of the lack of pastures, animals had starved during harsh winters. He described the French houses as log or frame with a shingle roof and stated that each family had a carriage.

The French lack of interest in farming was also fostered by the lack of markets for their produce. The British army in Detroit and Michilimackinac were their major markets as the cost of shipping the produce to Montreal was prohibitive. Conversely, the French farmers at Detroit were a market for British and colonial goods. They paid for the merchandise with farm products that were in turn sold by the colonial and British merchants to the garrison for bills of exchange or to traders who paid in fur. Corn, peas, and other produce were shipped to Michilimackinac to provide food for the traders traveling to the northwest.

As the prime source of furs moved farther northwest of Lake Superior, Detroit became a British military post preventing American occupation of the Great Lakes and a farm community supplying provisions to the ever-increasing numbers of fur traders at Michilimackinac and northwest of Lake Superior. In addition, the farm boys found employment in the trade with the Indians during the summer, providing a needed source of cash for the families.

## SUGGESTED READINGS

W. J. Eccles, *France in America* (1990).
Marcel Trudel, *The Beginnings of New France, 1524–1663* (1973).

# 3

# The French Traders

The most profitable source of furs was the area surrounding the Great Lakes that had been part of French Canada. In 1760 this land was opened to British and colonial merchants, who perceived a golden opportunity to profit from a trade previously closed to them. But a small group of French merchants controlled trade in Canada, and the best that the incoming British and colonial merchants could do was to create business relationships with the French.

The French in Canada had established an effective process for bringing fur from the frontier to Montreal. The French in New Orleans had created a similar organization. Working for the merchants were French traders who had courted the Indians since the seventeenth century, buying their furs and selling them to French merchants in Canada and Illinois. Half of the furs went down the Mississippi River to New Orleans and then on to France, providing French hatmakers the fur to supply the European hat market. The other half went to Montreal. After 1760 these furs were exported to England to British hatmakers who competed with the Continental hatters.

The French traders were especially successful because they treated the Indians fairly and with respect. The French had been dealing with the Indians since the seventeenth century and in many instances had formed ties that dated back several generations. The French traders frequently took Indian wives—"country wives"—in addition to their wives in Montreal. After a century and a half of contact, many of the traders were of mixed blood.

The children of the mixed marriages bore the French names of their fathers and learned both languages from birth, giving them a tremendous advantage over the colonial traders who came later.

In contrast, the British army did not treat the Indians well at the forts. One of the leading complaints of the Indians was the lack of respect from the British army, possibly because the soldiers had nothing to gain from the Indians. Colonial traders angered the Indians by using rum to cheat them. Another cause of friction between the Indians and the colonists was the continual French efforts from both Illinois and Montreal to maintain their competitive edge in the fur trade. The pivotal point was instigating Pontiac's Uprising in 1763. To control the market, the French encouraged the Indians to resist the colonial traders, even to the extent of inspiring the uprising and supplying them with arms, ammunition, and provisions. The French effort to regain control of the fur trade in 1763 was successful. Pontiac's Uprising had a major impact on the fur trade. Before it, as many as 180 colonial traders, 24 Jewish traders, and 40 British Canadian traders have been identified annually. After the uprising, the numbers dropped sharply and fewer than 100 non-French traders per year have been identified, mostly in New York.

The French continued to encourage the Indian resentment in order to keep the colonists out and maintain their monopoly of trade. In March 1765 the Pottawatomis at Detroit reported that some Frenchmen, including the substantial merchants Godfroi and Maisonville, were encouraging the Miami Indians to attack the colonists. A few months later, in July, Dr. Richard Shuckburgh, a surgeon at Detroit and friend of Sir William Johnson, reported that even though the Indians wanted a peaceful trade with the British and the colonists, the French continued to urge them to resist. The French motivation in stirring up the Indians was to prevent the newcomers from competing for the fur. Much of the antagonism was created by French merchants in Detroit.

The ill feeling continued in 1767 when French traders left Detroit illegally without passes and went to Indian towns on the Wabash and Miami Rivers. The traders, including Lorrain, LaMotte, Potdevin, Capasin, Bartholomi, Bergen, and Richarville, easily succeeded in excluding the colonial traders. All of the efforts of the British army, the Indian Department, and the colonists were unsuccessful, and the French traders from Illinois and Montreal dominated the fur trade by 1768.

French traders obtained supplies and sold their fur in Montreal. Although the main port of entry to Canada was Quebec, ships could navigate the St. Lawrence River as far as Montreal. As soon as the river was free of ice in the spring, ships from Great Britain, New York, and Philadelphia moved up it. In 1768 fifteen ships arrived in Quebec from Britain; seven from southern Europe, Africa, and the West Indies; and seventeen from the thirteen colonies. The vessels from Britain averaged 150 tons and were full-rigged ships. The smaller ones from the colonies averaged 60 tons and were schooners and sloops. The seven from the other areas averaged 100 tons, both ships and schooners.

Ships that arrived before the river was clear waited at Halifax, Nova Scotia, and usually headed upriver in a convoy. Before the annual convoy, daring ship captains chanced sailing to Quebec to deliver their cargoes first. The merchants who received this early merchandise sold it at higher prices before the market was glutted.

In 1768 imports to Quebec from Britain included 195 tons of wine, 2 tons of tea, 7 tons of gunpowder, and a wide variety of manufactured goods. Usually about 30 tons of gunpowder (valued at about £9,000 New York, or $1,134,000) came from England each year. The wine and tea were for the French market while the gunpowder was traded to the Indians. The manufactured goods were for both the French and the Indians.

From the West Indies came 45,000 gallons of molasses and 150 hundredweight of sugar. The thirteen colonies sent 250,000 gallons of rum (worth £22,500 New York, or $2,835,000) and 3,000 bushels of salt. The salt was used to preserve beef for army rations and the rum was traded to the Indians.

The ships returned from Canada to southern Europe, Africa, Britain, the West Indies, and the thirteen colonies. The most important American export was fur and deerskin. Shipment of furs to England from Quebec was accomplished by a few ships before the ice blocked the river. In 1764 eight vessels (the *Ranger*, the *General Murray*, the *Canada*, the *London*, the *Nancy*, the *Little William*, the *Eltham*, and the *Royal George*) took 91,000 beaver, 30,000 martin, and 25,000 raccoon pelts and 15,000 deerskins. These shipments were the majority of the furs and skins exported from Quebec that year.

The French used rivers and lakes to move merchandise to the frontier and to return with furs. The St. Lawrence River was deep enough for seagoing vessels to move westward as far as Montreal. The French and, later, the British also built sailing ships on the lower Great Lakes. The schooner *Huron* was built on Navy Island in the Niagara River in 1761 and the sloop *Michigan*, in 1762. These armed vessels provided secure communication between Niagara and Detroit.

For the most part the French adopted the Indian canoe as a means of transport in Canada. Two types of birch-bark canoes were in common use—the master canoe and the Northwest canoe. The master canoe, which measured 35 to 40 feet long, 4 to 5 feet wide, and 2 to 3 feet deep, was used both on the lakes and on the Ottawa River routes. Paddled by up to eight men with two passengers, its capacity was 65 packs of from 90 to 100 pounds each, for a total load of 3 or 4 tons. On a trip up the Ottawa River, a canoe also carried 600 pounds of biscuit; 200 pounds of pork; 3 bushels of peas; 2 oilcloths to protect the goods from the weather; a sail and rigging; an axe; a towline; a kettle; a sponge for bailing; and gum, birch bark, and watape, a gummy substance used by Indians to seal the seams when a canoe was repaired. These provisions would last for ten weeks. In 1768 one master canoe carried eight men, 20 barrels of "de Boisson" liquor, 400 pounds of gunpowder, 1,400 pounds of ball and shot, and 12 fusils. Another canoe carried twelve men with 110 gallons of rum, 110 gallons of wine, 800 pounds of gunpowder, 1,400 pounds of ball and shot, and 6 fusils.

The rough wear on the master canoes, which cost £15 in Montreal, limited their use to a maximum of two years, and often only a year. The number of paddlers was apportioned according to the weight carried and the direction— with or against the current. Moving north on the Ottawa River the canoes carried at least six paddlers; moving south with the current, their number was reduced to four or five. Operating the canoes was hard work. Each night the canoes were beached and completely unloaded.

Portages between navigable streams were sometimes made using carts or horses, or the loads might be carried by Indian porters, as at Niagara Falls and on the Wabash route. However, the packs usually were carried on the backs of the canoe men. A sling was placed across a man's forehead to support one pack on his back. Novices carried a single 90-pound load and made many trips, but experienced men carried one or two additional packs placed atop the first to reduce the number of portages. Each man would have to carry at least six packs to the next stream, and the old hands were able to carry it all in two or three trips. The canoe was removed from the water immediately and allowed to dry as long as possible. It was the last item portaged because the drier the canoe, the lighter it was to carry.

For the trade northwest of Lake Superior a smaller canoe was used: 24 to 28 feet long, about 5 feet wide, and up to 2 feet deep. These canoes were paddled by four men and carried from 1.5 to 2 tons. Major Rogers estimated the average value of a Northwest canoe's cargo at £450 New York (£283.10 sterling, or $56,700) and listed a sample cargo:

18 bales of stroud, blankets, frieze, coats, bed gowns, coarse calicoes, linen shirts, leggings, ribbons, beads, vermillion, and garters

9 kegs of gunpowder

1 keg of flint steels and gun screws

10 kegs of British brandy

4 cases of ironwork and cutlery

1 box of silver work and wampum

2 cases of guns

2 bales of brass kettles

2 cases of looking glasses and combs

5 bales of tobacco

10 bags of lead buckshot and ball ammunition

The routes from Montreal to the Great Lakes used by the French were the Ottawa River, leading to Lake Huron, and the St. Lawrence River, to Lake Ontario and Lake Erie. The northernmost route, the Ottawa River, was used in the beginning of the seventeenth century by French explorers, followed quickly by French fur traders bringing European goods to the Indians.

The route began by wagon from Montreal to La Chine. Usually the goods arrived at Montreal in May and were divided into packs and small kegs ready to be taken by the annual flotilla up the Ottawa River. The departure of the flotilla, which included up to one hundred canoes, was a gala event in eighteenth-century Canada and was marked by farewells to some men who would not return for several years.

The canoes went up the Ottawa River to Lake Nipissing, the French River, and Georgian Bay. From there they went to Michilimackinac or Lake Superior. Although the trip from La Chine to Mackinac took thirty-five to forty days it was shorter and quicker than the lake route, even though there were forty portages between Montreal and Michilimackinac. The portages were necessary around rapids as well as to move from one river or stream to another. Another advantage of the Ottawa River route compared with the Great Lakes was avoidance of the storms that periled shipping on the lakes. Also, the Ottawa route opened earlier than the lakes in spring because westerly winds clogged the Niagara River with ice.

The longer winters and tedious navigation on the St. Lawrence and Ottawa Rivers hindered the Canadians. Montreal and Quebec had average temperatures below freezing from November to March, and during that time ice blocked the waterways. The Lake Erie route was blocked by ice for nearly six months. When the ice on shallow Lake Erie broke up in the spring, large quantities of broken ice floated east. The prevailing westerly wind piled it at the east end of the lake and jammed the Niagara River. Many days of warm weather were needed to melt the accumulated ice pack.

In December 1767 when Sir William Johnson ordered Major Robert Rogers to return to Michilimackinac, he was told to take the Ottawa River route, which was generally open some time before the ice cleared from the Niagara River. The Ottawa River route remained open later than the lake route in the fall, when the time of arrival in Montreal and Quebec was crucial in order to load peltry on ships bound for Europe before the St. Lawrence froze. The Ottawa River was more reliable, an important factor because delay could mean disaster if the furs had to be held in Canada until the next spring.

Prompt action paid dividends, whereas delay could mean financial disaster; therefore all activity had to be planned with an eye on the calendar and the map. Letters from that time comment on the weather and its effect on business.

An average of 100 canoes were licensed in Canada each year to trade with the Indians. The highest total found in my research was 123 in 1767. Most of the canoes went to Detroit (from 10 to 30), Michilimackinac (20 to 30), and Illinois (10 to 20). In the spring of 1761, 47 canoes went from Montreal to the interior, 37 went to Mackinac, and 10 to Detroit. In 1764 during the aftermath of Pontiac's Uprising, only 19 were licensed. After 1768 about a dozen went to Lake Superior and beyond.

Both British and French merchants in Canada relied on French canoe men. The merchants in Montreal, Detroit, Michilimackinac, and other posts hired *voyageurs* who steered the canoes and *engagés* who simply paddled the canoes to the interior to trade with the Indians and return with furs, often leaving one of their men to winter with the Indians to sell the remainder of the goods. The voyageurs and engagés were almost entirely French on the Ottawa River route and mostly French on the Great Lakes.

The number of Frenchmen on the frontier was limited. Fewer than 300 experienced voyageurs along with less than 600 unskilled engagés visited the Indian villages each year. The names of 370 French voyageurs and merchants who participated in the fur trade between 1760 and 1774 have been found in the records. Only a few remained in the trade for more than eight years. Some of the voyageurs, many of whom had Indian wives, were offspring of mixed parentage, called métis. The only non-French personnel mentioned in the records were a few Indians.

Colonel John Bradstreet, the British quartermaster in Albany in 1764, thought that the fur trade was of value only to the boatmen, including the voyageurs. Even the men who simply paddled the canoes were well paid: in Canada, £6 sterling ($1,200) or more for the summer; in Pennsylvania, £16 sterling ($3,200) for four months, plus rations; and in New York, more than £12 sterling ($2,400) per season in addition to food and clothing. Many took a trip or two to earn ready cash and then returned to other employment. These men were relatively assured of making money, while the traders risked both their money and their lives.

The new engagé was called a *mangeur de lard*, or "fat eater," because he was not accustomed to the rigorous diet made necessary by the small amount of provisions carried in canoes on the long trips west. The illiterate young country boys had little time for debauchery because hard work filled their lives. I have tabulated the names and employment of over 2,000 individual engagés during the period from 1760 to 1774. Considering that only about 600 unskilled men operated 100 canoes in a single year, this data is ample for statistical purposes. The engagés seldom served more than three years. Of the 2,000, less than 10 percent took four or more voyages during the fifteen years between 1760 and 1774, leading to the conclusion that the great majority of engagés were not professional and did not make the fur trade their lifetime occupation.

Most licenses contain the names of four or fewer paddlers, indicating that the canoes seldom carried more than six men. As young men reached an age when they could sign on, they often joined up with the same voyageur who had hired their older brothers. The same family names were linked to the same voyageurs year after year. The wages earned by the paddlers were an essential part of the well-being of the French farm families in the St. Lawrence Valley. The extra cash paid for purchases of special products such as tea, sugar, clothing, and shoes.

The men who remained with the Indians over the winter provided them with ammunition and other expendable items. The winterers, men who would spend the winter with the Indians, were quite different in character. They were an essential link in the trade, spending the cold months in the hunting grounds trading with the Indians and coming into the posts at the beginning and end of winter to dispose of furs and obtain more merchandise. An example was Gerrit Griverat, who in April, May, October, and November of each year from 1768 to 1773 obtained supplies from Rinkin & Edgar in Detroit. Experienced men were scarce, and novices who had not previously wintered among the Indians were not successful.

The life of a winterer was not easy. He was continually beset by the hardships of cold weather, insufficient food, and hard work and was in constant danger of being robbed or killed by the Indians. The correspondence of the period is filled with robbery incidents. Many winterers adopted Indian ways and married Indian women, whose families would provide them some protection. Their children in turn became winterers and carried on the tradition of buying merchandise from the canoes that came west every spring and paying with the furs accumulated during the winter.

The winterers were a thorn in any attempt to regulate the fur trade, as many could claim to be Indians and exempt from any rules. They had great influence on the tribes with whom they lived, defeating the efforts of the British to control the tribes.

In September 1762 James Sterling sent a Frenchman, Amable Foucher, from Detroit with two canoes of merchandise to trade at St. Marys. Sterling had originally asked his clerk, Morrison, to make the trip, but he refused and Sterling discharged him. Morrison's refusal was indicative of the great dangers facing a British trader who lived with the Indians over a winter. The French were somewhat safer as they had better relations with the tribes who could not always be trusted.

The influence of the winterers gave the French merchants the upper hand in the Canadian fur trade. Even if the British and colonial merchants offered more goods for the furs, they could not compete with the French unless they also offered large quantities of rum, which was detrimental to the trade. The French favored limiting the quantity of liquor that a trader might carry but opposed any rule restricting their activity to the military posts.

The fur business was not always profitable for the winterer because of the tremendous risks. The goods that he purchased had passed through many hands, and because of the high cost of transportation and the markup needed to cover the losses of others, these products had become very expensive. Furs obtained from the Indians were sold at a low profit because, again, transportation costs had to be added before the pelts were sold in London. On the other hand, with little or no capital an adventurous young man could, with luck, net £100 sterling ($20,000) in one summer, far more than a skilled tradesman could earn in a year. Such a lucrative opportunity enticed many to risk their lives in the woods.

French voyageurs who ran away after accumulating a large debt were a continuing problem. In June 1762 Sterling wrote to Lieutenant William Lesly in Michilimackinac to collect 84 French livres ($840) from Lavoin Chevalier, who had run away from Detroit. Sterling intended to send one or two canoes to Michilimackinac and Green Bay and would send Lesly anything that he needed. Isaac Todd in Mackinac received news in 1768 that M. Robins, a winterer, had collected seven packs of fur during the season but had not come in by the end of June. Fearing that Robins and his men had drunk all the liquor, Todd sent another trader to collect whatever pelts Robins might still have. Unfortunately, Robins already owed £1,360 sterling to another merchant who had first call on any pelts that came in. Furthermore, there was fear that Robins would trade the furs to Askin, who had gone out with liquor and goods during the spring.

These runaways were called *coureurs de bois* (literally, "trappers"), or vagabonds. The unlicensed trapper was a problem before the British came to Canada. He, too, wintered with the tribes, often living with an Indian woman and adopting the native way of life. Occasionally, one would come back to the settled area of Canada and recklessly spend his accumulated profits. There were several hundred of these vagabonds among the Indians in 1762. George Croghan, the Indian agent, described them as "an idle lazy set, a parcel of renegades from Canada much worse than the Indians." General Thomas Gage described Michilimackinac in the months of June and July as being inhabited by several hundred vagabonds, "many of whom have inhabited the Indian country from twelve to thirty years, differing little from the Natives except in color, and being more addicted to vice."

Between their annual visits to the posts the Indians relied on the winterers and vagabonds as their only sources of European merchandise. Each year during the late summer or fall, the vagabonds and winterers obtained their goods in Detroit, Michilimackinac, or at other posts, then returned to their home villages and resumed trade. Although the British objected to this method and attempted to concentrate all trade to the posts, the plan never succeeded. Johnson reported to the Board of Trade that vagabonds were still dealing with the Indians even during Pontiac's Uprising.

The French vagabonds continued to be a menace to the legal trade, obtaining supplies in Illinois after the British occupied the posts on the Great Lakes in 1761. The Illinois-based vagabonds competed with the traders from the St. Lawrence and Ohio Rivers and destroyed Johnson's plans for creating a well-regulated trade centered around the garrisoned posts.

In the late 1760s the French, fearing the growth of colonial competition to their trade, stepped up their campaign to distance the Indians from the colonists. The Illinois French encouraged the Pottawatomis at St. Joseph to kill colonial traders. The French were active along the Wabash River and the Ohio River trying to drive the colonial traders out. While the French continued to trade around Lake Michigan, the colonial traders from Michilimackinac feared to visit many areas.

The Illinois French tried to divert as much fur from Canada as possible. They were determined to keep the fur trade for themselves as it was exceedingly profitable to the traders and fur was a valuable commodity exchanged for French merchandise imported to New Orleans.

Canada had been the major French source of fur before 1762. An estimate made by the French in 1761 concluded that goods worth £60,400 Quebec were bartered to the Indians in Canada in the following areas:

| | |
|---|---|
| Niagara | £18,320 |
| Detroit | £14,580 |
| Miami River | £3,330 |

*(Continued)*

| (Continued) | |
| --- | --- |
| Ouiatanon | £2,500 |
| Michilimackinac | £10,420 |
| Green Bay and Sioux | £4,170 |
| Lake Nipigon | £1,250 |
| La Pointe | £3,330 |
| St. Joseph | £2,500 |
| Total | £60,400 ($8,456,000) |

The estimated value of fur exported was £135,000 Quebec ($18,900,000), double the value of the merchandise. This estimate was on the high side. In 1765 the customs value of fur exports from Canada to Britain was £39,034 sterling (the true value was closer to £80,000 sterling, or $16,000,000), less than the French estimate. The reduced amount may have represented the inroads that the Illinois traders had made diverting the fur to New Orleans. Another estimate stated that about 100,000 beaver pelts (worth £39,000 sterling, or $7,800,000, in London) were exported annually from Canada. Adding other furs and deerskin would have doubled the total value to about £80,000 sterling ($16,000,000) annually.

The average value of the merchandise in a single canoe in 1754 was 7,000 livres, or £400 Quebec ($56,000), and an average of 100 canoes went west, with an estimated value of £40,000 Quebec ($5.6 million). The total value of the goods sent west from Montreal in 100 canoes had increased to £48,960 Quebec ($6,720,000) by 1767. Governor Guy Carleton estimated that the value increased 9,000 livres (£360 sterling, or $72,000) in 1768.

Canada and the Northwest were growing markets for British manufactured goods. The impact of the changes is revealed in the trading licenses. The licenses for fur-trading canoes show an average cargo value of £400 Quebec ($56,000). In 1769, 77 licenses were issued to trade in Canada including Detroit (22), Michilimackinac (26), and "Canada" (22), and the remainder were for points northwest of Michilimackinac. The total value of merchandise and rum carried by these canoes was £27,720 sterling (about $5,500,000), and that did not include the value of the foodstuffs provided by the farmers in Detroit.

The total value of merchandise in 121 canoes that set out from Michilimackinac between July and September 1767 was £38,964 sterling ($7,792,800). The canoes from Michilimackinac went to the north and west.

Half of the canoes went to the Mississippi River and Green Bay and 32 went to the Northwest and Lake Superior. Only 29 went to the older established areas around Lake Michigan and Lake Huron. The value of goods sent west increased from £4,170 sterling in the 1761 estimate to a remarkable £18,214 in 1767, indicating a major movement of merchandise to Illinois.

| Destination | Canoes | Value of Goods |
|---|---|---|
| Lake Superior | 18 | £7,481 |
| Northwest via Lake Superior | 14 | £5,117 |
| Lake Huron | 5 | £1,275 |
| Lake Michigan | 24 | £6,875 |
| Green Bay | 43 | £13,364 |
| Mississippi River | 17 | £4,850 |
| Total | 121 | £38,962 |

The value of merchandise sent to Lake Superior increased somewhat, from £4,580 in the 1761 estimate to £6,392 in 1767. The Lake Michigan total increased from £2,500 to £5,117. In the 1760s the value of goods at Michilimackinac itself was £18,280 sterling ($3,656,000) compared with only £10,420 Quebec in the 1761 estimate.

French traders heavily outnumbered British traders at Michilimackinac. The French traders used the Ottawa River route from Montreal, which was inaccessible to the New Yorkers and Pennsylvanians because the canoe trip via Lake Erie and Lake Huron was not economical. Even though schooners sent by Detroit merchants supplied Michilimackinac with provisions, rum, and other bulky cargo that was sold to the Montreal-based traders, the colonial traders could not compete with the Montreal traders for furs.

Most of the traders listed in petitions at Michilimackinac were French. Most of them had a history in the fur trade. Nicholas Bezze had a license for a canoe for Michilimackinac in 1767 and may have been the same Bezze selling provisions to the British army in Montreal in 1765. J. Carrignant had a license to take two canoes to Green Bay in 1767 with security provided by Frobisher. Neither Bouillerese nor Poultney have been found in other records. Louis Chabollier was a charter member of the general store at Michilimackinac and in 1766 signed a petition in Montreal requesting permission to winter. In 1769 Chabollier had a license to take a canoe with £469's worth of goods to Michilimackinac, and he continued to trade in the Lake Superior area in the early 1770s.

There were five members of the Chaboillez family in the fur trade in 1767. In that year four of them had licenses to take canoes to Mackinac. In 1770–74 Augustin Chaboillez had licenses to take canoes to Michilimackinac. In 1779 he was running a general store there.

Duperon Baby took a load of furs to Fort Pitt in 1761, which he tried to sell for goods. Although arrested for illegal trading, he was allowed to return to Detroit. He helped the Detroit garrison during Pontiac's Uprising in 1763. In 1764 he requested, but was denied, permission to trade with the Indians before the ban had been lifted. In 1765 he signed a petition in Montreal, and another in Detroit in 1767. In 1767 he had twelve canoes at Michilimackinac and traded in the Lake Superior area. In 1768 he met John Lees on Lake Ontario on the way to Niagara. During the Revolution Baby organized Indian war parties in Detroit to attack the colonists on the frontier for the British.

Nicolas Marchessaux had five canoes under his care in cooperation with Boyer and Bissonett in 1765 and signed petitions in Montreal in 1765 and 1766. He was in Michilimackinac in 1767 and secured the license of Barsolon and Hartebise. In 1772 he took two canoes to Green Bay.

Pierre LeDuc was in Michilimackinac in 1761 and in Green Bay in 1763. He supplied goods to Captain Howard in Michilimackinac in 1765. In 1766 he signed a Montreal petition and in 1767 wintered at St. Joseph, taking two canoes. In 1769 he took a canoe to Illinois.

Jean-Baptiste Guillon was a native of France and an officer in the Canadian militia in 1760 and 1767. His son took a canoe to Michilimackinac in 1769 and two canoes to Illinois in 1778 by way of St. Joseph. In 1780 he had two canoes in Michilimackinac.

Unfortunately, the name Joseph Caron was not found in any other document, but Nicholas Caron took a canoe up the lakes in 1770 and a canoe to Detroit in 1774. François Mouton took a canoe to Detroit in 1769 with security by Joseph Mouton of Montreal. In 1768 John Lees met a Mouton on his way from Oswego to Niagara. Aimable Auge signed petitions in Montreal in 1765 and 1766 to permit wintering. Michel Auge provided security for Jean-Baptiste Bissonet (Bisionette) in 1772. Bissonet took canoes of goods to Michilimackinac for various French merchants in 1761, 1767, 1770, and 1771, and to St. Joseph in 1772.

During Pontiac's Uprising, Louis Chevallier hid two colonial traders, Fred Hambuck and Richard Winston, from the Indians at St. Joseph in 1763. He signed a petition in 1765 in Montreal. In 1767 he was in Michilimackinac and provided security for Courtois, who took two canoes of merchandise to St. Joseph. In 1779 Chevallier ran a general store at Michilimackinac.

Leonard St. Pierre was in Green Bay in 1763 stirring up the Indians against the British. In 1767 he wintered at St. Joseph with a canoe secured by John Porteus. In 1772 he was in Michilimackinac corresponding with Lawrence Ermatinger, a Swiss merchant who traded in the Northwest. F. Joiliette (Joilliet) had his provisions seized in 1765 by Captain Howard for breaking the rules. He also signed a petition in Montreal that year.

Pierre Cardinal lived in Detroit in 1769 and traded at Michilimackinac the same year. In 1770 he provided security for Jacques Cardinal. Charles

Boyer traded at Michilimackinac in 1760 and 1761 and at Toronto in 1763, each time for different merchants. Bissonette provided security for Chabouillet in August 1767. Neither Soulleyney nor Petite Derreoice has been found in other eighteenth-century documents describing the fur trade.

In general the French traders were men of substance with assets sufficient to guarantee winterers and minor traders. They remained in the fur trade for at least eight years and moved freely about the Great Lakes posts and the area northwest of Lake Superior. They seldom operated stores, but instead dealt with the Indians only during the summer. They had business ties with a number of Montreal merchants who would finance their voyages if necessary.

By 1767 the pattern of commerce was shifting to the West. Niagara drew furs from the tribes around Lake Erie and Lake Ontario. Detroit was the center for the tribes south and west of the fort. The Miami River and Ouiatanon served the tribes on the Miami and Wabash Rivers in Illinois. Michilimackinac traded with Indians from upper Lake Michigan and Lake Huron. The French at Green Bay traded with tribes in the Fox and the Wisconsin River valleys and the Sioux Indians west of the Mississippi. St. Joseph, on the southeast shore of Lake Michigan, drew Indians from south of the lake.

The primary destination of the canoes sent up the Ottawa River was Michilimackinac. After the post was captured by the Indians in 1763, it was reestablished in September 1764 by two companies of the 17th Regiment. In 1765 the garrison was a detachment of the 17th Regiment under the command of Captain William Howard, whose first priority was making peace with the Chippewas, the Ottawas, and other tribes. The Indians had been deprived of goods for two years, and in 1765 the merchants at Michilimackinac petitioned Howard to quickly reopen trade, which in former years had produced £90,000 sterling. The number of canoes sent up the Ottawa River to Michilimackinac rose during the period 1765 to 1768.

The French were active as well on the shores of Lake Superior. La Pointe was on the south shore of Lake Superior, and Lake Nipigon was in the area northwest of Lake Superior. In 1762 the British army had established posts at Sault Ste. Marie, Kamanestaque, and Chequamegon, but these were closed by Pontiac's Uprising. In 1765 at Chequamegon Bay (on the south shore of Lake Superior), Alexander Henry found the Indians wearing deerskin trousers again because they had no source for the much more comfortable woolen trousers. Deerskin becomes extremely stiff after being soaked and then dried, a common occurrence when canoeing, as the Indians did constantly around the Great Lakes. Wearing deerskin was a clear indication of their desperate need for European goods in 1765.

In 1767 the trade at La Rivière, LaPointe, and Chequamegon (near present-day Ashland, Wisconsin) was estimated at eight canoes (about £4,000, or $800,000), a very lucrative trade at much less risk than the Northwest. On July 7, 1767, a convoy of fourteen canoes left Michilimackinac bound for Lake Superior under the control of five French traders, two of whom were supplied by English merchants and three by French merchants, with goods valued at £5,117 sterling ($1,023,400). During the next few days five more canoes under four French traders, all supplied by French merchants, left Michilimackinac bound for Lake Huron with merchandise valued at £1,275 sterling ($255,000). The average value of a canoe varied from £365 ($73,000) for the Lake Superior canoes to £255 sterling ($51,000) for the Lake Huron canoes.

The expansion of commerce by all parties in the Northwest began as soon as peace had been restored in 1764. During the 1760s the area northwest of Michilimackinac was explored and trade opened with new tribes of Indians. A temporary abundance of game in the area south of Detroit created by the limited amount of hunting and trapping during the Seven Years' War and Pontiac's Uprising, soon dwindled. As the demand for fur increased new sources were needed. The rivers and lakes northwest of Lake Superior led to hunting grounds that had not before been exploited. There was competition from the Hudson Bay Company where Indians of the area brought some pelts to various of its "factories," but the amount was minimal considering the potential of the area. The Indians preferred that traders come to them, which suited the French traders from Michilimackinac whose dealings with the tribes were more amicable.

Time was the crucial element in the Northwest because of the long cold winters. Lake Superior was almost free of ice by June 10, but as early as the end of September the onset of winter again made canoeing very risky. In contrast, Lake Michigan and Lake Huron had a longer season, opening about May 20 and remaining navigable until the end of October. Lake Erie was open even earlier, usually from April 15, and was navigable to the end of November. Traders from Montreal came to Michilimackinac in June to meet winterers from the Indian villages and provided them with new merchandise. Other traders paddled to Grand Portage and elsewhere in Lake Superior to meet the winterers and the Indians. In September the French traders returned from Lake Superior to Michilimackinac, paid some of their bills with pelts, and continued on to Montreal via the Ottawa River route with most of their fur. Some winterers came to Michilimackinac in the summer to obtain a fresh supply of merchandise and to pay their debts. In late August 1769 Benjamin Roberts, then in Michilimackinac, waited for a later ship to take him to Detroit because people who owed him had not yet returned from the Northwest.

Henry has left us an account of the mechanics of trading in the Northwest in the 1760s. In 1765 he purchased four Northwest canoes and goods worth £1,250 sterling ($250,000), an average per canoe of about £312 sterling. He hired twelve men (only three men per canoe) at £150 ($30,000). Fifty bushels of corn were acquired for provisions for £62 10s. ($12,500). The entire investment of £1,462 10s. sterling ($292,500) was obtained on credit. Rather than paying cash for the equipment, supplies, and wages, he promised to pay a total of 11,700 pounds of beaver pelts valued at 2s. 6d. ($25) per pound with a total value of £1,462 sterling.

In 1780 an estimate of the cost of a venture of a master canoe from Montreal to the Northwest was £750 sterling ($150,000), double the cost of Henry's canoes. The dry goods at Montreal cost £300 sterling plus an additional charge of 50 percent, for a total of £450 sterling. Two hundred gallons of rum and wine cost another £50, for a total value of £500 ($100,000) in goods. The cost of taking the canoe from Montreal to Michilimackinac was £160. Taking the canoe to Grand Portage was an additional £90 including wages and provisions for eight canoe men and two clerks who would winter with the Indians and trade the goods for fur.

The cost of returning the fur to Montreal was another charge. In 1768 the average freight charge to move a ninety-pound pack from Michilimackinac to Montreal by way of the Ottawa River was £1 10s. sterling ($300). Slower but much cheaper, the less valuable deerskin could be shipped by schooner to Oswego and then on to Albany and New York.

The exchange of merchandise between the traders and the Indians usually was made on a credit basis as well. When the Indians visited a post they needed credit to obtain supplies of ammunition, clothing, weapons, traps, and other necessities for the coming year. They seldom had enough furs to exchange, and the traders would extend credit to individual Indians, hoping to be repaid in pelts during the coming year. The missionary David Zeisberger commented that the Indians were fond of buying on credit, promising to pay when they returned from hunting. Some traders took the risk, hoping to receive all the furs when the Indians returned. However, the Indians ignored their debts if they found unscrupulous traders and sold the fur to them. As a result, traders learned to give very little on credit.

The winterers usually returned to pay their debts because the undesirable alternatives were remaining with the natives or going off to Illinois. A man who did not pay his debts became an outlaw, so custom favored the man who came back, even if he could not pay his complete debt. Returning to repay credit was encouraged because the rule was that the most recent debt was paid first, and all previous creditors could share only in the remaining assets. Therefore, a creditor could obtain credit for the next year even though he was unable to pay for everything. This practice varied from the standard form of bankruptcy in which all creditors received a percentage of their debt from the assets of the creditor. The more lenient rule allowed a winterer, having the misfortune to lose everything, to obtain a full outfit on credit based on confidence in his ability to deal profitably with the Indians and on the assurance of priority repayment to the merchant, regardless of any other outstanding debts. The theory behind this lenient custom was that if the trader could obtain additional credit, he eventually would repay his old creditors, at least in part. In addition, this custom reflected the great demand for men skilled in the Indian trade. It took many years for a man to learn the languages of the tribes and their customs. A man who was known and trusted by the Indians could deal far more advantageously than a stranger not knowing the rules or the language. An experienced hand, regardless of his credit standing, was far more likely than a beginner with good credit to return with a large shipment of furs.

Because of the risks and the many hands through which goods and furs passed before the final sale of the fur in London, the profits were not as great as might be assumed. For example, a bundle of tobacco from Brazil purchased in Lisbon and sent to London would be purchased by the agent of a Montreal merchant. The tobacco was shipped to Montreal where it was placed in ninety-pound packs. The Montreal merchant would engage voyageurs to take the tobacco and other items to Michilimackinac to be transferred to a Northwest canoe and sent to Grand Portage. From there it would be taken up the smaller rivers into the wilderness to be traded to the Indians for fur. The fur would then follow the path in reverse until it reached the agent in London, who would sell the fur at auction and export it to Continental Europe. At that point credits would begin to flow back to all those who had taken part. Because prices fluctuated greatly throughout the transaction, fortunes could be made, lost, and remade within a few years. High wages and other expenses contributed to small margins of profit. The cost of liquor, provisions, canoes, and repacking the goods from the ships plus the wages of the voyageurs were half of the total investment.

In the 1760s there were more French than British merchants in Quebec and Montreal, and most of the actual conduct of the trading venture remained in French hands. In 1767 the French in Mackinac still outnumbered the British four to one, but the British sent more in value, £22,000 sterling's worth compared to only £16,000 sterling by forty French traders.

The French handled their dealings with the Indians more skillfully; moreover, they had knowledge of the territory and a well-established system of exchange with the Indians. Because of their past close association, the French had remarkable influence over the Indians. The British tried unsuccessfully to eliminate the practice of trading in the Indian villages. The French ignored the rules and traded wherever they wished even though they had obtained restricted licenses. Only in 1770s did the British learn to deal with the tribes and begin encroaching on the French.

The British, with the advantage of a greater supply of capital, better business organization, better London contacts, and greater government protection, were finally able to obtain a larger share of the wholesale trade than the French. To the north beyond Montreal the French continued to dominate numerically. The Indians remained dependent on the French traders. When war broke out in 1774, the Indians around the Great Lakes and north of the Ohio River had no choice but to continue their alliance with the British in Montreal, for without them the Indians could not survive. The British soon employed the Indians in raiding parties who offered their services in return for European goods.

# 4

# Settlers

The American colonies in 1760 had 1.5 million people, including 400,000 slaves, compared with 11 million people in the British Isles. The American population was increasing rapidly—nearly doubling every twenty years—creating a major export market for British products. The frontier fur trade provided a commodity, along with tobacco, rice, and lumber, that could be sold in England to balance the colonists' purchases of British manufactured goods.

The frontier in the mid-eighteenth century was roughly defined as the territory straddling the Appalachian Mountains. It included land east and west of the line drawn by the Proclamation of 1763, the watershed created by the mountains. By 1775 one-fourth of Americans lived in villages and on farms away from the coast. In Pennsylvania and South Carolina, half of the residents lived on the frontier.

Although western New York was sparsely settled with military garrisons at Niagara, Oswego, and other points, the Mohawk Valley had a considerable agricultural settlement and towns were developing at Schenectady and Albany. The population of the colony of New York, according to the census of 1756, was 96,765, with 17,424 people in Albany County and the remainder living within eighty miles of New York City. The census of 1771 recorded the population of the colony as 182,247, of whom 47,375 lived in frontier counties. These statistics indicated a rapid growth in the comparatively undeveloped areas of New York within a period of only fifteen years. Expansion at this rate created a busy market for the merchants of Albany and Schenectady.

The population of Pennsylvania, according to estimates, grew from 217,000 in 1760 to 276,000 in 1770. Although most people lived in the immediate area of Philadelphia and along the Delaware River, nearly 40,000 settlers lived in western Pennsylvania in 1760. The Province of Quebec, according to one estimate, had a population of 65,000 in 1762, concentrated in the St. Lawrence Valley. Using an estimate for New York of 117,000 in 1760, the combined population for the three provinces was 399,000 in 1760 with fewer than 70,000 beyond the coastal area. Even though only a small percentage of Americans lived on the frontier, they soon formed a growing threat to both the Indian population and the fur trade.

Fewer than 4,000 pioneer families lived east of the mountains on the western fringe of the settled areas of New York and Pennsylvania. Their farms were grouped in settlements with as many as fifty families for self-protection from the Indians. Because of the absence of roads (with the exception of Forbes Road from Philadelphia to Fort Pitt), the settlers farmed along the river valleys, of the Susquehanna and its tributaries in Pennsylvania and the Mohawk in New York.

Many of the small towns grew around millstreams. In the mid-eighteenth century a swiftly flowing stream was essential to turn the wheels of water mills, which were the major source of power prior to the steam engine. Hilly areas provided fast-moving streams. Weather was also a factor. The streams were dry in the summer and frozen in the winter.

As an example, a sawmill and a gristmill were built on the Natchaug River at Mansfield Hollow in Connecticut in 1728. The area became a center of cloth production, and in 1761 there were bolting, fulling, and flaxseed-oil mills related to wool and linen production. In 1760 mulberry trees and silkworms were imported and silk production began.

Another example is New Hope, Pennsylvania. The town was established on two 500-acre tracts of land on the Delaware River granted by William Penn to Richard Heath in 1710. A stream fed by the Great Spring flowed swiftly through the site year round, providing waterpower for three mills. In 1719 a ferry established a crossing for travelers between New Jersey and New York, and in 1734 the Ferry Tavern was established. On maps of the period the town is identified as Well's Ferry.

The first farmers in the New Hope area took their wheat on packhorses to Gwin's Mill, on the Pennypack River. Later a gristmill was built on the Great Spring stream that served the farmers in the area. In 1712 a fulling mill was built to process woolen cloth, which indicates a good number of weavers in the area. In 1740 a sawmill was built on the stream, followed in 1744 by a forge that probably used waterpower to operate hammers. In 1758 a rolling and slitting mill was built that used waterpower to roll iron into sheets and slit it into narrow strips to be made into nails. Later a foundry was constructed using pig iron shipped down the Delaware River from a furnace at Durham.

Thomas Smith ran a general store near New Hope in 1771, and later there were wool-carding machines, a flaxseed-oil mill, and additional sawmills and gristmills, all within a few miles of the ferry. The rapid current of the Great Spring stream, the major attraction of the town, provided a dependable source of waterpower for the numerous mills.

Small towns such as New Hope provided essential services to the farmers by grinding their wheat into flour and carding and fulling wool cloth from the family looms. They made iron tools and iron strips for nail makers, and they sawed lumber for homes and boats. The colonial farmers spread westward from the coast in the mid-eighteenth century.

The settlers were predominantly the younger sons of farm families on the seaboard and former soldiers. Some were immigrants from the United Kingdom and a few came from Germany. To settle a farm on the frontier required capital, farming experience, and military skills. Money was needed to buy land, the essential tools, and household goods. A typical settlement would include discharged soldiers to provide protection and younger sons with farming experience.

After the Seven Years' War many soldiers were enticed to remain in America because the British government offered soldiers fifty acres of land. Three Scottish regiments—the 77th, the 78th, and some battalions of the 42nd— were disbanded in America, and as many as 2,000 Scottish and Scotch-Irish soldiers remained in America. The Scotch-Irish were from northern Ireland, where many Scots had immigrated in the late seventeenth century. Also disbanded in America were four battalions of the 60th Royal American Regiment, made up of German enlisted men, mostly from Hanover, and British officers. The Germans had little desire to return to Europe, which was in continual turmoil, and as many as 2,000 of them remained in America. These discharged soldiers account for the many German, Scottish, and Scotch-Irish names among the settlers.

In the eighteenth century a regiment included wives and children of noncommissioned officers who were issued government rations in return for duties that included cooking, baking, and laundering and mending clothing. These family groups readily became settlers on the frontier.

The younger sons of farm families in the East were a persistent problem in farming because of the division of assets when the head of the family died. England solved the problem with the rule of primogeniture, which gave the land to the eldest son. The younger sons went into the army, the church, or civil service, options that did not exist in America. In America the parcel of land could not be divided as forty acres was the most economical and feasible size for a farm—ten acres under cultivation, ten acres of pasture, and twenty acres of woodland and untillable land. However, after a few generations in America these families did acquire some assets, and the younger sons would receive money or other assets rather than a share of the farm. New land on the frontier was available from proprietors in Pennsylvania and the Crown in New York. For a reasonable amount of money a forty-acre farm could be purchased. Two McCord brothers in the 1750s were able to buy land in the Susquehanna Valley. In New York the younger sons were more often descendants of the Dutch who had settled New York in the seventeenth century.

The immigrants directly from Europe often came as indentured servants. In the eighteenth century the enclosure movement in England forced many off the land. During the middle ages farmers in an agricultural village on a manor or estate farmed common land, each family having small strips scattered about and the right to graze their animals on the common land. The lord of the manor retained the right to many of the strips, which he farmed with hired hands, or which the local farmers cultivated as partial payment for their strips. While this system was adequate for centuries, new developments in fertilizing, cultivating, and rotation of crops were more successful when applied to large fields. Acts of Parliament divided these common lands, leaving the lord of the manor with a large body of contiguous land and the tenants with small farms. The lord could then practice the new techniques and increase the yield of his acres.

The inevitable result of the enclosure movement was that many people were driven off the land, as the farms could not be divided among sons. These younger sons received some portion of their father's assets and could emigrate to America as indentured servants. The frontier provided an opportunity for ambitious immigrants to obtain land and make a better life for their families.

Land jobbers jostled to obtain large grants from the British government in order to resell the land to the former soldiers, the younger sons, and the immigrants. However, until the West could be made reasonably safe for the settlers, there was little hope of selling forty-acre plots. The major concern of the potential pioneer in America was the acquisition of a farm.

The Virginia land statute of 1713 provided an insight into the process of land settlement on the colonial frontier. Before a patent or grant was made, the land had to be surveyed and classified as either "plantable" or "barren."

All land surveyed before 1713 was arbitrarily considered one-third tillable. Within three years of receiving a grant of fifty acres of tillable land, a settler had to clear and cultivate three acres. For every fifty acres of barren land, he had to acquire either three cows or six sheep or goats within three years. For small grants the proportions were maintained. With a grant of forty acres of which one-half was tillable, the settler had to cultivate only one or two acres within three years and have only one cow. The farmer was required to build a house at least twenty feet long and sixteen feet wide.

These requirements illustrate the rigorous life of the settlers, even though most of them had prior experience farming. Those who settled around Fort Pitt were Scotch-Irish and Germans from Pennsylvania. Some were farmers who had been forced out of Virginia by the speculators to create large plantations nearer the coast. In the early 1750s David McCord and William McCord received grants of land near Chambersburg, Pennsylvania, from the Penn family, the proprietors of Pennsylvania.

Early illegal settlements were opposed by the land companies because they were scheming to acquire large tracts of Indian land to sell to potential farmers. The first major land company was the Ohio Company, formed in 1748. The members of the Ohio Company were the most influential men in Virginia, including Thomas Lee, Thomas Cresap, George Washington, four Mercers, Governor Robert Dinwiddie, Daniel Cresap, and other Lees. Lawrence Washington, half brother of George Washington, succeeded Thomas Lee as president of the company in 1748.

Seeing the growing frontier as a major market, in March 1749 Virginia was authorized by the British Privy Council to grant 200,000 acres in the Ohio Valley to the Ohio Company. The company would receive an additional 300,000 acres if it settled one hundred farm families in the 200,000 acres within seven years.

In 1751 Christopher Gist was sent to the Ohio Valley by the company to locate suitable land. He selected a large area between the Monongahela and Great Kanawha Rivers, which was granted to the Ohio Company by the British Privy Council on March 28, 1754. However, the grant was not approved by Virginia. In another scheme, in February 1754 Governor Dinwiddie granted land to Virginian soldiers who had served on the frontier against the French. This claim set a precedent and would later be extended by succeeding companies as the legal basis for their claims to western land.

All settlement was halted by the war with the French in 1754, but by 1759, when the French had been driven out of the Ohio Valley, the Ohio Company resumed activity. The company needed settlers to profit from the land. In July 1759 Thomas Cresap, representing the company, offered the commander at Fort Pitt, Colonel Henry Bouquet, 25,000 acres (enough for 500 50-acre farms) on the condition that he find German and Swiss settlers. Conveniently, Bouquet was Swiss, and the battalion of the 60th Royal American Regiment at Fort Pitt consisted of German soldiers. At the end of the fighting the presumption was that the battalion of the 60th Regiment at Fort Pitt would be reduced from one thousand men to five hundred, and the other five hundred would be discharged if they wished. Therefore Cresap's land offer was reasonable. In the eighteenth century the wives and families of some of the soldiers accompanied a regiment. The dependents were issued government rations in exchange for providing services, including food preparation, laundry, mending, and other household tasks. Had Bouquet accepted the offer, he would have been in a position to encourage married soldiers to leave the army at the expiration of their enlistment and settle with their wives and children on a farm near Fort Pitt. These soldiers as ideal tenants for Bouquet would have established a powerful quasi-military colony around Fort Pitt.

The annual rental on 500 fifty-acre farms, roughly £2,500 Pennsylvania ($300,000) would have made Bouquet a wealthy man. He properly refused the offer because settlement on the Ohio River was prohibited by the Treaty of Easton in 1758, which promised the Indians that their land would not be settled.

Not to be denied, in September 1759 George Washington and George Mercer of the Ohio Company planned to meet with Virginia governor Francis Fauquier to petition London to renew the land grant offer made ten years earlier, in 1749. Fauquier forwarded the request to London in December 1759, but the proposition was complicated by the Virginia grants to officers who had served on the frontier during the war. On March 13, 1760, Fauquier informed the Board of Trade in London that prior to presenting their claims the officers wanted to survey the land near Fort Pitt. To add to the confusion, both Pennsylvania and Virginia claimed the territory around Fort Pitt. The Virginia military bounty grants of 1754 were also in conflict with the grant to the Ohio Company. The land situation was chaotic around Fort Pitt.

Settlement was permitted in New York and northern Pennsylvania. In New York the colonial government was granting land in the Mohawk Valley even though it was prohibited by the Board of Trade on November 11, 1761. Settlers in the spring of 1762 also were moving into the Wyoming Valley in eastern Pennsylvania despite the prohibition. Sir William Johnson tried to quiet the Indians while General Jeffrey Amherst, the British army commander in America, hurriedly rejected the Pennsylvania land grants. In April 1762 the Board of Trade again registered definite opposition to settlement on Indian land.

Land barons continually campaigned to obtain land from the British government. In October 1762 Amherst rejected a petition from Rutherford & Duncan to obtain land to settle families and a monopoly to trade in an area in New York. He stated that any permit to settle was given with no restriction on trade. Amherst revoked a grant of land to Sterling on October 20, 1762, on instructions from the Board of Trade.

Pennsylvania faced the problem of illegal development of small settlements by squatters who had no legal title to their land. Squatting on small parcels began after the French threat was removed when France capitulated in 1760. Many of the squatters who had served in the colonial militia against the French were knowledgeable of the area and its potential for farming. After Pontiac's Uprising was put down in 1764, the danger of Indian attack decreased. The land speculators and the fur traders sought to remove the squatters from land that they believed would eventually be granted to the speculators.

In Virginia a group of speculators convinced Governor Fauquier that the illegal settlers at Redstone, south of Fort Pitt, posed a threat to Virginia's claims in the area. Fauquier reported to London that the Indians were disturbed by this wholesale invasion of their land, and he warned the British government of the danger of Indian reaction to the settlements in May 1765. However, to the author's knowledge not a single murder was recorded by either side at Redstone from 1765 to 1767. At a conference with the Indians, convened by the Indian agent George Croghan at Fort Pitt, the tribes were assured that the only legal settlers west of the mountain were those on the road to Fort Pitt who provided lodging and supplies for the army and other travelers. Accepting the explanation, the Indians at the conference were very cooperative, agreeing to return any prisoners and to escort Croghan on his proposed trip down the Ohio River. There was no indication of hostility or threat of war at the time.

In 1765 Pennsylvania began the Application System for new settlers. A farmer or land speculator applied to the land office for a survey with the intent of settling on a tract. When the survey was completed, the applicant submitted a claim and was granted the land for £5 sterling for each 100 acres, with a maximum grant of 300 acres. The tax rolls of the portion of Cumberland County that later became Bedford County include the names of many merchants involved in the frontier trade, such as Baynton and Wharton, Daniel Clark, Robert Irwin, William Trent, and Edward Shippen Jr., all of whom were speculators and did not fit the category of settlers. The settlers usually had two horses and two cows, and several had indentured servants or slaves. George Woods had two servants, seven horses, and four cows. Only a few had sheep—Adam McCartny had nine, John Watson, three, and John Ramsey, five.

In the eighteenth century, the usual frontier farm covered as much as forty acres. A farmer with a single share plow and one or two horses could cultivate up to ten acres. Another ten acres were needed for pasture for the horses and a few cattle. The remaining twenty acres were left idle as woodland to provide firewood and building material, as well as fruit trees and bushes. Often the new landowner had to clear the land of trees, a painstakingly slow project lasting some years. The most desirable farms were those with the proper mix of trees and open land. The assumption of forty-acre farms was carried on in the survey of the Northwest Territory in the 1780s, which remains the basis of land descriptions to this day. Forty-acre farms still exist in the Midwest, although many have become part of larger operations. Today large-scale farmers often rent the land of several small farms while their owners occupy the buildings. In land zoned as agricultural in southeastern Wisconsin, the minimum parcel of land that can be sold is thirty-five acres.

Most frontier farms were small family subsistence farms. The family raised enough to feed themselves and have a small surplus to exchange for the luxuries of tea and sugar along with necessities such as clothing and shoes. The cultivated area was limited by the available labor. The yield was low, from ten to fifteen bushels of wheat per acre. In the eighteenth century an average adult consumed a pound of bread per day. A family of four needed more than a half ton of flour per year. A bushel of wheat weighed sixty pounds and produced forty-eight pounds of flour. A family would have to cultivate more than four acres of wheat to raise fifty bushels to provide the half ton needed for their own use plus seed for the following year, pay the miller to grind the wheat into flour, and pay the land owner. For centuries the arrangement between a tenant farmer and a landowner was equal division of the crop. Therefore a farmer who did not own his land had to produce twice the amount of wheat needed to feed his family for a year and for the other purposes, more than a ton. If a settler owned the land or was squatting illegally, his needs would be one-half of the sharecropper's.

A horse consumed more than a ton of grain and nearly two tons of hay each year. With a yield of fifteen bushels of wheat per acre, a farmer could feed his family, two horses, and some cows with seven acres under cultivation and several acres of pasture for livestock. A few additional acres of woodland provided fuel. Several more acres of wheat were needed to provide a surplus to exchange for other goods. Fifteen acres under cultivation produced enough to survive. Additional acres would have required more men to plant and harvest the crops.

Any surplus produce, corn, flour, vegetables, and hay was sold to local inns, stables, and army garrisons or shipped east to Philadelphia. Farmers sold some of their produce to obtain cash to buy clothing and other necessities. A bushel of wheat sold for six shillings Pennsylvania in the 1760s ($34.50), so thirty bushels of wheat would bring £9 Pennsylvania ($1,035), not enough for many luxuries. In 1768 flour was selling for ten shillings per hundredweight in Philadelphia and a half ton brought only £5 Pennsylvania ($575). In New York flour sold at £1 13s. New York ($220) per hundredweight. However, the cost of grinding the wheat and taking the flour to market reduced the return to the farmer. The excessive quantity of wheat, flour, and cattle that the farmers had to sell was more than the market demanded, and therefore the prices were very low.

The Indians and the army were major markets for provisions and liquor. The liquor came from the seaboard, but the frontier farmers provided a good share of the food. The daily ration for each soldier was a pound of meat, a pound of flour, and a half pint of rum. Given the stress of frontier life, the demand for liquor was inexhaustible and limited only by the means of the consumers to pay. The demand for rations for the army was continual, and the Indians had to be fed from time to time during a bad harvest or a large conference. For that reason the settlers had a ready market for their surplus grain and vegetables.

The land was plowed with a single-share steel plow pulled by either a horse or an ox. Weeds were held in check with frequent use of the hoe by the older boys in the family. A scythe with four wooden fingers acting as a cradle was used to harvest the wheat. All of this hard work required endless hours and limited the amount of land that could be cultivated.

A typical frontier home was constructed of rough-hewn logs notched at the end to form the corners. The cracks between the logs were filled with clay. The roof was clapboard. The furniture included a bed with a straw mattress, a table, and three-legged stools. The fireplace provided heat and was used for cooking. The major utensils were an iron kettle and a frying pan. The house measured approximately twenty feet by twelve feet. Some were divided into two rooms, but one room was more common. As many as nine people lived in a small cabin.

Because of the rough life on the frontier, both the Indians and the pioneers wore out their clothing, blankets, and guns at a much faster rate than eastern farmers and city dwellers. Firearms and clothing were in continual demand on the frontier even though the farmers had very little disposable income to purchase merchandise. The American frontier was primarily a market for British imports and colonial products including rum, ironware, flour, and preserved meat. The most profitable markets for the merchants were the townspeople, the Indians, and the army.

The large number of settlers and small-town residents composed a considerable market for miscellaneous tools and other items, but it was relatively static. Some tools were imported from Europe for the farms of America. In 1769 Michael Gratz imported long straw-cutting knives from Germany with the aid of Edman Boghm and Son as well as iron plate eighteen inches wide. In 1761 John Sanders of Albany ordered thirty-six broadaxes, a dozen frying pans, augers, draw knives, adzes, and other carpenter tools in quantities of one to three dozen from John Bonbonous in London. William Clarkson purchased cutting knives, scythes, and other tools from William Dawson. However, most tools were made locally; for example, a hundred hoes and a hundred Indian axes were sold to Johnson as gifts to the Indians in 1770.

Glass for windows and tableware was a luxury usually imported from England. There was a small glass factory in Lancaster in 1767 producing what John Penn considered glass of poor quality. When the Sons of Liberty enforced the nonimportation rule in 1769, only the local, poor-quality window glass was available.

England had long been the world center for wool manufacture and wool was its leading export. Before 1750 wool was the dominant cloth made in England, offering more employment for its manufacture than any other industry except agriculture. Very little cloth was made in the colonies because the imports from England were cheap and better than homespun cloth.

The Industrial Revolution with its new machines in England improved the quality of woolen cloth and made it even cheaper to manufacture. Manufacturing cloth was the major industry of England, centered around the towns of York, Lincoln, Louth, Stamford, Beverly, Winchester, Oxford, Nottingham, Leicester, Gloucester, Exeter, Coventry, Norwich, and London.

There were five steps in producing woolen cloth: carding the wool to straighten the fibers, spinning the yarn, weaving the cloth, fulling the yarn to thicken it, and dyeing. All of these steps were done in the homes of the workers except fulling and dyeing, which were performed in small workshops or mills. In the domestic system, the cloth was woven from yarn spun by a weaver's wife and children in their cottage, an unhealthy environment with small windows. The loom filled the room and the weaver lived and worked there along with his wife and children. Carding was done by boys, and the wife and girls worked the foot-operated spinning wheels. The purchase of these implements could be afforded by one man who remained an independent operator and sold his finished product at markets. The cloth was sold by the piece at cloth halls or on the streets of the towns. For the most part, a weaver would have only a single piece to sell. Each week cloth merchants walked up and down the rows of tables, buying a piece here and there. The merchants would then have the cloth treated at a local fulling mill. In Halifax each Saturday all of the streets of the town were lined with tables of cloth.

Before the laborsaving machines, the number of workers needed to manufacture cloth from a pack of short-staple wool in 1737 was 56: 1 sorter, 4 scribblers, 30 spinners, 4 winders, 8 weavers, 4 burlers, and 5 fullers. The ratio of workers was different in the worsted trade. More spinners were needed to keep pace with the weavers, and fewer workers were required for the fulling and dyeing. In 1736 the number of workers making worsted was 158: 6 combers, 120 spinners, 10 throwers or doublers, and 22 weavers.

The workers in the domestic system were poorly paid. A female spinner earned 4d. to 6d. per day ($3.35 to $5). In Leeds the day laborers were paid from 2s. 6d. to 3s. ($25 to $30) per week. As long as these low pay rates merely supplemented farm income, they were of minor importance, but the impact was serious when a family's total income came from spinning. Parents would be forced to put all their children to work in order to survive.

Little skill was necessary to prepare the yarn, but four times as many people did the weaving. Half the weaving was actually done by unskilled people. A wife and two or three children could card and spin enough yarn to keep a weaver busy. The simple and inexpensive new machines increased the productivity of the cottage weavers. Notable was the flying shuttle, developed in 1733 by John Kay, but not widely used until 1760. It moved mechanically rather than being thrown by hand and not only increased the speed of the operation but enabled the weavers to create a wider strip of cloth.

The increased production of the looms, however, created a shortage of yarn. Before the flying shuttle, four spinners could supply one weaver, but twice as many spinners were needed to keep up with the flying shuttle. Weavers were forced to go from house to house passing out wool to be spun into yarn. Some homes specialized as spinners, and others had several looms.

The increased demand for yarn led to the spinning jenny, patented by James Hargreaves in 1767. The spinning jenny was a simple device used in the cottages to spin eight threads at once. Later models used in factories twisted eighty threads simultaneously. Within a few years, the spinning jenny had replaced the spinning wheel even in the cottages. The spinning jenny produced yarn suitable for the woof but not strong enough for the warp.

The water frame developed in 1769 by Richard Arkwright produced a tough, coarse yarn. In 1779 the mule, developed by Samuel Compton, combined the jenny and the water frame to produce a finer thread. Carding by hand to straighten the fibers was replaced by a machine, developed in 1748 by Lewis Paul, which accelerated that operation considerably.

Woven cloth required fulling and other processing before use. The manufacture of cloth centered around towns because of the need for water-powered fulling mills. Fulling was essential to produce heavy-weight, good-quality wool. Before the mills, the cloth was placed in a long trough or large vat in a heated combination of water, soap, fuller's earth (hydrous aluminum silicates), and animal urine and for three to five days was trampled by several men, called walkers, with their bare feet, which caused the short-scaled fibers to shrink, interlock, and mat. The walkers, generally a low-class, disorderly group of men, worked naked.

The mills replaced walkers with a hinged beam operated by a man to pound the cloth. An upright post was set at the side of the fulling trough and a heavy mallet was hinged to the upper end of the post. The mallet was then swung down to beat the cloth against the side of the trough. The fuller moved the cloth along the trough to be struck by the mallet operated by a second man. In the sixteenth century, the mallet was replaced by a trip-hammer attached to a water mill.

The water-powered fulling mill had two large heavy oak hammers that pounded the cloth forty times per minute. The machine processed the cloth in minutes, compared with hours. The process shrank the cloth as much as 50 percent, producing a heavy, dense fabric. Lighter-weight woolens (worsted, says, serges, biffes, and stamforts) were given a less arduous fulling that served mainly to clean the cloth.

Because great power was needed to turn the camshafts that operated the hammers, the fulling mill required waterpower from a fast-flowing stream to operate an overshot water wheel. Undershot waterwheels had enough power to grind grain but not to operate fulling mills. Because hilly terrain had more fast-moving streams, the West Country (Devon, Somerset, Gloucestershire, Worcestershire, Wiltshire) and East Anglia (Suffolk and Essex) became significant centers.

After the cloth was shrunk, it was "rowed"—stretched by ropes and pulleys—and dried on the grass. Burlers then raised the nap on the cloth with weavers' teazels. The burlers were replaced by gig mills that had teazels set on large drums turned by waterpower or by winches. The final step, dyeing, was usually done in a workshop by hired dyers who could process the output of a large number of weavers.

The increase in production in the West Riding county of Yorkshire was probably typical of the other cloth-making regions. In 1740, 100,000 pieces were made annually; in 1750, 140,000; in 1760, 120,000, a drop because of the sharp decrease in military purchases; and in 1770, 178,000, over 75 percent more than in the previous thirty years, reflecting the impact of the early machines and a rapidly expanding market.

Linen was the major alternate to wool in the eighteenth century. In the mid-eighteenth century, 25 million yards of linen worth £1 million sterling were imported annually into England, mostly from Germany. Linen was made from flax that grew in wetlands. The young plants from seeds of a previous crop required constant weeding, usually by children whose small, bare feet did not damage the stalks. After maturing the crop was harvested. Some seeds were saved for next year's crop and the rest were used for flaxseed oil. Linen came from the stems, which were beaten to remove the soft matter leaving the tough fibers, which were chopped and dried. The fibers, "tow," were then spun into thread on spinning wheels much smaller than the spinning wheels used for cotton and wool. Women and children did most of the spinning. The thread was bleached in solutions that varied according to the desired degree of whiteness. The thread was then woven into cloth on a loom, usually operated by the man of the house. The finished piece of linen was sold to a merchant who had the cloth bleached and, in some cases, dyed in factories called bleacheries.

In the early eighteenth century the Dutch sold much of the world's linen. In bleacheries in Haarlem, the Dutch dyed linen from Berg, Elberfeld, Bremen, Osnabruck, Münster, Hanover, Hesse, Brunswick, Silesia, Ravensburg, Juliers, Cleves, and East Friesland in Germany, as well as Poland, northern France, and the southern Netherlands.

The place of manufacture often gave a type of linen its name. Coarse linen came from Russia. The chief sources of the low-grade linen were Hesse and Osnabruck. The fine linen for sheets came from Holland as well as Ghent and Bruges.

The linen from Juliers, called garlics, was used for shirts that were ruffed with muslin. Prior to 1770 garlix from Hamburg dominated the British market, but British suppliers substituted the cheaper Irish linen for shirts. By 1750 the manufacture of linen was carried on in Belfast, Newry, Londonderry, Dublin, and other Irish towns, and 20 million yards worth £1 million sterling were exported in 1770. In 1765 Baynton and Wharton sold a piece of Irish linen to Alexander McKee, a fur trader in Fort Pitt, for £9 Pennsylvania. The Scottish linen industry was also growing, and in 1760 12 million yards worth £500,000 sterling were manufactured.

Linen was widely used in frontier commerce. Among the items ordered from John Blackburn of London in 1770 by Sir William Johnson were fifty pieces (about 20 yards each) of garlix valued at approximately 12d. New York ($6.30) per ell (about a yard), 8 ells of hessen at 9d. per ell, 418 ells of "oznabrigs" valued at 8d. per ell, and 625 yards of Irish linen at 16d. per yard. Stringer's account listed thirty pieces of garlix at prices ranging from 24s. 6d. to 45s. and seven ells of Pomeranian linen. In 1769 Michael Gratz sold E. McKay ten pieces of linen for £27 Pennsylvania. John Sanders of Albany ordered the following from Moses Franks in 1760: two pieces of best osnabergs, two pieces of striped caliminca, two pieces of garlix at £2 New York ($252), six pieces of garlix at £1 New York ($126) per piece, and four pieces of flowered calico.

A variety of the decorative fabrics were "nonsopretties" (a braid or tape), crepe de dames, prunellas, imperials, croon crasses, and perpetuanas. Daniel Clark's order sent to Quebec and Montreal listed poplin, various colors of damask, and three gross of nonsopretty at 4d. and 5d. a gross of finer cloth.

The potential market for merchandise and the profits to be made from selling land created great interest among American merchants. Baynton and Wharton planned to expand its market to Illinois in 1764. The enthusiasm of the Philadelphia merchants to begin selling merchandise to the Indians was not shared by the people who lived on the frontier and had suffered from numerous attacks in 1763 as part of Pontiac's Uprising. Occasional Indian attacks on Pennsylvania traders continued in 1765. In June 1765 the Seneca Indians killed a trader near Fort Pitt. William Dice and another colonist were killed by three Indians earlier near Redstone.

The dangers of settling on the frontier were exemplified in the McCord family. Fort McCord was built in 1756 on land granted to William McCord on May 24, 1753, in Lancaster County as part of a line of forts on the frontier to defend against Indian attacks. On April 1, 1756, 26 people were killed or captured by the Indians with French support at Fort McCord. The McCord women were recaptured in a daring raid at Kittanning in September 1756 by militia under Colonel John Armstrong.

Four McCord children were captured by Indians in 1758 at Derry (now Hershey) Pennsylvania. James McCord was taken to Detroit, then Montreal and England and was exchanged for French prisoners. In 1763 another Fort McCord in Perry County was attacked by Indians during Pontiac's Uprising when McCord and family members were killed. The McCord children were among the 240 women and children freed after 1763. During the uprising, 1,500 very frightened settler families abandoned their homes and more than 2,000 were killed or captured.

The frontiersmen, rightly, were especially concerned about the sale of guns, ammunition, and knives to the Indians. One of the most salable items was the "Indian gun," a small-caliber, smooth-bore fowling piece, or fusil, that was light-weight and easy to carry, compared with the heavy military musket. The fusil had enough power to wound a deer and also could be used in warfare.

In January 1765 the British were faced with a dilemma. The settlers objected to providing arms to the Indians, who only months ago had been killing families on the frontier. On the other hand, the Indians needed the weapons for hunting. If the British and colonial merchants did not supply the Indians with guns, knives, and ammunition, the tribes would turn to the French from Illinois, who would instigate even more trouble to maintain their Indian alliances and promote hostility toward the British. At Fort Pitt in February 1765 Croghan conferred with the Shawnees concerning resuming trade. The Shawnees promised to release white captives in return. Croghan planned to distribute a large amount of goods as presents but deferred until the Indians had complied with the terms of the agreement. Croghan had £1,200 sterling's worth of presents and £2,000 in cash to purchase more, a total of £3,200 sterling ($640,000).

In June 1765 General Thomas Gage urged Lieutenant Governor John Penn to open the Indian trade officially, despite the objections of the fearful settlers on the frontier. The Indians had met all terms of the agreements negotiated by Croghan in February. If goods were unavailable at Fort Pitt, Gage said the Indians would deal with the French in Illinois. By the end of June Penn reopened trade, but the frontiersmen were still threatening to attack the convoys.

Johnson had promised the Delaware Indians that trade would be reopened as a condition of peace on the frontier, a promise he was also making to the Chippewas and the Shawnees. Anticipating the resumption of trade, in February 1765 merchants sent goods to Fort Pitt. The first convoy of eighty-one horse-loads was dispatched by Robert Callender. As the convoy was bypassing Fort Loudon, a barrel broke and some of the alarmed frontiersmen observed that it was filled with scalping knives. On March 6, 1765, a hundred armed men with blackened faces calling themselves the "Black Boys" followed the convoy to Great Cove on Sidelong Hill five miles from Fort Loudon, whipped the horse drivers, killed three horses, and burned sixty-three loads of goods valued at £3,000 Pennsylvania ($345,000). The attackers kept the other eighteen loads, mostly liquor. Later some of the attackers were captured and taken to Fort Loudon, but because the local residents favored the action of the prisoners they were released. However, the question remained what was to be done with their rifles, an indication that they were Pennsylvania frontiersmen, who usually carried rifles.

When taken before a local grand jury in April 1765, the matter was dropped because of insufficient evidence. The defense claimed that the attack had been committed by men from Virginia. The Black Boys could not be found in May. The merchants claimed that the merchandise was not intended for the Indians, which was illegal but, rather, for the army at Fort Pitt. William Allen, the justice of the peace at Fort Loudon, stated that too many goods were being sent and that five or six horse-loads would have supplied the garrison at Fort Pitt. Gage believed that many members of the grand jury actually had been involved in the riot. After the attack the settlers in the area maintained a scout on the road to inspect convoys for any Indian goods.

Johnson was concerned that the unhappy frontiersmen would continue to obstruct the movement of merchandise unless the army provided an escort. Baynton and Wharton asked the British army for escorts. When the first escorted convoys went forward, shots were exchanged by the soldiers and the attackers, opening a dispute between the army and the local residents. The Indians did not believe that the Pennsylvania merchants could supply them at Fort Pitt so they went to Detroit with their fur, leaving Baynton and Wharton with unsold merchandise at Fort Pitt.

The other source of profit on the frontier was land. An enormous opportunity opened up with the British acquisition of Canada in 1763. Before the Seven Years' War, few American merchants had enough capital to conduct large commercial operations in the West. However, their opportunities changed during the war when commercial activity expanded between 1754 and 1763 to supply the British army in America. The war created fortunes for many businessmen. The land west of the mountains, the spoils of the war with France, were ceded to Britain in the Treaty of Paris in 1763. The new land offered two opportunities for investment—trade with the Indians, or land development by acquiring large tracts and selling small farms to settlers.

The American merchants especially turned their attention to land when the combined efforts of the Illinois and Montreal French traders ended any hope of large profits from the fur trade. To acquire the large tracts needed to produce major profits demanded a complex organization with lobbyists in London and political influence in New York, Pennsylvania, and Virginia.

From 1763 on there were mixed feelings in London, whether to maintain the area west of the mountains as an Indian preserve or open it to settlement. In May 1763 the Board of Trade ordered the removal of a settlement on the Susquehanna River in northern Pennsylvania as an illegal incursion onto Indian land. However, the London government did encourage some settlement in America. On August 5, 1763, the Board of Trade recommended new settlements in Florida and Nova Scotia, offering discharged soldiers grants of land. Field officers received 5,000 acres; captains, 3,000; subalterns (lieutenants), 2,500; noncommissioned officers, 100; and privates, 50 acres, slightly larger than the usual single-person farm. To receive title, the discharged soldier had to live on the land and could not sell his claim. The generous gift of a 50-acre farm to the soldiers was more than adequate to maintain a family. In May 1764 Gage commented to General Frederick Haldimand that discharged officers of the Fourth Battalion of the 60th Regiment refused to purchase commissions and instead preferred to apply for the very favorable land grants in Canada. None had applied for land in New York.

Even though the Proclamation of 1763 prohibited settlement beyond the mountains, speculators continued to purchase land from Indians who did not have legal title to it. The settlers were eager to obtain any land, even though other Indians objected to the purchases as fraudulent. The payments to the Indians who sold to the speculators were small and quickly spent. Pontiac's Uprising caused a temporary hold on land acquisitions, but they resumed in 1764.

When Baynton and Wharton and other Pennsylvania merchants began to lose money in the fur trade, to rebuild their fortunes they turned to schemes involving land from the Indians. Throughout 1764 the merchants who had lost money in the Seven Years' War and Pontiac's Uprising—"the Suffering Traders"—continued to press their demand for compensation. Croghan, the Indian agent at Fort Pitt, was employed by Baynton and Wharton to further their plans. Croghan asked permission from Sir William Johnson, who was also involved with Baynton and Wharton, to go to England to seek compensation for the traders' losses in the form of a land grant.

Croghan represented both Baynton and Wharton and the partnership of Franks, Simon, Trent, & Company, the other major player in the Pennsylvania fur trade. While Croghan presented the case to the Board of Trade in London during 1764, Trent, Callender, Baynton, Morgan, and Samuel Wharton gathered the names of those who had suffered losses and in some cases purchased the right to present their claims. The Indiana Company was developed to pursue the claims. John Hughes held in trust seven shares. One share each went to William Franklin, John Baynton, Samuel Wharton, George Morgan, and William Trent; Callender had a half share; and Croghan had one and a half shares. Traders who had claims were offered 30 percent of the value of the claim, though some were paid as much as 50 percent. However, they were to be paid only after the land grant was made and approved by King George III. Each of the traders provided details of his losses. Baynton and Wharton listed its losses in 1763 as £4,369 Pennsylvania ($524,280). As another example, Winston at Fort Chartres detailed his loss to the Indians at Ouiatanon on the Wabash River in 1763 at £2,415 New York ($275,310). The high value of these claims attests to the significance of the business.

Croghan was unsuccessful in obtaining the support of the British government for the scheme and returned from London in late 1764. Baynton and Wharton nevertheless did not abandon land speculation and was busily buying parcels of land in Pennsylvania. The total purchases from November 1, 1763, to February 18, 1765, were £5,570 Pennsylvania ($670,000). Those who sold land to the partners were an unusual group—men in the Indian Department, merchants, and some small landowners:

In 1764 the British government asked Johnson to obtain Indian reactions to a new western boundary for New York and Pennsylvania. The promoters of the Suffering Traders seized on this opportunity as a means to obtain a land grant. On January 5, 1765, a memorial from the Indiana Company was sent to General Gage asking Johnson to present a request to the Indians for compensation. The memorial was signed by Trent, Levy and Company, Callender, Alexander Lowrey, Thomas Mitchell, Thomas Smallman and Company, John Gibson, Margaret Welsh, Patrick Allison, and others.

Johnson's position was that the Indians were not solely responsible for the losses in 1754 because the French had been involved as well. However, he did support compensation from the Indians for the losses in 1763. As a result of Johnson's decision, the claimants split into two groups, those who had earlier losses in 1754 from Virginia, and those claiming compensation for the losses in 1763.

The Indiana Company, backed by Baynton and Wharton, included only those claiming losses from 1763 and excluded the claimants of losses to the French in 1754. The group known as the "Suffering Traders of 1754," of course, became competitors of the Indiana Company. The leaders of the 1754 group, Murray, Franks, and Company, were archrivals of Baynton and Wharton. The Franks group prepared a list of claims for losses of £30,920 Pennsylvania ($3,710,400), a substantial sum of money, to support its request for a major land grant, which was presented to Johnson by David Franks, Joseph Simons, Levy Andrew Levy, and William Trent.

The Indiana Company's next step was to gain the support of the Indians and their agreement to sell their land. At a conference with the Delaware and Iroquois Indians held in May 1765, the tribes agreed to give land to compensate the traders and to sell additional land to Johnson in return for resumption of trade. Croghan informed Benjamin Franklin, who was representing the Indiana Company in London, that the Shawnees, Delawares, Wyandots, and others had agreed to give land to the colonial merchants as compensation for their losses during the uprising. Johnson also supported the Indian offer. The Indiana Company forced the issue and compiled a new list of twenty-one claims for compensation, a total of £80,862 Pennsylvania ($9,703,440), nearly three times the sum presented by the 1754 group. Although Gage supported the proposed purchase with the cooperation of all concerned, the Board of Trade burst the balloon when, because of lack of funds, it was unable to purchase the land from the Indians.

Later that year, in October 1765, the Indiana Company was again actively pressing its claim in London. By 1766 Baynton and Wharton really needed a boost in its financial affairs because the partnership was deeply in debt as a result of the failure to capture the Illinois business from the French. In November 1766 it owed Richard Neave in London £6,400 sterling ($1,280,000) and needed the land schemes. To achieve this end it continued to press the demands of the Indiana Company. A boon to its cause was

Johnson, who, as a secret partner of Baynton and Wharton, promised to support the efforts of the Indiana Company. He urged London to fix a new boundary with the Indians to facilitate the purchase of land by the Indiana Company. In a letter to the Board of Trade, Johnson also supported the petition of the Suffering Traders (including the Indiana Company) for compensation from the Indians as gifts of land.

Meanwhile, another problem was developing in 1765. A group of Virginia settlers illegally began farming in Indian territory. In the summer of 1765 squatters moved into the Monongahela Valley at Redstone Creek. Alexander McKee was sent from Fort Pitt with some Indians to remove the Redstone settlement but was unsuccessful, and it became a point of contention between the Indians and the colonists. The Virginia governor and the merchants associated with Baynton and Wharton convinced the British government that the situation at Redstone was dangerous. In August 1765 London ordered that the illegal settlements be removed by Virginia and Pennsylvania. If needed, Gage was to supply troops.

In July Gage had offered the Pennsylvania government the troops stationed at Fort Pitt to remove the settlers because he had received information that the Indians demanded their removal. But the governor would have to issue the order. Pennsylvania ordered the settlers to leave in September 1765, and Virginia did the same in July 1766. Governor Fauquier of Virginia suggested that they allow the Indians to deal with the settlers. However, the settlers remained and Gage blamed the inability of the colonial governments to act.

In September 1766 the settlers were still at Redstone. The Earl of Shelburne, the British cabinet member in charge of colonial affairs, ordered Johnson, Gage, and the colonial governors to maintain the boundary set in the Proclamation of 1763 and remove the settlers. He also ordered action against the dishonest traders who were going to the villages and disturbing the Indians, an indication that he was being influenced by Benjamin Franklin representing the Baynton group. The group opposed visits to the Indian villages by either the French or the colonists as they undercut the Baynton stores in Pennsylvania and Illinois.

When the Pennsylvania Assembly refused to provide funds to drive out the settlers, Lieutenant Governor Penn issued a proclamation on September 23, 1766, ordering the settlers to leave. Fauquier made a similar proclamation on October 24, 1766, but both were ignored. In December Gage ordered the troops at Fort Pitt to drive out the settlers as authorized by both Virginia and Pennsylvania.

The army was able to remove the settlers but the solution was short-lived. By January 1767 the settlers had returned to Redstone, and Penn admitted to Shelburne that he had no solution to the problem. The farmland was so desirable that squatting was a chance worth taking. Shelburne believed that punishing the settlers to please the Indians would solve the problem and refused to consider any alternatives to relieve the pressure of the settlers crossing the mountains. In February 1767 Shelburne requested information concerning the punishment of the illegal settlers.

A new player arrived in 1767 when Colonel Michael Cresap of Maryland arrived in Redstone and began trading with the Indians at prices lower than at Fort Pitt. The Indians were not disturbed enough to discontinue trading with the settlers at Redstone. Fauquier was more concerned with Cresap's gaining influence with the Indians and proposed to refer all Indian grievances to Johnson. He merely expressed the need to prevent settlements at Redstone without offering any solution. Gage referred to the settlers as bandits.

Johnson continued to report Indian dissatisfaction. In September 1767 he told Gage that Indian chiefs loyal to him had reported a conspiracy to oppose the settlers and the growing Indian anger at the traders who cheated and insulted them. In another report Johnson insisted that illegal settlements be removed along with dishonest traders. He suggested that missionaries be sent to the Indians to bring peace.

By December 1767 the opponents of the Redstone settlement had convinced Gage that the settlement was the major Indian grievance and that something must be done. Lieutenant Governor Penn had promised to do all that he could to force the settlers to leave, but he had been unsuccessful in the past. In January 1768 the Pennsylvania Assembly passed a law subjecting anyone to the death penalty who did not leave Indian land after a thirty-day notice. Gage hoped that a similar law would be passed by Virginia. However, in March Gage had no hope that the Pennsylvania law would do any good without the assistance of the army to remove the settlers by force. Virginia had refused to pass a similar law. In April 1768 Gage stressed that the army would have to do the work.

The Croghan group continued to overstate the problem of the settlers. Croghan reported that he had been threatened and asked Gage for thirty soldiers for protection. Although Penn was convinced that there were 150 families in the Redstone area, in fact there were only approximately 50 in the three settlements at Redstone, Guesses Place, and Turkey Foot. As part of the panic, traders at Paxton, near Fort Pitt, were forced to sign affidavits that they had not sold gunpowder to the Indians, even though its sale was legal and in fact necessary if the Indians were to hunt efficiently enough to feed themselves and have time to trap fur-bearing animals.

The incursions of settlers into Indian territory upset the peaceful relations with the tribes. Rather than ignoring the settlers, as they had the colonial traders, the Indians reacted violently to the settlements after 1768. In retaliation for the intrusion the Indians began to rob and kill settlers and colonial traders that ventured onto their land.

The Croghan group attempted to take advantage of the chaos. The Illinois Company was formed and achieved some success in December 1767. Johnson continued to hammer home that the British government must pacify the Indians or face all-out war on the frontier. Benjamin Franklin used the loss of two boats on the Ohio River and Indian unrest in pressing the need for a new boundary. Parliament's opposition to westward expansion finally collapsed under the pressure. The Board of Trade on December 23, 1767, informed Shelburne that in view of the Indian threat expressed by Gage and Johnson a new boundary acceptable to the Indians was to be drawn.

While the main competition for land in western Pennsylvania was between two groups of merchants—one led by Baynton and Wharton and the other by David Franks—who competed vigorously with each other in the Illinois market as well, a group of former Virginia militia officers including George Washington, Thomas Walker, and William Crawford claimed land in the Monongahela Valley on the basis of Virginia grants for service in the Seven Years' War. All three of the groups sought to restore their fortunes by obtaining land grants from the British government.

In late 1767 Shelburne came to the conclusion that the solution to the problem on the frontier was the establishment of three new colonies rather than trying to keep the settlers out of the area and allowing it to remain as an Indian preserve. Shelburne believed that the formation of three colonies— one around Detroit, another in Illinois, and a third in the Ohio Valley—would benefit Britain as new markets for British manufactures. Another concern was the threat posed by the French influence on the Indians and the fear of French-sponsored attacks on the frontier. Money for the creation and governing of the three colonies would come from quit rents to be collected from the settlers. In September 1767 Shelburne presented the concept of quit rents (an annual payment to the British government for the land) to the British cabinet, but the cabinet observed that because the Americans were slow to pay such rents the idea was not practical.

In October 1767 Shelburne outlined his reasons for favoring the three new colonies. First, the colonies would improve the regulation of the fur trade. The colonies also would protect the frontier from French and Spanish intrigue from Louisiana west of the Mississippi. Furthermore, the colonies would form a barrier against any French-inspired attacks. By encouraging the colonists to settle the frontier, they would be less likely to invest in manufacturing in competition with England. The farms in the new colonies would provide food for the army on the frontier at less cost than the current method of shipping the rations from the seaboard colonies. Later Shelburne suggested to Gage that the new colonies would end the illegal export of furs to France via New Orleans. Shelburne saw the three new colonies as a panacea to solve many issues.

The proposal for new colonies ran into a storm of objections in the British government. Lord Clare, one of its opponents, did not believe the colonies could stop the illegal export of furs from New Orleans. The Board of Trade took the matter of the new colonies under consideration in January 1768 and was concerned about the enormous expenses in the West. The board believed that the new colonies, rather than improving its regulation, would destroy the fur trade, which was not as profitable as had been expected. Sir William Johnson was concerned that the three new colonies would make matters worse and pleaded that nothing be undertaken until the Indians had been consulted. Johnson's opposition may have been prejudiced by his association with the Baynton and Wharton land scheme, because the new colonies would replace its proposal for the Illinois Land Company.

Baynton and Wharton continued to cherish hope that the Illinois Land Company, at least one of its projects, would succeed. In February 1768 it asked George Morgan to remain in Illinois until the land deal came through. In March it assured Rumsey that the new colony would be approved shortly and that Rumsey would make great profits. In April Morgan believed that the new colony would enable Baynton and Wharton to wrest the fur trade in the Mississippi Valley away from the French. However, the Illinois project died in the face of British opposition. By March 1768 the idea was blocked in the cabinet. Hillsborough, the new secretary of state for America, was opposed because of the expense. Instead he proposed to abandon the western forts and transfer the troops to the seaboard in Canada, New York, New Jersey, Pennsylvania, and Florida. Hillsborough transferred Indian regulation from the Indian Department and the army to the colonies. Johnson exaggerated the danger of Indian resentment and linked the single murder and robbing of two boats on the Ohio River to the argument that regulation was necessary to confine the traders to the posts. According to Johnson, a new colony was needed in Illinois to restrain the French influence on the Indians, a relationship that caused the trouble. By closing the western forts, the colonies became responsible for peace on the frontier rather than relying on the British army. His summation was that if the colonial traders created problems, the colonial governments would have to solve them.

In defeat the Baynton group turned to other land schemes with Croghan, Joseph Spear, Trent, Jeremiah Warder, and Peters and Clark. During 1767 the Baynton group, the Franks group, and the Virginia group presented a variety of plans to acquire land west of the mountains. All of the groups used the potential conflict between the settlers and the Indians as a reason for opening legal settlement of land in the West. Each group tried to use the Indians and the settlers to further its schemes to acquire vast tracts of western land.

Baynton and Wharton launched the Vandalia project to establish a new colony roughly in what is now West Virginia. The land was to be ceded to the land speculators associated with Baynton and Wharton by the Indians at a conference at Fort Stanwix in 1768. The conference was similar to a political convention. While the majority of attendees ate, drank, and listened to speeches, the real work was done in small meetings involving the colonial representatives, the Indians, and the agents of Sir William Johnson as well those of Baynton and Wharton. Based on the results of these meetings, the Baynton and Wharton group of Pennsylvania merchants, represented by George Croghan, in effect dictated the actions of the Indians. As a result the Indians offered to sell a huge tract of land to the British government and also requested a specific grant to the Suffering Traders (the Baynton and Wharton group) to compensate those merchants who had lost merchandise during Pontiac's Uprising. With the connivance of Croghan, the Indians in attendance offered land for which they had no real claim.

The British government refused to accept the Fort Stanwix agreement, and Hillsborough's plan was followed. Many western forts were closed and the regiments sent to the seaboard where they later fought with the American patriots. This action left the frontier without protection.

Although the taxation disputes created by London were the primary issue in the coastal cities, on the frontier the issues were Indian unrest created by French intrigue, British rules that hindered the colonial traders, and the refusal of London to permit settlement west of the mountains. The Indians found strong support from the French in Illinois and Canada and from British Canadians who reflected the policy of the London government's intention to prevent the westward movement of the Americans. After a few years of comparative quiet, the Indians were aroused by the actions of the settlers and the land barons. The colonists became the enemy of the Indians after 1765. In deference to Indian concerns, the London government opposed westward expansion, angering the colonial merchants. The Indian-settler conflict remained until the Revolution, after which American policy favored the settlers and damned the Indians as the fur trade was no longer a priority.

# 5

# The New York Traders

Trading with the Indians in New York dates back to the seventeenth century. The Dutch who settled New Amsterdam had competed for furs with the French in Montreal since the seventeenth century. New Amsterdam became English territory in 1664 and was renamed New York after a war with Holland. British merchants moved into New York but the Dutch continued to trade.

After the French capitulated at Montreal in 1759, the Dutch spread out and began trading at Fort Niagara, Detroit, and even Michilimackinac. Albany enjoyed the advantage of cheap West Indian rum, superior English cloth and kettles, and lower prices than the French were able to offer the Iroquois along the Mohawk Valley and at Oswego. The Iroquois of New York became middlemen, purchasing goods from the Dutch and English and in turn supplying the tribes farther west.

The merchants of Albany and Schenectady were also involved before 1760 in the illegal trade with Montreal by providing the French with low-cost English goods in return for furs. The Albany traders sent goods to Montreal using Lake Champlain and connecting rivers. Indians were used as the middlemen in the trade, and several Dutch families made considerable fortunes. The Dutch traders had the advantage of cheap rum and ready access to British merchandise. In the 1760s the Dutch still dominated the New York trade although British and other colonial merchants were taking over the wholesale business of importing from England, as the Dutch had few contacts there. A number of discharged soldiers also began to compete with the Dutch as well.

An intense internal rivalry developed in New York between the Dutch versus the other colonists and the British merchants. The colonists had little respect for the Albany Dutch. The British thought very little of these "low lived rascals" who would cut one another's throat for a raccoon skin. The antagonism between the Dutch and the other colonists was apparent in a letter by Sir William Johnson: "The Dutch are grown so imperious since ye present administration, that in short there's scarce any bearing with them." Elsewhere, Johnson described Oswego traders as Dutch from Albany, Schenectady, and the Mohawk River who in general were very ignorant and practiced parsimony in diet, clothing, and all other expenses. They had no ambition to build the trade but were content to sell the contents of a small canoe (worth £372 New York, or $47,000) in the three or four months that they traded at Oswego. The remainder of the year they spent idle in their homes, living on the small profit made in the summer.

Johnson complained of unscrupulous storekeepers who provided cheap rum to get the Indians drunk and then made enormous profits from the remainder of their goods. The Albany merchants were often criticized for the fact that a much higher percentage of their trade was in rum, as compared with the merchants from other areas. The Albany traders "intent upon gain, right or wrong, sell them spirituous liquors; and after making them drunk, cheat defraud and overreach them in bargains. Any wonder the Indians fight back?" In Detroit, Captain James Stephenson commented that the traders, most of whom were from New York, "were a sad set, for they would cut out each other's throat for a raccoon skin." In the face of such damning contemporary comment, little more can be said. Trading with the Indians could be dangerous, and only adventuresome men dared involve themselves.

Because the Albany traders floated their cargoes from Albany by rivers and lakes with only a few short portages, rum was far easier to transport than on other routes such as the Ottawa River route, which had numerous portages between Montreal and Michilimackinac. The route from Philadelphia to Fort Pitt consisted of many miles on horseback. West of Fort Pitt only horses could move on the Indian paths north of the Ohio River. The eight-gallon kegs weighing 64 pounds apiece were difficult to carry over long portages or on horseback. Even though the profit per pound was less on the rum because of the cost of moving it, the ease of water transportation made it more profitable in the case of the Albany traders. Some traders would arrive in Detroit with their canoes loaded only with rum, even though an effort was made to require that only a fraction of the cargo be made up of rum.

The Albany traders usually dealt at the forts, where soldiers could cope with unruly drunken Indians. The Iroquois complained of traders who took rum to the hunting grounds to get the pelts before the Indians could take the furs to the forts. The solution suggested by colonial merchants was to restrict trade to the forts. If the French were restricted to trading at the posts, then the colonial traders would be able to undersell them. The colonials were reluctant to visit the Indian villages for fear of being robbed, as the Indians could easily kill a trader and take all of his goods. However, that robbery seldom did occur is evidenced in the fact that the names of the same traders appear in the records year after year; likewise, few lost their lives.

Farmers of Dutch descent also served as canoe men and teamsters, just as the farm boys from the St. Lawrence Valley served the French merchants. Merchandise was transported from the Hudson Valley to the West by canoe men and wagon masters who usually had Dutch names. In addition to filling the roles of petty merchants, boatmen, and teamsters, the Albany Dutch were also merchants. Many had reputations extending across the Atlantic, and family connections among the merchants in Albany, New York, and London were as important to the Dutch as to the British.

Unlike the French in Canada, the Albany merchants had good connections with England. They had ties with New York correspondents, with English agents, or directly with the English suppliers. The Sanders family of Albany obtained merchandise in London, Amsterdam, and the West Indies as well as from Lawrence Vander Spiegal, their agent in New York City, and sold many supplies to the British army in the New York campaigns during the late 1750s. John Sanders of Schenectady, the most active member of the family during the period from 1760 to 1774, imported fabrics, tools, gloves, hats, nails, household utensils, and many other items from London, while returning ginseng, furs, and coin in payment. His correspondents in London were Champion & Hayley, James Bonbonous, Moses Franks, John Steel, Champion & Dickinson, and Henry Jordice. Sanders traded with customers in Schenectady and along the Mohawk River valley, many of whom described themselves as fur traders on various petitions during this period.

David Vander Heyden of New York dealt with his brother, Dirk, in London. Gerrard G. Beeckman of New York had his younger brother, William, in Liverpool as his correspondent, and Jacob and John Beeckman were merchants in Albany. Perhaps the most prominent Dutch merchant was Jelles Fonda, a former agent of Johnson. Fonda's headquarters was in the Mohawk Valley and supplied many of the canoes that carried merchandise from Albany to Detroit.

Typical of the early colonial traders was Hans Leger from Albany, who received a pass in October 1760 from General Thomas Gage at Montreal to trade with the Indians in dry goods only (no rum!). However, Daniel Claus, Johnson's Indian agent in Montreal, had advised Gage that Leger was a petty trader who seldom dealt honestly and would be a disgrace to the British.

In addition to the Dutch, the Irish, the Scottish, and the English were active in New York, along with men whose families had been in America for one or more generations. John Askin, an Irishman who later succeeded in the Michilimackinac trade, had his beginnings in Albany in the 1760s. Daniel Campbell, a Scot, was a prominent Schenectady merchant who established a sizeable business in Niagara and Detroit. John Macomb, an Albany merchant who later gained prominence in Detroit, was active in Niagara from 1761 to 1766. James Phyn, a Scot, entered a partnership with John Duncan and Peter VanBrugh Livingston in 1763 that employed James Sterling in 1762 to take over dealings in Detroit. John Porteus of Detroit and Sterling were added to the partnership in 1765 to open business in Michilimackinac when Livingston and Walter Rutherford, who had joined the partnership in 1762, dropped out. Alexander Ellice provided it with capital. Phyn & Ellice subsequently became one of the major trading companies on the frontier, based in Schenectady.

The major customers of Phyn & Ellice were not the Indians but the army, the Indian Department, and traders who dealt with the tribes and the inhabitants of the posts in the West. Through the firm's agents, such as Sterling and Porteus, their trade extended not only to Detroit but also to Michilimackinac, the Mississippi River, and into the area northwest of Grand Portage. Phyn & Ellice even cooperated with its rivals from Montreal by supplying them with heavy goods in Mackinac. Their major advantages in developing their thriving business were the capital provided by Ellice and the convenient transportation system via the Hudson River and the Mohawk River–Oswego–Lake Erie route.

The expansion of trade with the Indians in the Albany area was indicated by the increasing tempo of correspondence of John Sanders, a New York merchant. In July 1761 Sanders was corresponding with Moses Franks regarding an invoice for £125 New York ($15,750), with James Bonbonous about two invoices for nearly £85, and with Champion and Hayley about an invoice for £110. In November 1761 Sanders wrote to Champion and Hayley that he had sent the firm a hogshead of beaver and peltry to sell at the best advantage. The estimated value of the shipment was £186 New York ($23,430). He also ordered a shipment of goods including cloth, muslin, garlics (a type of cloth), chintz, handkerchiefs, calico, and needles. On the same day, Sanders sent a bill of exchange to Franks for £104 sterling ($20,800) and ordered Robert and Richard Ray of New York to buy for his account frieze, serge, suiting, taffeta, boys' stockings, and mohair suiting. Also in

November, Sanders paid John Bonbonous £100 sterling and ordered nails, broadaxes, frying pans, and other dry goods. Despite the departure of most of the army to the Caribbean in June 1761, Sanders was able to pay all his debts in full either in sterling bills of exchange or by shipment of furs.

The primary point of contact between the Dutch and the Indians was Oswego, at the eastern end of Lake Ontario. It had been the chief trading point for the Dutch before 1760, with eighty traders. Johnson estimated the total value of merchandise traded annually before 1760 as £20,000 sterling ($4 million). He set the markup rate at 50 percent at Oswego, 70 percent at Niagara, and 100 percent at Detroit. Therefore, a small canoe of merchandise should have returned £558 New York ($70,300) in fur and a profit of £186 New York ($23,436), enough to maintain a family.

The most prominent merchant at Oswego was Henry VanSchaack. VanSchaack moved to Oswego in 1759 from Albany and began trading in 1759. He imported English goods and sold them in Niagara and Detroit. By 1768 the Dutch settlers created a monopoly for carrying the canoes and cargo over the portage using packhorses and horse-drawn wagons. In the 1760s the Mohawk River route continued to be significant despite the competition from Montreal and Quebec. In 1767, 20 percent of the peltry and skins from Michilimackinac were sent to Albany.

Much of the merchandise from Albany did not stop at Oswego but was sent on west to Niagara and beyond. Bradstreet estimated that 180 canoes each with £170 sterling's worth of merchandise left Albany. Eighty stopped at Oswego with £13,600 sterling, and 100 canoes continued west with £17,000 sterling (or $3.4 million) in merchandise.

Niagara was the next important post along the Mohawk River route to Michilimackinac and was also linked to the Montreal route by Lake Ontario. In 1726 a stone storehouse was built by the French at Niagara to compete with the British post at Oswego. After Niagara's capture by the British, Edward Cole from New York and John Van Eps from Schenectady were among the first to travel there in May 1760 to open trade with the Indians.

Fort Niagara was located at the mouth of the Niagara River on Lake Ontario with a garrison of more than one hundred men. It was the focal point in commerce on the lower lakes, guarding the portage around Niagara Falls, and served as the major trading post in the 1760s. The army closely supervised trade with the Indians who arrived at the post in the spring. An area on the beach where the traders could deal with the Indians was established. Soldiers were posted to prevent any disturbance.

The amount of trade conducted at Niagara was estimated at ten canoes' worth of goods in the 1760s, valued at approximately £3,750 sterling ($750,000) plus the sizable quantities of presents distributed by the Indian

Department. The total trade averaged more than £4,700 sterling. The Albany merchants made considerable profits from selling rations to the Fort Niagara garrison and presents for the Indians to the Indian Department. In May 1768 a single payment of £772 New York ($97,000) was made for sixteen boatloads of provisions. In June 1768 Phyn & Ellice was preparing another large order for the garrison and the Indian Department. The presents were distributed by the commissaries, who purchased the goods from the local merchants. The opinions of the French and New York traders were divided over the role of the commissaries at Niagara. The French petitioned Johnson, claiming that the commissaries were discriminating again them. These charges were challenged by the New York traders, Peter Ryckman, Volkert VanVeghter, William Hare, Alex Fraser, Jacob Nukerck, and Groesbeck.

Many Indians traveled to Fort Niagara each summer to trade furs with the dozen or so traders usually there during the 1760s. Edward Cole of New York City and Justice Van Eps of Schenectady went to Niagara in May 1760 to trade with the Indians. In 1761 the British grant to Walter Rutherford for the exclusive right to trade at Fort Niagara was protested by Johnson. All trade was halted by the Indian rebellion in 1763. After Pontiac's Uprising, Rutherford's monopoly was ended and more traders were given passes to trade at Fort Niagara, including those with both English and Dutch names. In 1765 Henry VanSchaack, Edward Cole, and Daniel Campbell joined in a venture to trade at Fort Niagara. In 1766 passes to trade at Niagara were given to Alexander Fraser, Peter Ryckman, Barret Visscher, Garret VanVeghter, Ephraim VanVeghter, William Hare, Thomas Visscher, Garret A. Rosseboom, Thomas Williams, Edward Pollard, Harms Vandell, Garret-Teller, and Henry Williams.

In 1761 Peter Van Brugh Livingston of New York City; Walter Rutherford, a former captain; and John Duncan, a former lieutenant in the 44th Regiment, formed a partnership with James Sterling and approached Sir Jeffery Amherst, the governor-general, for permission to establish a settlement on the southern end of the portage at Niagara. They stressed the great advantage of having forts established at both ends of the Niagara portage as the French had. Rutherford inferred that the proposal had been discussed with Johnson before communicating with Amherst, but in May 1761 Johnson called this plan bad policy because Indian land would be taken and that would prove to the Indians that the British intended to drive them out of their country.

However, in July 1761 James Sterling received a grant for 10,000 acres on Navy Island, a large island in the Niagara River above the falls, on condition that he build a storehouse. This was a huge grant equal to two hundred 50-acre farms, four times the number of farms at Detroit! By the end of July 1761 the storehouse was completed and stocked with goods.

Albany merchants protested the favorable position because Sterling was intercepting the Indians coming to use the portage road from Lake Erie to Lake Ontario. In October 1761 Johnson echoed the objection.

Another petition in January 1762 by the Albany merchants attacked the privilege given to Sterling and his partners, Rutherford and Duncan. Sterling monopolized the trade, contrary to the promise of a free trade. In February 1762 Johnson reported to Amherst that he had received a memorial signed by fifty Indian traders protesting Sterling's trading house. The traders wanted permission to trade at Little Niagara on Lake Erie along with Sterling to give the Indians a greater choice and to share in the profits. Amherst responded that he had never granted exclusive privilege to any person to trade at Little Niagara. Everyone was free to carry on the trade there if agreeable to regulations. On April 21, 1762, Johnson wrote to Captain William Walters at Niagara that no monopoly had been granted at Niagara and that all were free to trade under the rules. Sterling was forced to share the trade with the others.

Most of the Indians who traded at Fort Niagara were Iroquois from western New York. In 1770 a Seneca traded furs for silver armbands, and later fifty Chippewas went to the fort. Some Indians also arrived from the west side of the Niagara River. The post commander commented on April 30, 1765, that the Indians from north of Lake Ontario had not yet arrived at the fort.

To the loss of the Niagara merchants, many Indians traded before they reached the post. In the early 1760s Sterling intercepted them. In the late 1760s the Indians from the Lake Erie area were intercepted by Edward Pollard's trading post at Little Niagara at the south end of the portage around Niagara Falls. In 1768 Phyn & Ellice sent a cargo in three canoes to Pollard worth £591 New York ($75,000) as well as a previous cargo worth £451 New York ($56,800). Pollard had also ordered 200 gallons of rum worth £115 New York ($14,500) from John Macomb. Pollard was doing very well in 1768, ordering £1,042 16s. New York ($131,400) in goods from Phyn & Ellice. Delivery was delayed by winter weather, but the goods were expected to arrive in the spring of 1769. Pollard also ordered rum from Macomb worth £115 7s. 8d. New York ($14,450). At 3s. 6d. per gallon the order would have been for more than 200 gallons. Pollard's aggressive business activities, combined with the competition from Toronto on the north shore of Lake Ontario, brought trade at Fort Niagara to a standstill in June 1766.

Traders at Toronto also purchased fur from the Indians before they reached Fort Niagara. In 1766 General Gage was trying to enforce the rule of confining the trade to the posts at Niagara. The interpreter at Fort Niagara,

Jean-Baptiste DeCouange, reported that trading was occurring at Toronto in January 1766. The two trading posts on the north shore of Lake Ontario were Frontenac and Toronto. Thomas Dunn and John Gray had leased the posts for fourteen years in 1762 for £400 per year, which gave them a monopoly of the trade at those two locations. In August 1766 Governor James Murray prohibited trade on the north shore of Lake Ontario except for Dunn and Gray.

In early 1767 Sir William Johnson reported to General Gage that two illegal traders, Joseph Bryan and James Morisson, had been arrested at Toronto but that there were several more traders on the north shore intercepting the Indians and ruining the trade at Niagara. Benjamin Roberts, Johnson's Indian agent at Niagara, let them pass to trade farther west without punishment. Gage requested that Acting Governor of Quebec Sir Guy Carleton punish the two traders and prevent others from trading without permission. In 1770 Ferral Wade and Michael Keyser were trading openly at Toronto and had acquired 112 pounds of beaver and 70 pounds of deerskin plus many other furs. They had already sent 120 pounds of beaver to Albany for sale. The Indians wanted everything the traders had, but there were no small items left. Wade and Keyser needed more goods as they intended to spend the winter there. They wanted Jew's harps and red strouds and were expecting two canoe-loads of goods. A great trade was at hand, with a gallon of rum selling for one beaver, a stroud for three beavers, and a kersey (a type of garment) for three beavers. Evidently Wade and Keyser were trading with Johnson's permission but asked him for a pass to validate their activity and make the British army officers leave them alone.

The problem of traders at Toronto was a continuing irritation to the merchants at Niagara. In 1766 Roberts, Johnson's agent at Niagara, reported that the traders at Toronto and Pollard at Little Niagara, south of the fort, intercepted the Indians and that not much trade was conducted at the fort.

The Niagara merchants protested trade on the north shore as the Indians were intercepted before they paddled across the lake to the fort. Signing the petition in March 1766 were Henry Williams, Alexander Fraser, Peter Ryckman, Hugh Boyle, Thomas Williams, Harmanus Wendel, Garret-Teller, Ephraim VanVeghter, William Fease, and Edward Pollard. Henry Williams, Thomas Williams, and Hugh Boyle were among the traders who signed petitions at Detroit. William Fease also signed another petition on 27 March 1766. Alexander Fraser, a former officer in the 78th Regiment who had traveled to Illinois with the Indian agent George Croghan in 1765, was a partner of Abraham Van Eps in September 1765. William Hare was an Indian Department officer in 1764 with Henry Montour. Hare signed four other petitions in 1766 and 1767. Edward Pollard was an active trader at

Niagara from 1765 to 1768 dealing with Phyn & Ellice and Norman McLeod and selling goods to the Indian Department agents. Garret A. Rosseboom was a New York trader who moved to Canada in the 1760s. In 1763 Rosseboom was a partner of Abraham Lansing at Green Bay and in 1766 was active at Niagara. Peter Ryckman had been in Albany in 1764 and was in Niagara in 1766 and 1767. He returned to Niagara in 1772 and was captured by the Indians. Garret-Teller, originally from Schenectady, was in Niagara in 1762, went to Detroit in 1763, and traded in Niagara in 1766 and 1767.

Another petition contained the names of additional traders. Ephraim VanVeghter was in Niagara in 1762 and received a pass to trade at Toronto that year. In 1763 he was in partnership with a Wendell who was killed by the Indians at Big River near Niagara when VanVeghter was wounded. He was trading in Niagara in 1766 and 1767. Garret VanVeghter was trading at Niagara in 1766 and 1767. Barret Visscher was peddling rum at Niagara in 1762 that was confiscated by the British army. In 1764 he was in Albany protesting the regulations limiting trading to the posts as well as the use of rum. In 1766 he was trading at Niagara. Thomas Visscher (probably Thunis Visscher) moved to Canada in the 1760s from New York and traded at Niagara in 1766 and 1767. In 1768 John Lees met three canoes owned by two Dutchmen named Visscher as well as George Meldrum and Thomas Williams, all of who were named as either Detroit or Niagara merchants. Harmanus Wendell, a justice of the peace in 1762 in Albany County, was captain of a sloop on the Hudson River in 1763. In 1764 he was in Albany protesting the British rules confining the fur trade to the posts and in 1766 was at Niagara.

There was a mixture of Dutch and English names on the petitions. All of them opposed the British rules that in effect gave the fur trade to the French who had evaded the rules by giving rum on credit to métis (French Indians) who wintered with the Indians and acquired the furs as they were brought in.

On October 8, 1767, Norman McLeod, another agent of Johnson, complained that only one Indian had traded at Fort Niagara since September 22. The traders passing through from Detroit all complained about the competition from Illinois, where traders were free to winter with the Indians and were coming up the Miami River. Traders from Canada received passes to trade in Illinois but traded all of their goods along the way and never reached Illinois.

By 1769 relations between the Indians and the army were deteriorating. No Indians were allowed in Fort Niagara, and at the post the Indians were allowed to sell only venison for bread. A sentry had threatened a Seneca chief with a bayonet, and the Indians were very dissatisfied with their shoddy treatment.

Detroit, the next major post beyond Fort Niagara, had 300 dwellings and as many as 2,500 people including the garrison in 1760. Inside the fort 70 or 80 houses were laid out in regular streets. Most of the French lived on 60 farms, each having a narrow frontage on the Detroit River. The farms stretched ten miles on both sides of the river, which was 900 yards wide.

In 1761 Captain Daniel Campbell described the fort as large and in good repair with two bastions facing the river and one facing the land. On each bastion a three-pounder cannon and three small mortars were mounted. The fort was surrounded with palisades, all in good repair. When the Indians laid siege to the fort in May 1763 only 120 men were willing to defend it, including 100 soldiers of the 60th Regiment and 20 English traders. As a result of the haphazard reinforcements to defend the fort against Pontiac the garrison consisted of small companies from three regiments. In early 1765 Lieutenant Colonel John Campbell of the 7th Regiment arrived to take command. In the fall of 1766 he was succeeded by Captain George Turnbull of the 2nd Battalion of the 60th Royal American Regiment.

Detroit was a substantial market for New York traders. In addition to trading with the Indians there was a demand for rations and rum for the army, supplies for the French farmers, and presents for the Indians. As the use of sailing vessels on the lakes increased, Detroit became relevant as a source of provisions for the army and the French traders in the Great Lakes area. The army also purchased a variety of merchandise from the merchants. To repair the fort in 1763 James Sterling sold the army construction tools worth £261 New York ($33,000). In addition the army purchased presents worth £156 New York ($20,000) for the Indians in the fourteen months ending November 1763 from Sterling. Sterling was only one of nearly twenty merchants supplying the troops at Detroit. In 1767 Johnson sent Croghan to Detroit with £1,000 sterling ($200,000) to pay for Indian Department expenses, primarily gifts for the Indians.

After the uprising was quashed in 1764 Detroit resumed its role as a center of the fur trade, serving the routes leading south to the Ohio River valley by way of the Maumee River and the Wabash River and also St. Joseph, located on the east shore of Lake Michigan. The value of the fur trade at Detroit was estimated at seventeen canoes (£6,375 sterling, or $1,275,000), compared to only £3,187 for Fort Niagara. Most of the goods were sold to traders and winterers who visited the fort in the spring. Although many Indians lived near Detroit during the summer, few others traveled to Detroit compared with Michilimackinac, Fort Pitt, or the posts in Illinois.

In September 1767 a group of merchants in Detroit signed a memorial to Sir William Johnson to remove the restriction of trading to the posts. Included in the list were Henry VanSchaack, Thomas Williams, William Edgar, Richard McNeal, Samuel Tymes, Pierre Fleurimont, Duperon Baby, Jean-Baptiste Chapaton, Isaac Todd, and Philip DeJean. Four of the names were French, one was Albany Dutch, one Jewish, and the other four men were colonists.

Two months later another group of merchants in Detroit signed another memorial to Johnson. Included were Henry VanSchaack, Williams & VanAlen, and Rinkin & Edgar, all of whom had signed the earlier petition, plus George Meldrum, Hugh Boyle, Peter Pond, Joshua Rand, Henry Williams, Cornelius VanSice, Jacob Lansing, Allen McDougall, John Magill, James Sterling, John Porteus, and Benjamin James. The second memorial included more Albany Dutch names but no French names.

Combining the two lists, we find that four men were from Schenectady and Albany and could be considered Albany Dutch. Henry VanSchaack, originally from Albany, had established a trading post at Oswego in 1759 and was very active in the frontier trade, traveling between Detroit and Albany. In 1765 he was a partner of Edward Cole and Daniel Campbell at Niagara and had close ties to Sir William Johnson. In 1767 VanSchaack accepted two bills of exchange for £775 New York ($97,650) for Indian Department purchases. In 1768 he left Detroit and transferred his Indian Department business to Allan McDougall. In 1769 VanSchaack was on the verge of bankruptcy.

Cornelius VanSice has not been located elsewhere. Jacob VanSice was a freeholder in Schenectady in 1771, however, and may have been a relative.

Jacob Lansing, an Albany trader, sold black wampum to Johnson in 1759. Lansing signed several petitions concerning the rules of the fur trade, including one in Albany in 1764. In 1762 he had protested the privileges of Rutherford and Duncan at Niagara. His relative, Myndert Lansing, was an importer in the West Indies and paid Spanish dollars for cargoes received from Madeira, London, and Amsterdam.

John VanAlen, Henry Williams's partner, sold goods to Johnson in 1763 and purchased wampum in 1765 from Henry Holland of New York. Holland was the supplier for Myndert Schuyler and the Lansings of Albany.

Eight other signers came from New York but did not have Dutch names: Thomas Williams, Henry Williams, George Meldrum, William Edgar, David Edgar, David Rinkin, Samuel Tyms, and John Porteus. Thomas Williams was a former officer in the New York militia and a trader at Detroit dealing with William Edgar as late as 1776. He made a claim for payment from Johnson in 1762. In 1766 he signed another petition protesting the restriction to the posts. In 1768 he brought a canoe to Detroit along with two owned by the two Visschers from Albany and George Meldrum.

Henry Williams, an Albany trader, had 240 gallons of illegal rum confiscated in Niagara in 1762. He was a partner of VanAlen in 1767. In 1762 and 1767 he signed petitions as a Niagara trader. In 1764 he signed a petition opposing restriction of trade to the posts in Albany. As a dealer in rum, Williams could profit only if allowed to trade in the Indian villages beyond the control of the British army.

George Meldrum was a Schenectady trader who brought a canoe-load of goods to Detroit in 1768 in partnership with Thomas Williams. In 1776 he was in Detroit to sell grease to William Edgar for shipment to Michilimackinac. He was not a major player.

William Edgar, one of Detroit's most influential merchants, was associated with Thomas Shipboy of Albany; Robert Callender of Philadelphia; Jean-Baptiste Chapaton, a French trader; Chapman Abrams and Isaac Todd, prominent Jewish traders; and Simon McTavish, a Scottish trader, along with many others, including a relative, David Edgar.

David Edgar of Schenectady was in the Indian trade with William Edgar. In 1767 he sold ninety-three steel traps to the Indian Department that he had obtained from Daniel Steel of Albany. Edgar sent goods to both Detroit and Michilimackinac.

David Rinkin was in partnership with David Edgar. Rinkin ran a store in Michilimackinac in 1779. Samuel Tymes was a Schenectady trader.

John Porteus went to Quebec in 1764 and in 1765 was an agent for the Duncan Rutherford group. He assisted Sterling in the Michilimackinac trade in return for one-fourth of the profits. In 1766 he signed a merchant's petition in Montreal. In 1767 he provided security for two canoes to go to Michilimackinac, and in 1768 he was in Detroit representing both Duncan and Phyn & Ellice of Schenectady. He became a partner with Phyn & Ellice in 1769 to manage affairs in Detroit and Michilimackinac and was also a partner in building a sloop in 1700 with Tymes, Sterling, and others. In 1774 he was responsible for closing out the partnership of Porteus and Phyn & Ellice. John Porteus was a minor character working for the larger merchants.

Two former British army officers, James Sterling and Richard McNeal, were important traders from New York. Sterling was the major player in Detroit. He came to America with the British army and served as a commissary for General Frederick Haldimand from 1759 to 1760. He was popular with the French, settled in Detroit, and married a Frenchwoman, Miss Cuiellierrie, in 1765. The commandant at Detroit had noted in 1761 that he was the only trader from New York who sold goods other than rum. In 1761 Sterling was the agent for Duncan, Rutherford, and Livingston at Niagara and he became a partner in 1764. In 1763 he warned the British of the impending uprising by Pontiac. In 1767 Sterling claimed that he traded £100,000 sterling ($20 million) annually, which would have put him in the same class as Baynton and Wharton of Philadelphia. In 1770 he built a sloop in company with a number of partners.

McNeal, a former captain in the 78th Regiment during the Seven Years' War, was at Venango, a trading post on the Allegheny River north of Fort Pitt, in 1760 with Colonel Henry Bouquet. In 1765 he was in Montreal and was associated in trade in Detroit with Rinkin and Edgar in 1769 and with Isaac Todd in 1766 and 1769, jointly providing security for a canoe of goods bound for Detroit.

Another group were the four French merchants, Pierre Fleurimont, Duperon Baby, Jean-Baptiste Chapaton, and Philip DeJean. Fleurimont advised Sir William Johnson regarding interpreters in 1763 he was active in the fur trade. In 1765 Fleurimont brought ninety packs of fur to Montreal that he sold for 1,000 Spanish dollars ($40,000). In 1766 he was at Fort Erie disputing with the British army over trade restrictions. He had a canoe in the trade between Montreal and Quebec in 1767 under Des Voyce and another in 1768 valued at £560 ($112,000).

Baby, a member of a prominent Canadian family, came to Detroit in the 1750s. In 1761 he was in Fort Pitt selling fur to the Pennsylvania traders but was in difficulty with the British army because he attempted to trade with the local Indians without a pass. In 1763 he sided with the British during Pontiac's Uprising. Later, he went to Montreal and attempted to get a pass to trade in 1764. He signed a petition opposing restrictions on trade in 1765. In 1767 he went to Michilimackinac with a canoe of goods under Antoine LeFortune and sent another canoe to winter in the northwest worth £500. In 1768 he sent two canoes to trade via Lake Erie from Fort Niagara.

Jean-Baptiste Chapaton came to Detroit in 1718 and remained a leading merchant through the Revolution. He sided with Pontiac in 1763. In 1769 he purchased 1,000 pounds of gunpowder, indicating that he had a substantial business.

Philip DeJean came to Detroit from France in the 1750s and was a prominent merchant through the 1760s. In 1767 he was appointed a justice of the peace in Detroit, an indication that he was a leading citizen.

Isaac Todd, a Jewish merchant, came to Montreal in the early 1760s and in 1765 and 1766 signed petitions protesting restrictions on the fur trade as a merchant of Montreal. In 1766 he was arrested by the British army for illegal trading at Toronto and ordered to return to Montreal. Instead, he remained at Toronto and ordered a fresh supply of goods from Montreal.

In 1767 he provided security for three canoes bound for Michilimackinac. In 1769 he provided security for twelve canoes bound for Michilimackinac and had contacts with William Edgar, Rinkin and Edgar, and Peter Pond. Although Todd spent most of his time in Montreal and Michilimackinac, he probably signed the petition in Detroit because of his business interests there.

Hugh Boyle came to Detroit in 1764 from Pennsylvania, where he had been trading on the frontier since 1761. In 1764 and 1765 he sold supplies to Captain John Butler at Fort Niagara. In 1765 he signed a petition as a Niagara trader. While wintering in 1772–73 Boyle was killed by a French employee. He was not a significant player.

There were five others who signed the memorials but did not fit any of the categories. Peter Pond was born in Connecticut in 1740 and had served in the militia in the Seven Years' War. Still a young man after the war, he went to Detroit to trade in furs. In 1770 he was asked to go on a trading venture to the Northwest valued at £4,600. Pond purchased the goods in Montreal and sent them with Todd to Michilimackinac. He recorded his experiences wintering in the Northwest in a journal that gave a vivid picture of the fur trade. Pond was a minor merchant in 1768 when he signed the petition in Detroit.

John McGill, a Scottish merchant, came to Montreal and wintered in the Indian country in 1770. He provided security for a canoe to Michilimackinac in partnership with Urbin Tessie valued at £1,200 Quebec ($168,000), an extremely valuable cargo. In 1772 he signed for two canoes for Michilimackinac. He had a brother in the fur trade and was a man of substance, considering the value of his canoes.

Benjamin James was in Detroit in 1766 and supplied Jehu Hay, an agent of Johnson, rum, pipes, Jew's harps, and other articles to be used as presents to the Indians. He was at best a minor trader. No other mention of Joshua Rand or Allen McDougall was found.

The analysis of the men who signed the two memorials offers an excellent cross-section of the merchants in Detroit. Many moved freely among Montreal, Michilimackinac, Niagara, and Albany. All found common cause in objecting to the restriction of trade to the posts, which most ignored to some extent in the coming years. Their major competitors were the French from Illinois who wintered with the Indians. Other than Sterling, none was a major player in the same category as Baynton and Wharton or the Gratz brothers of Pennsylvania.

The merchants of Detroit were unhappy in the late 1760s. They expressed their concerns in the November 1767 memorial to Johnson protesting the restriction of trade to the post because it favored the illegal traders from Illinois. Free trade would enable everyone to trade with the Indians, and even the Illinois traders would come up to Detroit to buy the cheaper English goods. Having the traders go out among the Indians did not increase the danger as the Indians could rob the traders on their way to Detroit on Lake Erie anyway. Free trade was being practiced at Michilimackinac without danger. Another problem was too much liquor. Brandy was given to the Indians at a low price and discouraged them from hunting. The solution proposed was that merchants from Quebec and New York be limited to carrying only half their cargo in liquor, and the remainder in dry goods. Merchants with good reputations, the signers believed, should be allowed to winter with the Indians but with only fifteen gallons of brandy. The signers of this petition were primarily French traders.

The last major post on the Great Lakes in the 1760s was Michilimackinac, where trade was dominated by the smaller traders, some of whom brought only a single canoe of goods to the fort each summer. The traders sent their furs to Montreal via the Ottawa River and to Albany by lake schooners. In 1767, of forty-two fur shipments from Michilimackinac, twenty-nine went to Montreal and thirteen to Albany. In 1768, as another example, Isaac Todd informed William Edgar in Detroit that Daniel Chabert de Joncaire wished to send his fur to Montreal and his deerskin to Albany.

General Gage described the Michilimackinac trade as a gathering of several hundred vagabonds in June and July to sell their fur and buy merchandise for the next winter. Some had lived with the Indians for periods ranging from twelve to thirty years and had adopted their lifestyle. In 1765 Louis Cadot accompanied eighty canoes of Indians from Lake Superior and expected thirty more canoes to follow, all coming to Michilimackinac to trade furs accumulated during the winter. Baptiste Cadot had bribed them with gifts of tobacco. In response to the Indians' request, Captain William Howard, the post commander, gave Jean-Baptiste Cadot permission to winter with the Indians the next year.

In 1765 a petition to Captain Howard concerning wintering was signed by five New York traders, one Jew, and twenty-two Frenchmen. The Jew was Ezekial Solomon, and the New Yorkers were Joseph Howard, Edward Chinn, Henry Bostwick, James Stanley Goddard, and Benjamin Frobisher. The Frenchmen were Nicholas Bezze, J. Carrignant, Chabeillet (perhaps Augustin Chabollier), Bouillerèse, Poultney, Louis Chaboulley (Chabollier), Duperon Baby, Marchesseaux, Pierre LeDuc, Jean-Baptiste Guillon, Joseph Caron, François Moutron, Aimable Auge, Jean-Baptiste Bisionette, Louis Chevalier, Leonard St. Pierre, F. Joilliet, Pierre Cardinal, Charles Boyer, Jean-Baptiste Bissonette, Soulleyney, and Petite (Joilliette) Derreoice. The heavy proportion of French merchants indicates the dominance of their role at Michilimackinac compared with Detroit and Niagara.

Solomon, who had been a partner of Goddard, was trading at Michilimackinac in 1760 before the British army arrived. He had a number of partners who were active in the trade from 1760 until 1774. During Pontiac's Uprising, four of his partners were captured by the Indians and the partnership lost £18,000 sterling ($3,600,000). During the Revolution he operated a store at Michilimackinac.

As for the colonial traders from New York, in 1763 Howard asked for compensation for losses during the uprising. In 1764 he was trading at Michilimackinac and he continued there until the 1770s. Chinn, trading in Montreal in 1761 and in Michilimackinac in 1763, was taken prisoner by the Indians at St. Joseph later in 1763. In 1765 he was back in Michilimackinac selling merchandise to the army. Active in the fur trade until the 1770s, he married a daughter of Forrest Oakes, a prominent Montreal trader.

Bostwick was trading in Michilimackinac in 1760 and also supplied the army there in the 1760s. In 1766 he obtained a permit from Captain Howard at Michilimackinac to winter with the Indians. Goddard was a partner of Solomon and was trading with him in Michilimackinac in 1761. He was also a partner of Forrest Oakes and William Grant in 1761. In 1765 Goddard went to Green Bay on a trading venture and in 1776 he went there to recruit Indians to attack the colonists on the frontier.

Frobisher started in the fur trade in 1765 and took two or more canoes to Michilimackinac and Grand Portage annually through 1774. In 1769 he had nine canoe licenses. In June 1769 he purchased corn and flour from Rinkin and Edgar at Michilimackinac.

Other traders were active in the outlying posts. Evan Shelby and Edmund Moran were captured at Green Bay in 1763, but Moran escaped and went to New York, where he sold furs worth £2,000 sterling. Moran did not abandon his hopes to make a fortune in the fur trade, and in September 1764 he was on his way to Fort Pitt with eighteen horse-loads of goods. He accompanied Bouquet's army to the Tuscarora camp in October 1764, leaving most of his goods at Fort Pitt, but by October 21, 1764, he had already sold nine horse-loads to the army and expected to sell the remainder.

At Michilimackinac, many Indians came to sell their furs in the summer of 1765 despite the French lies that the British would kill them as retribution for Pontiac's Uprising. Several hundred winterers also made their annual trip to the post after spending the winter in the Indian villages. The Indians had been deprived of merchandise during the uprising and were sorely in need. By the end of June 1765 over 700 Indians were at Michilimackinac, most of them from north of Lake Superior. In a very successful exchange, they brought a large quantity of fur and the merchants had a good supply of merchandise.

Around the Great Lakes the Indians relied on the traders for luxury goods that were becoming necessities. When they did not have sufficient fur to purchase supplies for the coming year, the merchants extended credit, expecting to be paid in fur the following summer. The Indians seldom broke their word for fear of cutting off the supply of guns, ammunition, and clothes. Therefore, they were forced to maintain the trust of those traders who would supply them. The tribes were eager to restore a faith and credit operation in the exchange of furs when the colonists replaced the French. In September 1761 the Indians across the river from Detroit asked Sir William Johnson to grant them credit as the French had done. Although Johnson claimed that he could not force the colonial traders to sell their goods on credit and the Indians would have to establish a credit relationship, he finally did instruct the traders to grant credit.

In May 1763 Fred Hambuck, an agent of William Edgar of Detroit, reported that a canoe had come in from wintering with very little fur and the greater part of the goods unsold. "The trade is all over here and there is still a great deal of goods left in this Fort. Other traders being still worse off than myself having made considerable credits to the Indians last fall and but few of them paying their debts." Despite these examples of nonpayment, the Indians continued to obtain credit, as a margin could be charged to cover bad debts. The need for supplies and the lure of rum were incentive enough to bring the Indians back to the posts, and given a minimum of enlightened self-interest among the merchants, the hunters would be obliged to make some payment before obtaining additional merchandise.

Some transactions involved not only the Indians but also French inhabitants, the army, the Indian Department, and other merchants. One example of these complex transactions is a shipment of merchandise brought to Detroit in 1763. Apparently involved, although not specifically mentioned, were Edward Cole, a Detroit merchant who later became the commissary for the Indian Department in Illinois; Major Robert Rogers; Cezar Cormick, an Albany trader; and a man named Butler (probably John or Thomas, both of whom were associated with Johnson). The profit was more than 100 percent. Not indicated was who paid for the original cargo, but each of the partners shared equally, receiving one-fourth of the net £626. More than half of the goods were sold to the army and the Indian Department, and one-fifth of the cargo was sold to British merchants. Less than a quarter of it was exchanged for pelts, most likely with the French traders in the Detroit area

The traders from New York were universally disliked, and the colonial traders in general were not respected by the British army in Canada. In 1766 Governor James Murray of Quebec referred to the colonial traders in Canada as 450 contemptible sutlers and traders who were at odds with both the army and the French inhabitants. Guy Carleton, acting governor of Quebec, echoed the sentiment in 1767, referring to the British and colonial traders as disbanded soldiers or adventurers in trade who lacked frugality. Many had already left Canada and more would leave within the next few years. Johnson referred to the merchants in Quebec and Montreal as "dregs," discharged soldiers, and sundry persons from other colonies and Britain. They allied themselves with dishonest French and British agents and he classified all of them as "cheats."

Even the merchants in Detroit had a low opinion of the lesser traders in 1767. They stated that anyone with £50 New York ($6,300), the cost of a canoe-load of rum, could become a trader. One-third of the trade was carried on by men of low character who had only rum. As a result, the Indians were drinking all day instead of hunting for more furs. With fewer furs available, the price paid for them in goods increased and made the trade less profitable for the honest merchants.

In 1773 Major Henry Basset at Detroit complained that the traders were outcasts of all nations and the refuse of mankind. He wished for a police force that could punish those who cheated the Indians because the army had no authority to control the traders.

These harsh words were probably justified, and the fur trade in the Great Lakes area was a brutal, competitive business. The French had the advantage of a long history with the Indians. The Pennsylvania traders had the financial backing of wealthy Philadelphia merchants. The Jews had religious ties with traders all over the colonies who provided them with information, financial backing, merchandise at low prices, and an effective marketing network. The traders working for the New York City merchants had similar advantages— good financing, low prices, and efficient marketing. The Albany Dutch played the one card in their favor, the ability to deliver unlimited quantities of rum to the Indians at prices lower than their competitors because the Mohawk River–Lake Erie route involved a minimum of overland movement. The Indian desire for rum nearly equaled that of the British soldiers and the American colonists, creating a vast market of 10,000 customers compared with the few soldiers and colonists on the frontier. No amount of regulation or enforcement could prevent eager customers from obtaining rum, and the Albany traders profited handsomely.

# 6

# The Pennsylvania Traders

In addition to the French and New York traders, traders from Pennsylvania formed a distinct group. Before the Seven Years' War, fewer than 300 Pennsylvanians were dealing with the Indians of the Ohio Valley, including up to 21 licensed traders, each accompanied by as many as 10 horse drivers. Many of the traders had served in the Pennsylvania Provincial Regiment stationed on the frontier in 1759. The former soldiers observed that sizable profits could be made from the Indians. Colonel Hugh Mercer, the Pennsylvania battalion commander at Fort Pitt, heard that half the officers of the Pennsylvania regiment had resigned in 1759 to become sutlers or peddlers with the British army during the next spring. Of the 304 officers identified as serving in the Pennsylvania militia during the French and Indian War, 23 were later recorded in frontier business. These former officers and soldiers evolved as traders dealing with the Indians on the Pennsylvania frontier.

The traders in Pennsylvania were of two types—those who traded in the Indian villages, and the clerks who operated stores in the forts. The former risked their lives and their capital, while the latter worked as agents for merchants who took the financial risk. There was little danger in running a store in Fort Pitt. The customers of the traders included Indians, the army, the Indian Department, and farmers. The Indian Department purchased gifts for the Indians.

The Indian trader had to be of a very strong character because he not only faced danger but also harsh physical conditions, including the uncertainty of even obtaining food. The typical fur trader from Fort Pitt has been described as being rough, bold, and as fierce as the Indians, wearing a blanket coat or deerskin, and armed with a rifle, knife, and tomahawk. A man named Strump was described as wearing a light brown cloth coat, a blue greatcoat, an old hat, and leather breeches. Ironcutter, presumably his Indian companion, wore a blanket coat, an old felt hat, buckskin breeches, long trousers, coarse white yarn stockings, and shoes with brass buckles. These men had to keep in the Indians' good graces or they would be killed. Entering a village of unhappy Indians could pose a serious threat to their longevity.

The clerks traded only in the forts rather than risk their lives in the villages. The storekeepers tended to cheat the Indians because the army protected them. Also, the clerks often gave the Indians liquor to confuse them while selling their furs. At the same time, the Indians often stole from the storekeepers by setting up a ruse while their friends took small items.

Estimating the total value of the furs purchased by the Pennsylvania traders is difficult. Many of the furs were not exported legally but instead were used to pay Dutch smugglers in exchange for tea and manufactured goods from Europe. British laws controlled the colonial trade, and legally the Dutch could not carry merchandise into the American colonies or purchase fur. However, large quantities of tea, cloth, and other goods were smuggled into the colonies on Dutch ships. The official fur export figures show the discrepancy. Less than £50,000 sterling's worth of fur and deerskins were exported legally from New York and Pennsylvania combined, compared with £100,000 sterling's worth from Canada. The financial records of colonial merchants clearly indicate that far more fur was collected from the Indians in Pennsylvania and there was no local market.

The traders carried their merchandise on packhorses, usually having a string of at least a dozen and often more. Depending on the number of horses, the trader hired one or more Indians as handlers. A handler was required for each half-dozen horses. Each horse carried more than a hundred pounds, so a string of twenty horses carried more than a ton of merchandise worth more than £150 sterling ($30,000), compared with a Canadian canoe that carried nearly three tons of merchandise worth £375 sterling ($75,000). Some traders purchased a Pawnee female slave as a traveling companion.

A considerable number of men were employed to handle horses and perform other duties including rowing the boats on the Ohio River. Their names represent the many ethnic groups then living in Pennsylvania. The saddlers, horse drivers, and boatmen were hired by the season from among the farmers. These temporary occupations were undertaken by young men for a few years to obtain cash for their families. In contrast, wagon masters and carpenters were professionals whose names appear year after year in the records.

The chief route for frontier traders in Pennsylvania was from Philadelphia to Fort Pitt using the Forbes Road, which passed through Lancaster, Carlisle, and Bedford. The road was passable from Philadelphia to Carlisle by either one-ton farm wagons drawn by two horses or the heavier Conestoga wagons drawn by four heavy draft horses or oxen. West of Carlisle the road was poor and packhorses were used.

The objective of both traders and merchants was to profit from the sale of merchandise in return for furs. Although the potential profit margin was substantial, no one could make a fortune in one year. The traders ignored the rules restricting them to the posts and went directly to the Indian villages to buy fur and deerskin. The best plan was to establish customers in a village and return there every year to sell goods—either for pelts or on credit for the coming winter—and to collect any debts from the previous summer. By providing this dependable service, the trader could expect protection from the Indian village. Three or four years of successful trading might yield enough profit to buy land and lead a civilized life.

The trader used packhorses to carry the merchandise and returned loaded with deer hides. Although the process was slow and the profits small, the practice of trading in the villages hurt business at the stores in Fort Pitt.

The Pennsylvania traders are often cast in the role of prime villains in the accounts of unrest on the frontier. They were accused of using liquor to make the Indians drunk and then cheating them, causing the otherwise peaceful Indians to react violently. Colonel Henry Bouquet described these country traders in March 1761 as "the scum of the neighboring provinces who have no visible means to live except a license." A month later, Bouquet sternly reported to General Thomas Gage that he had the houses of traders destroyed in punishment for illegal dealings and sale of rum to the Indians. Mercer believed that the British army should prevent such "vermin" from coming west.

However, the motives of the wealthy eastern merchants who accused the village traders are questionable. The Indians continued to insist that the traders be permitted to come to their villages rather than going to the forts themselves. The upscale merchants operated stores in the posts under the protection of the British army and were losing business to the traders in the Indian villages. The powerful merchants recognized that the visits of both French and colonial traders to the Indian villages were their greatest competition, and the merchants did all they could to limit trade to the posts. The accusation that the traders abused the Indians by making them drunk and cheating them described the very same activity that took place in the forts, probably to a greater extent than in the Indian villages. It was safe to make the Indians drunk at the forts because the British army could stop them from attacking the merchants. In the Indian villages the individual traders had to deal fairly for their own safety, and providing too much rum could endanger their life.

In an attempt to prevent abuse of the Indians, Pennsylvania issued licenses, approximately fifteen each year, but many people traded without a license. Those who were licensed are seldom noted elsewhere as being involved in the Indian trade. They apparently obtained a license to open stores to deal with tribes living near to settlements, who came down from the hills from time to time to obtain liquor, ammunition, and other supplies.

Unruly traders spread out rapidly in the Indian villages west of Fort Pitt despite Colonel Bouquet's rule that no trade was to take place beyond the posts. In early 1761 William Trent, one of George Croghan's agents, gave a cargo to a French trader on credit to take to a British garrison on the Miami River at the request of the army.

In 1761 Croghan, as Indian deputy at Fort Pitt, and General Robert Monckton, the commander there, permitted trading in the tribal towns. In February 1761 Monckton allowed Pennsylvania traders to travel overland to Detroit if they conformed to the rules of trade set by Croghan. The rules were to sell at agreed prices, cultivate good understanding with the Indians, trade justly, grant credit, show their invoices to Captain Donald Campbell as soon as they arrived in Detroit, and follow Campbell's instructions on where to trade and what could be sold to the Indians.

Other traders came from Fort Pitt to share in the newly opened trade, including Trent and Alexander Lowrey. When Trent and Lowrey arrived in Detroit in May 1761, Campbell asked to see their invoices and the prices of the goods and then assigned them a location where they were permitted to trade.

Business expanded rapidly westward. Cargoes were taken to Detroit, Sandusky, the Lower Shawnee towns, and the Delaware villages by Robert Callender, Michael Teaffe, Lowrey, John Hart, and Hugh Crawford. The Pennsylvania traders were primarily concerned with the territory immediately west of Fort Pitt in 1760, but they soon spread out. Although there were thirty-seven colonial traders in western Pennsylvania in 1760, only one went to Detroit and none to Michilimackinac. In 1761 there were thirty traders in Pennsylvania, sixteen from either New York or Pennsylvania had reached Detroit, and one had gone to Michilimackinac.

Some of the traders from Pennsylvania did not reach Detroit, stopping instead at Sandusky on Lake Erie even though doing so was against Bouquet's rule. Campbell sent fifty men to bring the renegades into Detroit. He complained that the traders from Fort Pitt did not know how to trade with the Indians, and so they brought goods for the French inhabitants, rather than for the Indians. The traders soon sold all of their merchandise because Detroit had been cut off from French supplies for several years. By December 1761 the merchandise was gone and the Indians begged Campbell for supplies, but he had nothing for them.

In July 1761 a trader presented a general pass to Bouquet claiming that it covered any Indian settlement and therefore he need not remain at Fort Pitt. Although Bouquet refused to honor the pass, in November 1761 James Kenny, the agent for the Pennsylvania Commission, noted that many traders had already gone to the Indian towns. The effect of the posts-only rule was to confine the legitimate traders to the posts while vagabonds from all areas, especially Illinois, took over the trade.

The Pennsylvania traders did very well in the summer of 1761. In July 1761 Patrick Allison, who purchased his goods from Baynton and Wharton, had just returned from Fort Pitt and was in Lancaster waiting for his skins to arrive. He already had seven horse-loads of summer skins at John Harris's and would send the additional skins by the first wagon. His partner, Matthew McRae, was still in Fort Pitt intending to send thirty horse-loads of skins to Philadelphia in three weeks. In August 1761 Edmund Moran returned from a trading venture at Fort Pitt and joined his partner George Ross in Lancaster. The two planned to return to Fort Pitt to check on their furs.

Other Pennsylvania traders included T. D. Hambuck from Lancaster, a former officer in the Pennsylvania militia and a friend of Bouquet. In January 1761 Hambuck planned a trading venture to Detroit in partnership with Isaac Vandervelden, a young storekeeper in Lancaster who put up £500 Pennsylvania in goods for his half share. They planned to take six horse-loads of goods to Detroit to trade for twelve horse-loads of furs and then return to Fort Pitt. They had to arrive in Detroit early in the spring before the ice melted on the lakes and rivers, which would open the way to the advantage of the French from Montreal. If they arrived before the French, they could sell their goods and double their money before the French arrived and cut prices. The partners succeeded. Vandervelden returned to Fort Pitt in July 1761 with one thousand pounds of fur and skins, six horse-loads. Hambuck remained behind to sell the remaining merchandise.

The colonial traders complained bitterly of the posts-only rule in 1761, yet in 1762 General Gage along with Sir William Johnson, head of the northern sector of the Indian Department, remained convinced that the five posts—Kanamistigoua on Lake Huron, Michilimackinac, Green Bay, Detroit, and Ouiatanon—were adequate to carry on all trade. The result of the posts-only rule was a great loss for the Pennsylvania merchants and allowed inroads into the Ohio River trade by the French from Illinois.

Pontiac's Uprising in 1763 brought trade to a halt for nearly two years. In 1765 when trade was resumed, many of the new men at Fort Pitt were former Pennsylvania militia officers, including Robert Callender, John Clark, Hugh Crawford, Fred Hambuck, Alexander McKee, William Patterson, John Prentice, Thomas Smallman, and at least fifteen others. Many of the Philadelphia merchants employed these former officers to act as their agents at Fort Pitt. Among those who established trading stores at Fort Pitt in 1766 were Joseph Spear, John Gibson, Daniel Elliott, Alexander Lowrey, and John Boggs. John Hart was the agent for Field, Callender & Company in 1765.

The number of licensed traders in Pennsylvania was remarkably low. Only eighteen were licensed in 1765 and as few as ten in the following four years. Among the traders receiving licenses were William Trent, Joseph Simon, David Franks, and Levy Andrew Levy. Trent was a partner of Simon, Franks, and Levy, all Philadelphia Jews. The partners placed Trent in charge of the operations at Fort Pitt from 1763 until 1769. Fort Pitt became the depot for traders Trent sent as agents throughout the area west of Fort Pitt.

A prominent figure was George Croghan, who had been in the fur trade in the 1750s and became an Indian agent under the supervision of Sir William Johnson. Croghan had business relations with William Trent and Baynton and Wharton.

The Indian Department agent at Fort Augusta was the illustrious Thomas McKee, the father of Alexander McKee, who was also an active trader on the frontier. Thomas received a trading license in 1744. In 1760 he was a deputy agent in Johnson's Indian Department working for Croghan at Fort Pitt. In 1761 McKee was the Indian Department agent at Venango and Presque Isle on Lake Erie. In 1762 Johnson offered McKee a position in the Indian Department, and he moved to Fort Augusta in the Susquehanna Valley in northwest Pennsylvania. In 1763 McKee was robbed by the Indians and joined the "Suffering Trader" group of men who had lost goods to the Indians during the uprising. In 1764, while living at Lancaster, McKee asked Johnson for pay for himself and his son. Earlier, in Fort Augusta in 1765, McKee had received £35 from Croghan and goods worth £338 Pennsylvania ($39,000) from Baynton and Wharton, presumably to be given to the Indians. In May 1765 McKee was in partnership with Baynton and Wharton on a shipment of goods worth £1,753 Pennsylvania ($201,480) to be sold in Fort Augusta. In 1766 he was still at Fort Augusta distributing presents to the Tuscaroras for the Indian Department. In July 1766 Baynton and Wharton and McKee entered a new venture, taking £800 in goods from the Fort Augusta operation and £920 from stock in Philadelphia—a total of £1,720 Pennsylvania ($197,800)—and sending the supplies to Fort Pitt for sale at the store there.

A number of merchants were located in the small towns along the route to Fort Pitt. One of the most famous in later years was Arthur St. Clair in

Ligonier, Cumberland County. St. Clair was a Scot educated at the University of Edinburgh who had served in the 60th Royal American Regiment during the Seven Years' War from 1759 to 1762. He resigned his commission in 1762. He had married well into a Boston family in 1760, receiving a dowry of £14,000 sterling ($2.8 million). In 1764 he built a fine home and a gristmill in Ligonier. Later he was a major general in the Continental army and fought the Indians after the Revolution.

In 1768 Bernard and Michael Gratz provided St. Clair and Captain Limes with credit to trade with the Indians. In July they sent an invoice for £94 Pennsylvania ($108,900) to St. Clair and Limes and urged them to send any furs to Philadelphia as the Gratz partners needed the money. St. Clair and Limes would receive dry goods and liquor only if furs were received. Apparently St. Clair did not deal fairly with the Gratz partners, who complained that one of St. Clair's men came down with a load of deerskin and sold it elsewhere rather than paying his debts to them.

Joseph Dobson of Carlisle was an agent for Baynton and Wharton at Carlisle, where cargoes were unloaded from the wagons coming along the road from Philadelphia. The merchandise was repacked at Carlisle and carried on packhorses for the remainder of the trip. Before 1770 Carlisle had more people than Fort Pitt.

In October 1767 Morgan, a partner of Baynton and Wharton, paid Dobson £45 Pennsylvania for expenses related to the Illinois expedition. In 1768 Dobson gave a complete report to Baynton and Wharton informing them that he was trying to move their merchandise to Fort Pitt in time to go down the Ohio River with Colonel Andrew Wilkin's troops. He also reported a rumor that the Indians would stage another uprising on the frontier.

Ephraim Blaine was an agent for Baynton and Wharton at Fort Pitt. In 1761 Blaine sold goods illegally to Duperon Baby from Detroit, who was later arrested. For this violation, all of Blaine's goods were confiscated by Colonel Bouquet. Subsequently, Bouquet took sterner measures when he destroyed Blaine's house, returned Blaine's merchandise, and banished him from Fort Pitt. In 1766 Blaine was in Carlisle and asked Wharton to lodge a land claim for him based on his service in the Seven Years' War. In 1768 Blaine left Carlisle with Joseph Spear to deliver six wagonloads of deerskins to Baynton and Wharton in Philadelphia. During the Revolution, Blaine, at the rank of colonel, was commissary general for provisions for the Continental army.

Joseph Spear moved about the frontier in the 1760s. He was a long-time partner of Robert Callender of Philadelphia and represented the partnership on the frontier. In 1761 he was in Detroit, and in 1762 he had a pass to take liquor for the garrison to Detroit. He formed a partnership with Callender and also was associated with Fred Hambuck. In Detroit in May 1763 Spear lost a considerable amount of goods to the Indians during Pontiac's Uprising and became another Suffering Trader. Later in 1763 he was again in Detroit.

In July 1763 Spear purchased 654 shirts and other goods valued at £2,784 Pennsylvania ($320,200) on behalf of Callender, Spear, & Company. In 1764 he was working with Baynton and Wharton and purchased goods worth £75 Pennsylvania ($8,730) from them. In January 1765 Spear's partnership sold goods worth £3,470 Pennsylvania ($399,130) to Baynton and Wharton. Later in 1765 Spear lost a quantity of goods when settlers raided a shipment destined for the Indians at Fort Loudon. In 1766 he purchased goods worth £535 Pennsylvania ($61,525) for Baynton and Wharton but paid only £295 for them. In November 1768 Callender and Spear shipped enormous quantities of rum to Fort Pitt to be sent to Fort Chartres in Illinois. Callender left Carlisle with 2,000 gallons of rum loaded on 100 horses, and 40 horse-loads of dry goods. A week later Spear bought ten hogsheads of rum (630 gallons, or 26 horse-loads). Spear's associate, Alexander Lowrey, moved sixty horse-loads of rum and Indian goods to Fort Pitt in the same month.

In 1766 Spear formed a partnership with John Prentice, who had served as a captain until 1760 in the Pennsylvania militia during the Seven Years' War. In 1762 Prentice was trading around Detroit as an associate of Abraham Mitchell. In 1763 he was captured by the Indians at Sandusky with 100 horse-loads of merchandise. Although reported as killed, Prentice was freed by the Hurons at Detroit in May 1764. The partnership of Spear and Prentice had dealings with Thomas McKee and Baynton and Wharton in 1766 and 1767. In 1768 Prentice traveled to Philadelphia from Carlisle with Ephraim Blaine.

Among a random sampling of the traders at Fort Pitt are six traders at Fort Pitt who complained to Sir William Johnson in 1766 that they had established proper trading houses at Fort Pitt but that Baynton and Wharton had set up a trading post on the Scioto River and intercepted the Indians before they reached the fort. The traders were Joseph Spear, Daniel Elliott, Alexander Lowrey, John Gibson, Simon and Milligan, and John Boggs. Spear has been previously described. No other reference has been found for Daniel Elliott or John Boggs.

Alexander Lowrey was born in Ireland and came to America in 1727. He started trading with the Indians in 1748 with Joseph Simon of Lancaster. In 1761 he was in Detroit with William Trent. Bouquet did not trust Lowrey and warned Captain Campbell at Detroit to be wary of him. Lowrey was in difficulty because of poor trading practices in Detroit in 1761 and 1762. In 1763 he was trading furs at Fort Pitt, working with David Franks and Levy, Trent, & Co. He lost goods in Pontiac's Uprising. In 1764 he was again in trouble and arrested at Fort Pitt. Nevertheless, in 1765 his license to trade with the Indians was renewed.

John Gibson also lost goods in Pontiac's Uprising. In 1763 and 1764 he was a prisoner of the Delaware Indians but he was again trading rum in 1765 at Fort Pitt.

James Milligan was another of Joseph Simon's many partners. In 1766 he was representing the partnership at Fort Pitt and dealing with Alex Maisonville and Baynton and Wharton. In 1770 he was a partner of John McClure at Fort Pitt.

As mentioned above, wealthy merchants hired agents to operate stores in the frontier forts and the Indian villages along the rivers west of Fort Pitt. Baynton and Wharton obtained a license in August 1766 from the governor of Pennsylvania to establish a store on the Scioto River after having asked General Gage whether he had any objections. The store was opened in 1765 and served the Shawnee Indians, saving them the trip to Fort Pitt. This favoritism granted the Shawnees caused an uproar with the Delaware Indians.

George Croghan continued to be the major customer of Baynton and Wharton. By November 1766 the partnership had sent Indian goods worth £1,683 ($193,545) to the trading store Croghan was operating on the Scioto River in the Shawnee territory. Croghan's store effectively reduced the volume of trade enjoyed by the merchants in Fort Pitt. Later in 1766 Baynton and Wharton received a license from Pennsylvania to set up another store in the Shawnee territory.

Alexander McKee also protested the store on the Scioto River, in a letter to Sir William Johnson. McKee had served in the Pennsylvania regiment in 1757 during the Seven Years' War. He was an agent in the Indian Department in 1761. In 1762 he was trading with the Indians in the lower Shawnee towns and served as an Indian Department agent at Fort Pitt from 1763 to 1765.

Thomas McKee joined with Baynton and Wharton to establish a store at Fort Pitt in 1766 to sell to the British garrison and buy fur that the Indians might bring to the fort. For this purpose £1,200 Pennsylvania's worth of merchandise originally intended to go to Illinois was left at Fort Pitt. Baynton and Wharton contributed goods from their store at Fort Augusta and its stock at Fort Pitt. In June John Irwin was given charge of the Fort Pitt store and instructed to clear out the building and check the gunpowder, clothing, and other items for possible damage. Any fur that Joseph Spear should send from Detroit to Irwin was to be sent on to Philadelphia in Edward Morton's wagons.

For the most part, Baynton and Wharton's affairs at Fort Pitt were being managed exceptionally well. Joseph Dobson had sent 14 horse-loads of fur obtained locally, had 60 more horse-loads with Alexander Lowrey to be sent to Philadelphia, and would collect another 5 horse-loads from John Hart, for a total of 79 horse-loads, or seven tons of fur and deerskin. Hart was the agent for Field, Callender & Co. at Fort Pitt in 1765.

In September 1766 beaver and raccoon from Fort Augusta worth only £62 were sold to Andrew Tybout. Later that month Baynton and Wharton sold beaver and raccoon worth £156 Pennsylvania ($18,000) from Fort Pitt to Andrew Tybout in Philadelphia. These small lots could not be shipped profitably to Europe but were convenient to pay for smuggled goods.

Most sales to the Indian Department were for gifts to groups of up to four Indians. Because spring was the best time to sell on the frontier, the total sales had increased to £450 Pennsylvania by May 30, 1767, but still the volume was very low. The account of sales to the British army and the Indian Department at Fort Pitt for the period June 1766 to March 1767 was only £222 Pennsylvania ($25,530), a trivial sum considering that the store had been stocked with merchandise worth more than £1,700 Pennsylvania in 1766.

Baynton and Wharton must have had brisk sales at its Fort Pitt store in the first half of 1768. In March Samuel Wharton thanked Johnson for telling Croghan to purchase £1,200 Pennsylvania's worth of Indian goods at Fort Pitt from Baynton and Wharton. In April the store was without liquor, silver, shirts, guns, gunpowder, and lead. The goods Croghan needed for an Indian treaty would have to be purchased elsewhere. In May Croghan transferred goods worth £243 Pennsylvania at Fort Pitt back to Baynton and Wharton to be sold to Pennsylvania for Indian presents. Because the partners' store did not have enough stock to fill the order, Croghan provided the needed items from Indian Department stocks.

The Pennsylvania traders eked out a bare existence in the late 1760s, mainly by selling to the Indian Department. The majority of the furs were being sold to French traders from Illinois. Pennsylvania traders on the edge of the frontier struggled with the French to gain a foothold in the territory that was supposed to be theirs after the Seven Years' War. The persistent French never gave up and one way or another remained in control of the trade. Their long experience and intermarriage with the Indians gave them the advantage. Because of their close relationship, the Indians were easily influenced by the French and were used as a tool to resist the new owners of the Ohio Valley to the point that the colonial traders never gained supremacy until after the Revolution.

# 7

# The Merchants

The traders dealing on the frontier purchased their supplies from merchants in Quebec, Montreal, New York, Philadelphia, and Albany. The eighteenth-century American merchants were wholesalers with warehouses rather than shops who imported in bulk. The major trading firms ordered goods from England and either sold them to traders or hired agents to deal with the Indian tribes. Philadelphia businessmen financed small traders who went to the Indian towns with a small stock of merchandise and rum worth £400 sterling and returned with deerskins and pelts. These wealthy businessmen also acted as bankers for the others by meeting obligations, paying wages, acting as sales agents, receiving furs from the posts, and either selling in America or consigning shipments to a London agent for sale on the London market.

In contrast, those people in business locally were called shopkeepers or storekeepers, but the lines were blurred. Some merchants dealt in both wholesale and retail. Training came by apprenticeship or by entering the family business.

Partnerships and individual companies were the forms of organization. The partnerships were formed for a period of from two to seven years and were often renewed. Merchants also engaged in joint ventures whereby a number of individuals took part in a single shipment.

The most lucrative markets on the mid-eighteenth-century frontier were the fur traders, the settlers, the British army, the Indian Department, and the French. Many merchants had made fortunes during the Seven Years' War. In 1760 the thirteen American colonies were in the midst of a commercial boom created, in part, by the lavish expenditures for provisions and other supplies for the British army during that war. The iron industry was flourishing, as were shipbuilding, fishing on the banks of Newfoundland, distilling rum, meat packing (beef and pork), and lumbering. Although there were some unfavorable English regulations of economic life, the merchants were prospering under the protection of the empire.

A new market was opened with the conquest of Canada, and colonial merchants flocked to Montreal and Quebec in 1760. On September 13, 1760, after the Capitulation of Montreal, General Jeffery Amherst invited the colonists to Canada. There was a rapid influx of British and colonial merchants. Most of them went to Quebec and Montreal either by sea or by way of Lake Champlain. Merchants from Great Britain, Connecticut, New York, New Jersey, and Pennsylvania tried to profit from selling goods on the frontier. Some Jewish merchants came as well. Whereas location determined the affiliation of most of the groups involved in frontier commerce, the Jewish merchants overlapped all of the geographical divisions and, based on their religion and mutual trust, conducted business with one another and all of the other groups in all areas.

On October 22, 1760, Governor James Murray of Canada opened trade with the Indians to everyone with no restrictions except that the Indians were not to be cheated and no liquor was to be sold. Although direct trade with the Indians in Montreal continued in the 1760s, the major function of Montreal was preparing goods for shipment up-country and returning furs east to Quebec for overseas shipment. The investment in Montreal was substantial, considering the damage from a fire in 1765 was estimated at from £88,000 to £300,000 ($17.6 million to $60 million).

Wilson (probably William Wilson, who traded on the Pennsylvania frontier from 1768 to 1774) went to Montreal in 1760 to investigate business possibilities, and Sir William Johnson asked Daniel Claus, an officer in the Indian Department, to advise Wilson concerning trade with the Indians. Claus responded in November 1960 that Wilson was satisfied and intended to remain in Montreal over the winter. Wilson had sold nearly £400 Quebec on his first day of business and hoped to sell his entire stock to French merchants within several months. Claus feared that Wilson would have nothing left for the Indians when they came in from hunting.

The British and colonial merchants employed discharged officers from both the British army and the provincial militia who contributed experience in dealing with the Indians. Many were Scottish officers discharged in Canada and encouraged not to return to Britain, where they were in disfavor because of their support of Prince Charles, the Stuart pretender to the throne. Johnson described the British and colonial traders in Montreal as the dregs of society, former colonial militia officers and men from other parts of the British Empire, all of them cheats. The bad opinion of the British and colonial traders endured as late as 1773. The commandant at Detroit, Henry Basset, described them as the outcasts of all nations and the refuse of mankind.

As background to this resentment of the new people in the trade lies the deep-seated prejudice of the upper class in England against the Scots in the eighteenth century. The English officers disliked the Scots because of their support of Prince Charles, a Catholic, and the attempt to overthrow George II in 1745. Had Prince Charles succeeded and then reinstated the Catholic Church, many of the British who had obtained land as a result of the confiscation of church property by Henry VIII would have lost their estates.

The Scottish regiments had been formed during the Seven Years' War and were sent to America to rid Britain of some of the troublesome Scottish lairds and their followers. Another fortuitous step was to disband the regiments in Canada rather than return them to Britain. The former officers had experience on the frontier, but many of the Scots lacked business skill and left Canada by 1767. Eventually the British merchants in Montreal had to rely on the French to deliver merchandise to the Indians.

The French were not eager to accept the British as full partners in the fur trade, even though they were forced to deal with them when cut off from their French suppliers. Later, the more astute Frenchmen sought connections in London; for example, the Baby brothers, prominent merchants in Detroit and Montreal in 1764, ordered directly from Joseph Henry Guinand of London. One of the Babys wrote a merchant, Valade, in New York City that year referring to Guinand and Hankey of London as associates.

Not only did the French try to eliminate the British middlemen in Quebec by dealing directly with London suppliers, they were cool to attempts to share in the retail trade at the western posts where they were also reluctant to accept the British as partners. Of more than one thousand ventures recorded in the fur trade license records, only forty show a French–British partnership or indicate that a British merchant providing the bond or security for a French trader. In 1767 Governor Guy Carleton claimed that the French were willing to cooperate, but the records show little evidence in earlier years.

Despite determined French opposition, the British and colonial mercantile community grew in Canada during the early years. Many British and American merchants who came to Canada in 1760 had gained experience on the frontier in Pennsylvania or New York and moved to Quebec and Montreal to compete with the French merchants. Only a few Albany merchants moved to Montreal, preferring to operate from Albany and

Schenectady, moving goods to Canada on Lake Champlain during both summer and winter and using the Mohawk River to Oswego in the summer. Two other groups were Jewish merchants and discharged army officers from both the British army and the provincial regiments.

Although the winter was mild and the river had not frozen by late December in 1760, few goods arrived from Europe, and therefore prices remained high all winter. It was feared that prices would drop in the spring, however, because goods worth £80,000 sterling ($16 million) were on ships at Halifax and Louisburg waiting to go upstream when the ice melted on the St. Lawrence River.

Anticipating the opening of trade to British and colonial merchants, British merchants in England sent cargoes of goods to be traded; for example, John Noble of Bristol, England, sent a cargo of captured French goods worth more than £2,600 sterling ($520,000) to Montreal in 1760, and he advised the firm of Baynton and Wharton of Philadelphia to do the same. Many Philadelphia merchants, realizing the potential of the Canadian markets, sent cargoes of dry goods and rum for sale to the army, the French, and the Indians.

Among the merchants attempting to exploit the Canadian market was Daniel Clark of Philadelphia. On October 2, 1760, he sent cloth and other goods valued at £30 on board the brig *Boscowen* to Quebec. John Collins reached Quebec with a cargo from Baynton and Wharton of Philadelphia by November 1960. John Day also went to Quebec with another stock of goods for Baynton and Wharton.

By cooperating with the French, Collins hoped to acquire most of the furs reaching Montreal for Baynton and Wharton. By the end of March 1761 Collins still had not sold the dry goods brought from Quebec to Montreal in February, so he transferred the stock to another merchant to sell to the Indians in the ensuing months. Returning to Quebec in April 1761, Collins found the French still reluctant to purchase from the British and colonial merchants who were thus forced to sell their goods at public auction at low prices. Merchandise was growing cheaper every day as the influx of ships from London had arrived, and prices were lower than at New York.

John Day received a cargo in Quebec on May 20, 1761. Not finding a market there, he took the merchandise to Montreal and opened a store. Neither the soldiers nor the French had cash, so he traded for beaver pelts. More beaver was available, but the French were reluctant to sell because of their allegiance to France. Yet by June 22, 1761, Day had obtained 1,500 pounds of beaver pelts and £100 worth of other furs and hoped that by September he would be able to ship a large quantity to England.

In February 1761 Collins, in Quebec, analyzed the trade in Canada for his employers, Baynton and Wharton. The dry goods previously sent for sale to the army had not been sold because the troops were supplied directly from London and the French refused to buy English goods because French styles were preferred. The British merchants were not eager to purchase goods because they believed that peace would come in 1761, at which time many British firms would ship goods to Canada, causing a drop in prices.

Because of the mild winter, the river to Montreal would open for ships early in 1761, so Collins urged Baynton and Wharton to move its cargoes to Canada early, and asked it to fill the orders he had received from Montreal merchants with shipments directly from London. The merchandise had to arrive by September 1761 as the Montreal merchants came to Quebec in September and October to buy goods.

Because the French were intent on controlling the trade, the only role left for the British and colonial merchants was supplying the French in Montreal and the various posts. The experience of Baynton and Wharton in Quebec and Montreal reflected the problems the colonial merchants had even in supplying the French traders. In 1764 Collins and William Govett could not pay Baynton and Wharton for goods received. Samuel Eldridge tried with little success to collect some of the outstanding debts from Collins and Govet and McLeane and Stewart. Because the French would not buy the goods, Eldridge had to auction the merchandise for £6,652 Pennsylvania ($765,000). Adding to the conflict, although goods sent from Philadelphia sold for 45 percent more in Quebec, the cost of transporting the merchandise to Quebec was 30 percent of the Philadelphia cost, leaving a slim margin of only 15 percent.

In 1766 George Allsopp also tried to collect money owed to Baynton and Wharton by the French. Boileau owed £101 Pennsylvania in September 1766 and Allsopp planned to sue him in December. Jean-Baptiste Parent owed over £400 Pennsylvania but had placed his assets in the hands of trustees, which meant that Baynton and Wharton would get only a fraction of what was owed. Bondfield and Chartier was also bankrupt and paid only five shillings to the pound sterling (one-fourth the amount owed). Ginice paid only three shillings to the pound sterling. Collins and Govett still refused to pay although the partnership was still in business. Allsopp had some good fortune: Papin paid his debt in full. The court ruled in favor of Baynton and Wharton with regard to Ainslie's debt.

We can best understand the composition of the merchant class in Montreal by studying some of the individuals. In 1766 fifteen of the merchants of Montreal signed a memorial protesting the trading rules: Isaac Todd, Samuel Holmes, John Delisle, Michael Wade, John Thomas (possibly Thomson), John Jenison, James Finlay, Neall Lessey, Jonas DeSaulles, Joseph Torrey, William Haywood, Lawrence Ermatinger, David Clunie, Edward Harrison, and James Morrison. In addition, twenty-four French merchants signed the memorial.

Isaac Todd, a Jewish trader, appeared in Montreal in 1766 and in 1767 provided security for twelve canoes destined for Michilimackinac, a major share of the fleet of canoes that went west that year. In 1767 Todd was in Detroit and a year later he went to Michilimackinac to supervise his commercial activities, commuting from there to Montreal through 1773.

Samuel Holmes was an Irishman who was in Montreal in 1765 and 1766 but does not appear in later records. John Delisle, who attempted in 1761 to obtain New York provincial citizenship, was in Montreal in 1765 and 1766. Michael Wade may have been a member of the Wade family that included Francis, Ferrall, and Matthew Wade, all of whom were active in commerce in Philadelphia, Pennsylvania, and Montreal from 1757 to 1766.

John Thomas, or Thomson, was probably the Thomson active in the fur trade at Fort Pitt from 1761 to 1764. John Jemison may have been the John Jemison or Jameson who was a justice of the peace of Bucks County, Pennsylvania, in 1761, 1764, and 1770.

James Finlay was a Scot who came to Canada about 1760 and wintered with the Indians in 1766. By 1768 he was a prosperous merchant dealing with Hunter and Bailey of London. Jonas DeSaulles has not been found, but John Peter DeSaulles received a license to take a canoe to Michilimackinac in June 1769 with security provided by Thomas Walker of Montreal. Joseph Torrey signed another petition in March 1766, but no other record has been found.

Lawrence Ermatinger was a Swiss who came to Canada in the early 1760s from London. In 1764 he joined with Richard Dobie in financing a canoe to trade with the Indians. He was active in the fur trade from 1764 to 1774 and sponsored two canoes in 1769. His investment in 1765 was placed at £3,000 sterling ($600,000). He married in Montreal and had four children between 1766 and 1772.

Edward Harrison signed a petition in Montreal in 1765 and in 1769 provided security for a canoe taken by James Morrison to Detroit. Morrison also signed a petition in 1765. His chief interest was grain and groceries, but he also was in the fur trade. In 1767 he was arrested for trading illegally at Toronto and taken to Fort Niagara. In 1769 he took a canoe to Detroit and another to Fort Erie. In 1772 he married a Frenchwoman in Montreal. No other record has been found of William Haywood, Neall Lessey, or David Clunie.

Many of the names of the twenty-four French merchants who signed the memorial in Montreal in 1755 are illegible. Some of those who could be identified were Michelle Ange, Matthiot, Louis and Jacques Hervieux,

Chenville, Amable Curot, Paschal Pillet, and Christopher and Charles Sanguinet.

A woman, Michelle Ange, was a proprietor of a store at Michilimackinac in 1780 with one-half a canoe-load of goods. Matthiot also signed a memorial in Montreal in 1765. Louis and Jacques Hervieux are identified as Montreal merchants in the Ramsey collection in the Minnesota Historical Society, and both signed other petitions in 1765 and 1766. Chenville signed another memorial in 1765 and had licenses to take canoes to Michilimackinac in 1767.

Amable Curot was trading with the Indians on Lake Erie and Lake Huron in 1764. In 1767 he was trading on the north side of Lake Ontario. He took canoes to Lake Nipissing in 1769 and 1770. In 1778 he had a license for a canoe to Green Bay.

Paschal Pillet took two canoes with goods worth £900 sterling to Michilimackinac in 1774 and took one canoe to Green Bay in 1778. He was in Montreal in September 1778. Christopher and Charles Sanguinet were active in the fur trade from 1765 to 1774 and had licenses to send canoes to Michilimackinac in 1769, 1774, and later. They were prosperous merchants who provided their own security for their canoes.

These brief biographies indicate that the merchants remained in the fur trade for a long period. There were two hundred British and colonial merchants in Quebec and Montreal in 1764. After Pontiac's Uprising the number dropped to thirty merchants from New York, Pennsylvania, and other colonies. On May 18, 1765, a disastrous fire ruined many of the traders in Montreal. Governor Murray estimated the loss at £87,580 sterling ($17,516,000). John Welles, an agent for Baynton and Wharton in Montreal, estimated the loss at more than three times that amount. The merchants who survived learned an important lesson—that the fur business required discipline—and many of the early British and colonial entrepreneurs who either would not or could not adjust to conditions left Canada.

By 1767 the conclusion of peace terms with the Indians increased the number of British and colonial merchants in Canada to fifty. However, in 1769 seventy-seven licenses were issued to trade with the Indians but only ten were given to men with British names.

While Canada was the best-known area for the lucrative fur trade, New York, Pennsylvania, and New Orleans were also commercial centers with valuable ties to the frontier, the settlers, and the Indians. Philadelphia was the center for Pennsylvania merchants in frontier commerce. It was one of the largest cities in the British Empire and the economic center of the thirteen colonies. During the decade of the 1760s the value of imports from Britain to Philadelphia was nearly £400,000 sterling in all but two years. Exports to England varied between £25,000 and £40,000 per year even though crop failures in Britain from 1766 to 1772 expanded the market for Pennsylvania flour and wheat. In addition, iron worth £11,000 Pennsylvania ($1,265,000) was shipped annually to England. Less than £4,000 sterling's worth of fur and deerskin was legally exported to Britain, but as much as £15,000 sterling was illegally sent to Europe.

The major exports to the West Indies and southern Europe were flour and wheat worth £300,000 sterling ($60 million). Portugal returned Madeira wine and salt worth £30,000 sterling. The remaining balance was paid for with bills of exchange the Portuguese received for wine sold in Britain. The trade with Portugal was extremely favorable to Pennsylvania.

The trade with the West Indies was balanced by imports of molasses, which was distilled into rum in Philadelphia. Merchants in the West Indies also paid for Pennsylvania provisions and lumber with English bills of exchange that they received for sugar shipped to Britain. The bills were used by Pennsylvania merchants, for example, James and Drinker, one of the most prominent merchant houses in Philadelphia, to pay for their imports from Britain.

The frontier became a major market for Pennsylvania in the mid-eighteenth century. The British acquisition of Canada in 1759 opened a new market for the Philadelphia merchants for the sale of rum and British manufactured goods to the French and the Indians. In 1760 the Philadelphia merchants expanded their scope of business rapidly in Canada and began developing an extensive trade in the Ohio Valley with the Shawnee and the Delaware Indians.

Much of this commercial activity was in anticipation of a vast increase in trade with the Indians in 1761. Before 1760 the trade with the Indians was divided between the private merchants and a public company created on April 8, 1758, by the Pennsylvania legislature based on the Quaker conviction that private dealers were not to be trusted with the Indians, and that a government trading agency would protect them.

The nine-member Pennsylvania Indian Commission was appointed to barter with the tribes. The commissioners, many of whom were merchants, were James Child, William West, Amos Strettell, Thomas Willing, John Reynell, Joseph Richardson, Edward Pennington, William Fisher, and Joseph Morris. Appointed as agents for the commission were John Langdale, Josiah Davenport, and Robert Burchan. The profits were to be used to pay for missionaries and teachers among the Indians. The commission also operated as a wholesaler to the smaller traders who went to the Indian towns. It had stores at Fort Pitt and Fort Augusta on the Susquehanna River, at the location of present-day Sunbury.

The commission received a major portion of its capital from Amos Strettel, a Philadelphia merchant with family ties in London. It subsequently received cash through the auction of its skins and furs by Thomas Lawrence, the public auctioneer in Philadelphia. The major sources of its goods were merchants in Philadelphia, including Willing and Morris, William Fisher, Edward Pennington, Francis West, and Amos Strettel. From London, John Strettel supplied gunpowder and Daniel Mildred shipped cloth and gunpowder.

By 1762 the Pennsylvania Indian Commission had sold £22,000 Pennsylvania ($2,530,000) in merchandise to the Indians. From 1760 to 1764 it made a profit of £694 ($80,000). In 1765 its profit skyrocketed to £9,014 ($1,037,000).

Private merchants were not as quick to take advantage of the increasing business opportunities as was the commission. John and Peter Chevalier, Philadelphia merchants, supplied the army contractors (Plumstead & Franks, the firm that furnished provisions for the troops) through Joshua Howell, their agent at Fort Pitt before he was replaced on March 21, 1760.

John Baynton and Samuel Wharton were leading Quaker merchants in Philadelphia with an extensive trade with Europe and the West Indies and the major traders at Fort Pitt in the late 1760s. The partnership of Baynton and Wharton made major purchases in 1760 from those involved in frontier commerce, including Ephraim Blaine, a Fort Pitt merchant, for £171 Pennsylvania ($19,655); John and Peter Chevalier for £353 ($40,595); Callender and Spear, the Carlisle partnership, for £297 ($34,155); Francis Wade for £97; John Hart for £88; and James Becham of Lancaster for £97.

Trading on the frontier, though usually profitable, was a dangerous business and few were willing to gamble their lives and fortunes. Although the frontier trade would eventually prove disastrous to Baynton and Wharton, the stakes were high at the time and might have paid off in enormous profits. Baynton and Wharton were not fortunate. The partners recorded a net profit of only £9,861 Pennsylvania from October 18, 1763, to January 31, 1765. The records showed an inventory of goods on hand at £6,445 Pennsylvania ($741,000). During this period, 1763 and 1764, Pontiac's Uprising caused major losses to all frontier traders, and the small profit that the partners did make probably resulted from their exports of flour and trade with southern Europe and the West Indies. The total cash flow was £40,585 Pennsylvania ($4,770,000), a considerable sum. In the first nine months of 1765 they had a deficit of £3,940 Pennsylvania ($453,100), most in the first half of the year. By June 1765 Baynton and Wharton owed their supplier in England, Richard Neave, £26,080 Pennsylvania ($2,999,200), equal to six months receipts for the partnership. The financial problems of Baynton and Wharton continued. In February 1765 Samuel Wharton was trying to obtain bills of exchange from the Indian Department in advance of providing the presents.

In 1766 John Irwin was appointed as Baynton and Wharton's agent at Fort Pitt. His instructions were to clean out the store and check the gunpowder, clothing, and other goods. He was to accept the furs that were sent by Joseph Spear from Detroit and send them to Philadelphia in Edward Moreton's wagons. Irwin was also directed to prosecute John McClure for trying to hold on to furs belonging to Baynton and Wharton. Irwin was given considerable powers to represent the partnership in Fort Pitt.

In 1766 Baynton and Wharton through its agent, George Allsopp, was selling large amounts of rum in Quebec at 1s. 11d. Pennsylvania ($11) per gallon. Alsopp also paid Hide and Hamilton of Manchester, England (manufacturers of metal goods that had been sent to Quebec), £200 sterling ($40,000) on behalf of Baynton and Wharton. Alsopp expected to be repaid by Baynton and Wharton from the proceeds of a shipment of wine from Philadelphia.

To promote its sales on the frontier, Baynton and Wharton relied heavily on connections with Sir William Johnson, General Thomas Gage, and George Croghan, an experienced Indian agent who had the most knowledge of the area. Baynton and Wharton purchased goods in far larger quantities than the average merchant. Philip Kinsey sold Baynton and Wharton goods worth £342 Pennsylvania ($39,330) and Hugh Reilly goods worth £325 Pennsylvania in February 1766. George Morgan, a wealthy young Philadelphian, later joined the firm and became its representative in the firm's most ambitious scheme: supplying the army, the local inhabitants, and the Indians in Illinois. Although the firm received payment in a wide variety of ways, the assets that could be used to meet its obligations in England were furs, deerskin, and bills of exchange.

On the one hand, by August 1766 Baynton and Wharton had practically ceased its old business of fitting out ships and sending cargoes to London, Boston, Newfoundland, and other ports because of the long lag between investing the money in such ventures and receiving payment. On the other hand, the partners continued to invest more money in the frontier. In February 1766 the partners had 140 horse-loads (nearly thirteen tons) of goods on the road to Fort Pitt, including matchcoating, stroud, guns, gunpowder, shirts, half-thicks, rum, and knives. Another example is the purchase of French and English blankets worth £318 Pennsylvania ($36,570) from Henry White on July 1, 1766. In April the firm sent goods valued at £926 by wagon to Fort Pitt. There was a steady run of charges ranging from £20 to £150 for transporting goods to and from the frontier from March to May 1766. In May it paid Mease and Miller £202 Pennsylvania ($23,230) for transporting goods to and from Fort Pitt. In September Baynton and Wharton purchased from Franks and Inglis provisions worth £397 ($45,600) that were delivered to Fort Pitt.

The scale of the Baynton and Wharton operation can be measured by its list of liabilities and assets when the partnership stopped paying its bills in November 1767. At that time it owed over £100,000 Pennsylvania ($11.5 million). Its creditors preferred that the partners remain in business with the hope that their bills would be paid in full rather than only a percentage being paid if bankruptcy were declared.

Baynton and Wharton's assets were worth £40,000 Pennsylvania ($4.6 million) in September 1767. The partners claimed that if they were able to collect additional sums that were owed to them, they would have a surplus of from £30,000 to £60,000.

The trustees appointed to conduct the firm's affairs complained that the partners had taken too many risks, specifically in the early months of 1767 when the Illinois venture became the partners' sole concern. The partners abandoned the profitable business of outfitting ships and shipping flour and bread to the West Indies. Previously these two activities had been Baynton and Wharton's most active and lucrative interests.

The partners had been meeting their Philadelphia obligations by selling bills of exchange for cash to James & Drinker, Jonathan Zane, and other Philadelphia merchants. These bills were drawn on Richard Neave, who served as Baynton and Wharton's agent in London. The bills later came back, protested by Neave because of insufficient funds.

Baynton and Wharton finally collapsed when it lost the contract to supply the army in Illinois with provisions. In desperation the partners turned to land speculation and lost even more money as London repeatedly spoiled their schemes.

Baynton and Wharton were part of a network of fellow Quakers throughout the colonies and in Britain. Religious ties were an important factor in eighteenth-century commerce. John Reynell, another Quaker merchant, had a long-term financial relationship with Abraham Redwood, a Quaker in Rhode Island, receiving a bill of exchange for £40 sterling ($8,000) in 1748. Reynell was also a close business associate of William Redwood, a Quaker merchant in Newport, Rhode Island. Reynell was still trading on the frontier in 1759 and complaining of the restrictions imposed by Croghan. In 1760 Reynell was a member of the Pennsylvania Indian Commission. In 1767 he sold merchandise worth £920 Pennsylvania ($105,800) to Baynton and Wharton and in 1768 merchandise worth £254 Pennsylvania ($29,200).

Henry Drinker of Abel, James & Drinker had been trading on the frontier since the 1740s, and by 1766 that firm was one of the major importers of frontier merchandise. In 1767 both Drinker and James were among the leading merchants of Philadelphia who signed a petition. In 1766 the firm sold goods worth £908 Pennsylvania ($104,400) to Baynton and Wharton for the frontier trade. The firm was also in the West Indies trade to obtain bills of exchange to pay for the large imports of dry goods from England.

Other non-Quaker merchants in Philadelphia included John Inglis, a Philadelphia merchant who supplied horses to Colonel Henry Bouquet, the commander at Fort Pitt, in 1760 and in 1761. He too was in the West Indies trade and protested the duty on the importation of slaves. He sold provisions to Baynton and Wharton in 1765.

Daniel Clark, a Philadelphia merchant, wrote to William Neal in London acknowledging an order including merchandise intended for the Indians, and he placed another very long order for delivery in the spring of 1761. Clark also ordered a small quantity of goods from Holliday, Dunbar, and Company. In November 1760 Clark ordered a long list of fabrics from Daniel Mildred (who also supplied dry goods to the Philadelphia Chevaliers and the Pennsylvania Indian Commission). In December Clark sent a shipment of rum and sugar to William Baker in London to balance his account. John and Peter Chevalier of London were dealing with Baynton and Wharton and William West.

Robert Callender was another Pennsylvania merchant in frontier commerce. From 1758 to 1760 he provided horses for the British army at Fort Pitt, with as many as four hundred in a single shipment. In 1761 he was trading with the Indians at Sandusky and Detroit in partnership with Fred Hambuck, providing him with goods worth £1,500 sterling, including rum. Callender had received special permission to sell rum from his close friend Colonel Bouquet. In 1762 Callender carried 180 gallons of liquor for the garrison at Detroit from Fort Pitt after receiving a permit from Bouquet. In 1763 Callender was supplying a wagonload and ten horse-loads of powder to Bouquet and contracting for army rations at Shippensburg. During the uprising, Callender claimed he had been robbed of goods by the Indians worth £8,110 Pennsylvania ($932,650). He was among the "Suffering Traders" who hired Croghan to go to London to recoup losses to the Indians.

After the uprising ended, Callender continued trading in cooperation with Baynton and Wharton. In 1764 Callender and his partner, William Spear, paid Baynton and Wharton £36 Pennsylvania for merchandise. Callender traveled with twenty-five horse-loads of Indian goods Baynton and Wharton sent to Illinois in 1769. The goods were camouflaged as British presents to the Indians. Believing that the shipment contained weapons for the Indians, thirty white settlers in Indian disguise attacked the convoy near Bedford. Callender continued to trade with the Indians after Baynton and Wharton failed. In 1770 he purchased half-thicks, Irish linens, and other goods for £580 Pennsylvania ($66,735) from William West.

William Moore, another Philadelphia merchant, offered to serve under Colonel Bouquet to pacify the Indians west of Fort Pitt in 1764. Moore was a justice of the peace for Chester County from 1764 to 1770. He sold Baynton and Wharton merchandise worth £272 Pennsylvania ($31,340) in 1765. In 1768 he made another small sale to that firm.

After Pontiac's Uprising Pennsylvania merchants had difficulty on the frontier as London imposed regulations to prevent abuse of the tribes. In 1768 the army at Fort Pitt restricted trade to the fort and issued an order that any goods offered for sale to the Indians other than at the fort were subject to seizure by anyone, in the same manner as an abandoned ship. However, these efforts to control trading off the post were futile. Because few Indians would make the long trip to the fort, the merchants in desperation sent men to the Indian villages to trade illegally. In 1767 some merchants who remained at Fort Pitt protested that other traders were ignoring the rules and going to Indian villages. In January 1768 John Gibson and Daniel Elliott left Fort Pitt to trade with the Indians in the Delaware towns. In the spring of 1768 the merchants demanded that the army force merchants trading off the posts to return. Their plea was of no avail.

The problem of enforcing the posts-only trade rule continued to be a source of controversy. The merchants complained that they had established stores at Fort Pitt with the expectation that the Indians would come there to trade. Instead, unauthorized traders were going directly to the Indian villages to compete with French traders who came up the Ohio River from Illinois.

In the 1760s the merchants of Philadelphia continually lost ground in the struggle with the French for the Indian trade between the Ohio River and the Great Lakes. By the end of the decade the French had regained their monopoly of the fur trade. The merchants turned to land speculation as a means to restore their finances.

The merchants in New York City did not specialize in frontier commerce but had an interest in the local New York City market. The traffic up the Hudson River affected almost every merchant in the city either directly or indirectly.

The merchants of New York did not face illegal French competition but still could not compete with the Canadian French in the Great Lakes. New York City was the second leading port in the colonies. A merchant there was usually worth in excess of £2,000 sterling ($400,000). Anything less was not enough capital to conduct major purchases and sales.

Family connections between merchants in New York City and London were basic to the conduct of business. As an example, Jacob Frank of New York dealt with his son Moses in London. In May 1767 John Sanders complained to Moses Frank about the quality of a shipment of shalleen cloth. Jacob in New York responded to the complaint and demanded that Sanders pay Moses in London. Sanders did so but informed Moses Frank that although they had dealt fairly in the past, there would be no further business.

Sanders also dealt with the Cruger family of New York City. In 1765 Sanders sent 300 Spanish dollars to pay one of the Cruger accounts. In 1766 Sanders demanded payment from Henry Cruger, a New York merchant, of £355 New York ($44,850). The Cruger family was well entrenched in the transatlantic trade. John Cruger was a mayor of New York City. John Harris Cruger managed the family business in Jamaica; Telemon Cruger was in Curaçao; Nicholas Cruger was in St. Croix; and Henry Cruger Junior was in Bristol. The younger Cruger was Sir William Johnson's principal agent for the purchase of supplies for the Indian Department. John Cruger, Beverly Robinson, and Peter Van Brugh Livingston had the contract to provision Fort Ontario and were paymasters and commissaries to the New York militia.

The Beekman family provides another example. Gerard Beekman of New York had a younger brother, William, in Liverpool and another brother, John, in Albany. In the 1760s Gerard was in the wheat and flour trade, receiving the products from John in Albany and shipping to other colonies as well as to Halifax and Quebec. Gerard shipped flaxseed to Ireland via William in Liverpool. He also dealt with David Barclay & Sons in London. John Beekman supplied Sir William Johnson and John Lottridge with Indian goods.

Dirck Vanderheyden arrived in London from Holland in 1752 to represent his father's interests. His brother, David Vanderheyden, was in New York. The Vanderheydens shared the ownership of a ship with Philip Cuyler of New York in 1758. David continued to trade in Indian goods with Johnson, Van Eps, Fairservice, VanSchaack, and others from 1759 to 1766. In 1765 Vanderheyden claimed a loss of £6,000 Quebec ($840,000) in the Montreal fire but still had some goods to sell. In 1766 his house in New York was vandalized by a mob opposed to the Stamp Act, and he was forced to swear an oath to oppose the act as well. In 1767 David Vanderheyden advertised in the Quebec newspaper that he would sell furs and provide goods for Montreal merchants. Dirck was the chief London agent for Cuyler and also provided goods to John Sanders and Johnson. Dirck and David's brother Jacob, who married Jane Livingstone in Montreal in 1770, was Dirck's partner and active in the fur trade.

Peter Van Brugh Livingston, another leading New York City merchant, was active in the West Indies, North Carolina, and the frontier trade. Livingston was associated with John Duncan, a partner of Phyn & Ellice, and with Walter Rutherford at Fort Niagara. In December 1768 Phyn & Ellice sent him eleven packs of deerskin and asked him to either sell at the fixed price or hold the skins until he received further instructions. Evidently the partners feared that Livingston would sell the skins at a low price.

Philip Livingston, the father of Peter Van Brugh Livingston, had made a fortune in the West Indies trade during the Seven Years' War when he was part owner of seven privateers preying on French merchant ships. He continued importing molasses illegally from the French islands after the war, using it to distill rum. In 1768 another relative, Peter R. Livingston was dealing with Michael Gratz and Sampson Simson in the provisions trade and shipping to the West Indies.

The major frontier merchants included William Darlington, who supplied Sir William Johnson in the 1760s not only for his own household, but also for the Indian Department. Peter Hasenclever and Thomas Shipboy were wholesalers for lesser merchants on the frontier. Hugh and Alexander Wallace were associates of Conyngham and Nesbitt and shared ownership of four ships including the *Rainbow*, the *Kitty*, and the *Sally*. Phyn & Ellice ordered the Wallaces to pay off a debt of £39 sterling owed by the partners to Welch, Wilkinson, and Startin, as the Wallace firm was holding a bill of £68 payable to Phyn & Ellice.

Robert Adams had served with the 46th Regiment in the Seven Years' War. In 1764 he was sutler with Bradstreet's expedition to Detroit. Later, he provided Johnson with Indian goods and supplied gifts for the Treaty of Fort Stanwix in 1768. In August 1768 he promised to do his best to fill an order for blankets, aurora, fusils, silver lace to decorate coats and hats, and wampum. However, some imported items were scarce and Adams asked Phyn & Ellice to supply the wampum.

Adams was an associate of Jelles Fonda in the Indian trade. In 1769 Adams was involved in a trading venture with Fonda and a trader named Steel trading with the Iroquois. Adams and Fonda purchased the goods and hired Bernard Wemp to do the actual trading with the Indians. The venture apparently turned out well, as Johnson ordered Adams to pay Fonda £393 New York ($49,540) in October 1769.

The extent of Adams's activity can be measured by Johnson's order to obtain goods for Indian presents that were scarce as a result of the nonimportation agreement. Included were blankets, aurora (a type of cloth), fusils, silver lace for coats and hats, and 45,000 wampum beads. Adams also provided financial services to Johnson and was ordered to pay Fonda, on Johnson's behalf, £393 New York ($49,518), an amount to be added to Johnson's account with Adams. Both Adams and Fonda were also in farming and potash production. The close connection of Adams and Fonda was typical of eighteenth-century business.

North of New York City, frontier commerce was controlled by merchants of Dutch descent in Albany, Schenectady, and along the Mohawk River. After the British gained control of Canada in 1760 Albany merchants shipped their goods by sleigh from Albany to Montreal in the winter of 1760–61. The winter route to Canada north of Albany was frequently used when ice closed the St. Lawrence River. John Welles and Matthew Wade traveled from Philadelphia via Albany, stopping to see Sir William Johnson on their way. Other traders traveling to Montreal from New York were Dirck Vanderheyden and Samuel Stringer. On March 17, 1761, MacKenzie and Oakes, merchants in Quebec, wrote to James and Charles Crokatt regarding the vast quantities of goods sent to Montreal over Lake Champlain in sleighs. The result was a glutted market that would worsen after the arrival of the ships from Europe.

Most residents of Albany were Dutch, and they had political and commercial control of the city. Names such as Staats von Lantvoord are common in the Albany account books. Appointment as an officer in the local militia was an indication of political power. In 1767 all of the captains of the Albany militia had Dutch names and they included some of the merchants often mentioned in documents relating to frontier commerce. Among them were Abraham C. Cuyler, Hendrick M. Roseboom, John M. Veeder, and Jacobus Van Alen. The Dutch used their political power to stifle business by new non-Dutch merchants in Albany. Any new merchants were taxed heavily by the city. In 1759 four new merchants were taxed £100 New York ($12,600) each, which amounted to one-twelfth of all taxes paid to the city. When they refused to pay, their goods were ruthlessly seized by the city.

The leading Albany merchant was Jelles Fonda who was very active in the fur trade. In 1768 Samuel Stringer offered Fonda a large quantity of merchandise suitable for the Indian trade. Fonda had a large quantity of fur and was willing to pay cash for goods. He had served Sir William Johnson as an Indian agent from 1758 to 1760 but was removed by General Amherst in 1760. Fonda was also a land speculator, buying land from the Indians with liquor in 1763 in partnership with Rutherford and Duncan.

A small number of non-Dutch traders were in business in Albany in the 1760s. Richard Cartwright was trading in the area in the late 1760s with John Stevenson, Daniel Campbell, and Phyn and Ellice. He was involved in the political fight in the New York Assembly to prohibit rum being sent to Fort Niagara, which was supported by the Dutch traders. The measure was opposed by the non-Dutch traders, who wanted an unrestricted trade at Niagara to intercept the Indians and discourage them from going to Oswego, where they had traditionally traded with the Dutch who provided liberal quantities of rum. If there was no rum at Niagara, the Indians would paddle east on Lake Ontario to Oswego.

Campbell had been active in the frontier trade at Detroit and Albany since 1758. In 1763 he formed a partnership with Henry VanSchaack and in 1765 added Edward Cole to the group. Together they brought in thousands of furs that Campbell was to sell in London. In 1764 Campbell was in disfavor with Sir William Johnson, but he was able to make amends in 1765 and later managed the provisions for Johnson at the Treaty of Fort Stanwix. In 1769 Campbell was in difficulty with the Sons of Liberty for having Indian goods delivered to him in November. Campbell pleaded that if he were not allowed to acquire the goods, the Canadians would take over the fur trade completely.

Samuel Tyms was a lesser participant in the Albany trade. In 1763 he was dealing with Daniel Campbell for cloth. In 1766 he was in Detroit, quarreling with Hugh Crawford. In 1767 he signed a petition for trade with William Edgar. In February 1768 Tymes went to Detroit via Schenectady, where Phyn & Ellice urged him to pay some of his debt to Hayman Levy. Later in 1768 Tymes did ship furs to Levy in New York City via Phyn & Ellice. In 1770 Tymes was a partner of Campbell, John Porteus, and William Sterling, who built a sloop to transport cargo on the Great Lakes. Tymes, who died in Detroit in 1772, left many debts. Campbell settled his affairs.

Lachlan McIntosh was a Scot who emigrated to Georgia in 1736. Initially he was in business with Henry Laurens there, and he later moved to Albany. In 1768, after McIntosh became a merchant in Albany, he sent merchandise to Detroit. He evidently did not do well, as his canoes were ruined by lying two summers in the sun. McIntosh returned to Georgia, where he later served with the Continental army.

John Askin was an Irishman who came to America in 1758 and served in the Seven Years' War. In 1761 he became a trader in Albany and in 1765 he visited Michilimackinac. He later was in a disastrous partnership with Robert Rogers and was active in the fur trade northwest of Lake Superior.

All of these Albany merchants based their livelihood on trade with the Indians. They achieved a modicum of success because the French could not compete with them for the Iroquois market. However, the Albany merchants failed in their attempt to unseat the French domination of the trade west of Niagara.

Schenectady was the first stop after Albany and developed as a trading center because of the universal rule that whenever one "broke cargo"—transferred goods from one form of conveyance to another, for example, from ship to wagon—that point became a center of activity and a logical place to do business. During the transfer process goods often were separated into smaller lots for shipment or retailed to lesser merchants.

The goods moved from Albany by wagon were divided at Schenectady and an assortment loaded on canoes for the voyage via the Mohawk River to Lake Erie and farther west. The process of dividing the merchandise into canoe-loads required many business transactions and involved many people. Most of the population of Schenectady performed related activity, working as canoe men, making canoes, or packing goods. The most numerous were the canoe men employed by the merchants.

Many of the merchants at Schenectady were also Dutch, but the Scots and English were more visible there than in Albany. The list of captains in the Schenectady militia includes some of the colonial merchants in frontier commerce: John Duncan, John Glenn Jr., John Sanders, and Daniel Campbell. The remaining seven had Dutch names. Among them were Gerart Lansing and Nicholas Groot, who were also merchants.

One of the merchants at Schenectady was John Macomb, who supplied Johnson with Indian goods in the 1760s. In 1762 officers of the 46th Regiment told Daniel Claus, the Indian Department officer, that Macomb was not a fair dealer. In 1765 Macomb asked Johnson for an appointment in the Indian Department because he was tired of trade. He turned over all his assets to his creditors, including John Duncan, the partner of Phyn & Ellice; Greg Cunningham and Company, one of the richest partnerships in New York City and part owner of thirteen ships; and Alexander Wallace, another shipowner and merchant in New York City. However, Macomb was unable to pay all his debts. In 1769 Phyn & Ellice was dunning him for payment of three accounts.

The Schenectady firm of Phyn & Ellice has left us with the most detailed account of its activities. It sold to merchants in Albany, Detroit, and Niagara, who in turn sold the goods to traders who dealt directly with the Indians. The traders paid with fur. Its most important customer was the Indian Department. James Phyn married a daughter of a close friend of Sir William Johnson, thereby cementing the Indian Department business. In April 1765 the partners sold Indian goods worth £1,691 New York ($213,000) to Johnson, a major transaction. The amounts continued to be substantial: in October 1768 the partners sent Johnson a bill from Lieutenant Benjamin Roberts at Michilimackinac and other Indian officers for £2,144 New York ($270,000).

The partners were not always able to fill the large orders of the Indian Department. In February 1766 no Indian blankets were available in New York City because all blankets had already been purchased by merchants in Philadelphia for shipment to Pensacola to outfit the British army expedition up the Mississippi River to Illinois. Indian goods were difficult to obtain in 1766, but the partners were able to supply ammunition to the Indian Department in Detroit.

Originally the partnership included Duncan, but he retired in 1767 and demanded a large share of the capital. Not only did the firm have to pay

Duncan for his share of the partnership, but it also had difficulty liquidating debts left by Duncan, who had extended credit to some bad risks, such as Macomb. Duncan had made some poor investments too, and the creditors demanded payment from the remaining partners. The partners drew £3,000 New York ($378,000) on Hayman Levy of New York City to pay the debts, pledging furs as collateral. The furs could not be sold in New York, so Levy sent them to London, which delayed payment. Paying off Duncan placed the remaining partners in financial difficulty for several years. Alexander Ellice had provided more capital, a one-third share for £714 New York ($90,000), a small amount considering the magnitude of the debts left by Duncan (£3,000, or $378,000). The partners favored their Scottish countrymen in ordering. In 1767 they paid William and Alexander Forsyth of Aberdeen, Scotland, £327 sterling ($65,400) with three bills of exchange presumably obtained from sales to the army. The Forsyths were their suppliers, and one member of the Forsyth family was married to a relative of Phyn. The partners also sent Forsyth a bill for £600 sterling ($120,000) drawn by Peter Hasenclever, wholesaler and a banker in New York City, on Richard Wells of London, which the partners wanted paid to William and Norman Durward. The Durward firm was one of their suppliers in London, from whom they obtained glass, white lead, black cloth, pewter ink stands, and stockings. Later they also ordered a young black male slave and two female slaves from Durward, their contact with the slave traders. The partners also sent a bill for £45 sterling ($9,000) drawn by Captain Archibald Montgomery on James Myruk, probably a London banker, indicating that the partners were selling considerable quantities of merchandise to the officers in the army.

Phyn & Ellice had some difficulty collecting for the goods ordered by the British army at the trading posts. In December 1767 they asked Peter Silvester, who acted as an attorney for Sir William Johnson, to honor a bill for £322 ($40,660) for goods delivered to Lieutenant Benjamin Roberts, the commissary at Fort Michilimackinac.

The partners received many orders for goods from Detroit merchants, including William Edgar, James Sterling, and John Porteus, and forwarded the orders to Hayman Levy, their agent in New York City. Most payments were made in fur, which Levy usually sold in New York. In November 1767 the partners informed Levy that they had thirty packs of fur worth £600 New York ($75,600), which they hoped would be enough to pay off all of their debts. In December 1767 they were still trying to pay off Duncan for his share of the partnership. They had already paid him more than £2,300 New York ($290,000) but he wanted more. Sterling and Porteus had also paid £800 ($100,800) New York to Duncan for their dealing. They asked Levy to borrow £800 New York on the credit of the partners in order to settle with Duncan after his retirement. The partners informed Levy that they had orders from James Sterling and John Porteus, two of the most active merchants in Detroit.

Levy was cautious in his dealings with the partners. He complained of the quality of the fur sent to him and of settlement of the debt owed to Duncan. Levy preferred to be paid in cash rather than fur and also complained of the large order for British merchandise that the partners had placed with him because they were slow to pay and canceled orders. In December 1767 the partners had skins worth £3,000 New York ($378,000) and were willing to redeem themselves by giving them to Levy as payment for all their debts. In early 1768 the partners had difficulty even providing bread for the boatmen and had to borrow money from relatives in Scotland.

By January 1768 Levy and the partners were at odds. Phyn & Ellice had agreed to sell fur at low prices to Hayman Levy and to take goods in return from Levy rather than cash. In January Phyn & Ellice wanted to settle their account and receive payment for the furs that they had sent down at the highest market price. They demanded that Levy give them a sterling bill of exchange for the amount as they had an obligation to send their agent in London, Neale, Pigou, and Booth—£700 sterling ($140,000)—by the end of January. Were their assets not sufficient to cover the £700 bill, Phyn & Ellice promised to send bills drawn on the Indian Department in March and April.

In February the partners informed Neale, Pigou, and Booth that they would pay their balance, having sent Levy £3,000 New York ($378,000). Levy had been instructed to pay Benjamin Booth the £700 sterling in January, but he could not because he had trouble selling the fur. Therefore the partners sent Neale a partial payment of two sterling bills totaling £250 sterling ($50,000). One bill, for £100 sterling, was drawn by Claus, the Indian Department agent in Canada, on William Baker, the London banker who had the contract to supply money to the British army in America. This bill was evidently for Indian presents to be distributed by Claus. The other bill for £150 sterling was drawn by Captain Brown on George Ross, a London merchant, evidently for personal purchases by the army officer. In March the partners sent Neale, Pigou, and Booth an additional £300 sterling ($60,000) with a bill drawn by Levy on Hasenclever, Seton & Croftes, London bankers.

Levy was still reluctant and again complained of the quality of the fur. He had difficulty obtaining the sterling bill that the partners wanted. Levy wanted cash and the partners offered only fur. He also complained about the large size of the order for goods for the next season. By June 1768 the partners and Levy had settled their difference, but Phyn & Ellice complained bitterly about not receiving goods ordered from Levy and as a result canceled some of their orders. The partners offered Levy some elk pelts and a bale of small furs. In June 1768 the partners sent him the elk skins and a bale of furs, stating that if Levy did not want to buy them at the set price in New York, he should send the skins and furs to Neale. Later in the month the partners complained that they had not received merchandise from Levy and canceled part of the order. Relations deteriorated, and in September the partners complained that Levy was selling their fur in New York City for less than the price in Albany. Therefore, the partners requested that any furs remaining with Levy be returned.

In September 1768 Levy complained about the quality of a beaver shipment to him by the partners. At the same time the partners were angry that Levy had sold the pelts at lower prices in New York City than could have been obtained in Albany. Phyn informed Levy that he would go to New York and retrieve all of the remaining furs.

The rift was evidently smoothed over, because in November 1768 the partners informed Levy that the canoes were arriving in Schenectady every day with beaver, raccoon, and deerskin. The partners were buying all available fur, and after holding it until March would give Levy the first opportunity to buy. The partners expected to have peltry worth £2,000 New York ($252,000) to sell. Business must have improved, as the partners had added Alexander Ellice's younger brother, Robert, to the firm in late 1768 and moved into a larger building.

Phyn & Ellice turned to others for merchandise, providing fur and deerskin in payment. In December 1768 the firm sent Peter Livingston eight packs of deerskin and three packs of deer leather worth a total of £192 New York ($24,192). Livingston was instructed to sell at the fixed price. If they were not sold, Livingston was to hold the skins for further instructions. Clearly the partners were not entrusting Livingston with the decision, usually made by the agents, to sell at the best price available. In November 1768 the partners placed an order for 98 pieces of cloth, 800 blankets, 6 hundredweight of powder, and 35 hundredweight of lead with Benjamin Booth, asking that he order from his friends in London if he did not have the goods on hand. If delivery was made by April 1768, the partners promised to place more orders.

Phyn & Ellice also began to bypass the New York City merchants to order merchandise directly from Britain. In December 1767 they placed an order with William and Alexander Forsyth in Scotland for 24 dozen blankets; 200 pairs of men's shoes; 100 pairs of women's shoes; 110 pairs of fine men's, women's, and boys' shoes; stockings; and a long list of various cloths. This finer merchandise was obviously destined for the colonists, not the Indians.

In February 1768 Phyn & Ellice sent Sir William Johnson a list of Indian goods on hand and promised to order any more that he might need. The partners asked Johnson to provide them with any bills of exchange because they were short of money, as their former partner Duncan had not paid his share of outstanding bills. They currently had bills for £671 New York ($84,500) drawn on Johnson for Indian Department expenses by George Croghan, Edmund Pollard, Benjamin Roberts, and Michael Byrne.

The partners were in need of money in early 1768 and asked Isaac Vrooman, a well-connected political figure who had surveyed the land purchased by Sir William Johnson in 1764, to pay his debt of £165 New York ($21,000). In July 1768 Phyn & Ellice again asked Johnson for money because bills worth £900 sterling ($180,000) had bounced. The bills had been drawn by Peter Hasenclever, the partners' agent in New York, who went bankrupt. Hasenclever had drawn bills on the partners, and when he went bankrupt they were required to pay immediately. All the bills drawn on him were refused. The partners employed James Duane of New York to try to collect some of their money from Hasenclever.

Phyn & Ellice asked Johnson for immediate payment of bills drawn on him by his agents Norman McLeod, Benjamin Roberts, Michael Byrne, Jean-Baptiste De Couange (a French interpreter at Fort Niagara), George Croghan, Daniel Robertson, Edward Pollard, and Hugh Boyle for Indian Department expenses. The total was £1,134 including the £671 requested in February. Johnson was evidently just as slow to pay as the others.

In October 1768 Phyn & Ellice sent Johnson bills drawn on him by Roberts, John Duncan, McLeod, and Byrne for Indian Department expenses at Niagara, Detroit, and other posts. The total was £2,144 New York ($270,170) and probably included the bills presented in July. Payment would have meant a major influx of cash for Phyn & Ellice and the amount is an indication of the high level of business they conducted with the Indian Department.

In November 1768 Johnson asked Phyn to provide him with Spanish dollars. Phyn obtained promises for 300 Spanish dollars that he could send to Johnson in exchange for New York currency as soon as he received the money from Johnson. Phyn also asked John Monier and Richard Cartwright to search for more Spanish dollars. That month the partners reported that the canoes from the West were coming in every day but mostly with deerskin. Nevertheless, they expected to receive shipments worth £2,000 ($252,000) by April 1769.

In 1768 business was bad. The British and the colonists were in great difficulty. In December Phyn & Ellice complained that they had received no returns, either bills or furs, from James Sterling, Lyme, John Farrell, and Robinson, all of Detroit. They had received bills of exchange from Henry VanSchaack, presumably obtained from the army in return for supplies. VanSchaack acted as a broker, receiving a large bill of exchange from the army and in turn paying the army accounts with various merchants in Detroit. The implication was that the British and colonial merchants were continuing to sell to the army, but the fur trade had been usurped by the French.

In 1769 the nonimportation agreements and strife on the coast made supplying the Detroit merchants with trade goods impossible. Phyn & Ellice informed Alexander Macomb in Detroit that they would not be able to fill his order, nor the orders of Porteus, Sterling, and James Cassety. Porteus had ordered four canoe-loads of goods, but there was nothing available—no goods, no rum. Neither were there men to paddle the canoes. The fur trade at Detroit was at a standstill and the business with the army and the Indian Department had been curtailed by the lack of merchandise to sell. As in Pennsylvania, the New York merchants had lost the battle for the fur trade to the French. Unlike Pennsylvania, there was little opportunity for land speculation. The only market left was the British army in the Great Lakes.

Centuries of persecution had created closer ties among the Jews than place of residence or national background. During the eighteenth century, personal relationships and confidence between buyer and seller were essential to all transactions, as there was no guarantee of quality, shipment dates, or date of payment. Jews in America and Europe dealt among themselves, just as the Scots in Montreal turned to their relatives, Phyn & Ellice, to supply them from Schenectady when profitable, and as the Quaker merchant John Reynell of Philadelphia turned to William Redwood of Newport, Rhode Island, because of religious and business ties. Trusting the person with whom business was transacted was essential, and the strong religious and family ties among the Jews made their success possible. Nevertheless, Jewish firms also dealt extensively with others in the fur trade, often acting as agents for the sale of furs.

The international ties of the Jewish community strengthened the position of its members in frontier commerce because the trustworthy network provided the capital, assembled the merchandise in Europe, moved it to American and Canadian ports, and transported the cargoes up the rivers and lakes to the frontier. The furs obtained in exchange and the credits received from the army in return for provisions returned through the same chain.

The Jews engaged in the frontier trade with the Indians, the British army, and the French settlers. Ezekial Solomon, a Jewish merchant, reached Michilimackinac in 1760, preceding Alexander Henry and the army. The Jews were interested chiefly in Michilimackinac, Illinois, and western Pennsylvania, representing approximately 10 percent of those involved in these areas, but their per-person capital was higher than the French Canadians' and many of the western Pennsylvanian merchants'. Simon, Franks, and Levy was the major competitor to Baynton and Wharton in supplying goods to the Indian Department.

New York City was the first center of the Jewish community in America, and from there Jews moved to Newport, Charleston, and Philadelphia during the eighteenth century. The New York City community began as a Sephardic one, although by the end of the eighteenth century, Ashkenazic Jews from Germany, Poland, and eastern Europe had arrived in increasing numbers. Among the families in America were Franks, Levy, Seixas, Isaacs, Gómez, de Lucena, Hendricks, Hayes, Myers, Simson, Judah, and Pinto. Hayman Levy was the most prominent individual in western commerce, and at one time he claimed to be the largest fur dealer in the colonies. Although this claim was open to question, Levy was the agent for Phyn & Ellice and received most of that firm's furs, acting in turn as its agent in obtaining supplies from Europe and other colonies. With these connections, Levy's relative share of the peltry coming down the Hudson River must have been far greater than any other merchant in New York City.

Many Jews, most of them Sephardic, came to Philadelphia between 1730 and 1750. Some had come from Portugal by way of Holland and England, where their relatives and associations had formed good business connections. David Franks and his brother, Moses, moved from New York City to Philadelphia in 1740 and during the following year formed a short-lived partnership. On May 16, 1760, a partnership to deal with the Indians that lasted nine years was formed at Lancaster by Joseph Simon, William Trent, Levy Andrew Levy, and David Franks. Joseph Simon was the leading merchant of Lancaster. Jacob Henry also entered the partnership before 1754. The Jewish merchants had other ties too. Trent was already indebted to Simon and Franks for £4,082 Pennsylvania ($470,000) and gave them a mortgage on his land. The firms of Simon, Trent, Levy, and Franks and Baynton and Wharton were the two major companies supplying the frontier during the 1760s. Joseph Simon and Levy Andrew Levy from Lancaster and Isaac Levy and David Franks from Philadelphia claimed losses to the Indians of £28,000 in 1763, indicating a sizable investment in western commerce.

Franks had excellent political connections in London and was a subcontractor supplying provisions to the British army. Through their London influence, David Franks and his father, Joseph, of New York City, held the provisions contract for the British army, and during the Seven Years' War, they handled more than £750,000 sterling ($150 million) in provision contracts. In April 1760 David Franks had the army provisions contract in partnership with William Plumstead and had accounts with Joseph Simon, Levy Andrew Levy, and Levy & Company. In 1764 David Franks, John Inglis, and David Barclay were the contractors for army provisions. Food for the regiments on the frontier was purchased locally by the contractors and their agents. In 1766 the contractors paid Baynton and Wharton £397 19s. Pennsylvania ($45,770) for rations for the army in Illinois. There is a prior entry for £300, also for rations.

Among the Jews arriving in Philadelphia during the war was Michael Gratz, who came as a clerk to his brother, Bernard Gratz. Eight Jews signed a nonimportation agreement in Philadelphia in 1765: Bernard and Michael Gratz, Benjamin Levy, David Franks, Samson Levy, Hayman Levy Jr., Mathias Bush, and Moses Mordecai. Bernard and Michael Gratz were major factors in the frontier trade. Bernard Gratz at Philadelphia wrote to Moses Frank in London regarding the sale of £86 in wampum to the Pennsylvania Indian Commission, and also dealt with Joseph Simon of Lancaster and Levy Andrew Levy in April 1760. Michael Gratz had transactions with David Franks of £300 Pennsylvania ($34,500).

Bernard Gratz came from Silesia, then a part of Prussia, to escape the severe persecution of the Jews by Frederick the Great. He first went to London and worked with Solomon Henry in the lumber, sugar, and fur business, dealing with David Franks of Philadelphia. Gratz was employed by Franks in the frontier trade when he arrived in Philadelphia in 1754. In 1760 he was dealing with Henry Solomon in London, Isaac Martin in Savannah, and with Joseph Simon and Levy Andrew Levy. In 1760 Bernard formed a partnership with Michael Gratz.

The Gratz partners were active in many facets of trade in the 1760s, dealing with Jacob Henry of Newport and Robert C. Livingston, John Harris Cruger, Isaac Adolphus, and James Kennedy of New York City. In April 1765 the partners provided Edward Ward with rum for the Indian trade. In July 1765 they received an order for four pipes (500 gallons) of whiskey from James Cunningham, their agent in Quebec. Beginning in 1766 Bernard and Michael Gratz competed with Baynton and Wharton for the Illinois market, working with Joseph Simon and Levy Andrew Levy. In August 1768 the partners sent two horse-loads of rum and four wagons of merchandise to Eneas Mackay at Fort Pitt. They outfitted William Murray at Carlisle in 1768 to trade in Illinois.

In 1769 Bernard and Michael Gratz sold George Croghan £1,000 Pennsylvania ($115,000) in Indian goods. By 1772 the partners were the principal creditors of Croghan and had power of attorney to sell his lands in New York to satisfy Croghan's debts.

Because the Jews constituted a tightly knit group of merchants in Pennsylvania and in other commercial centers, there was some resentment.

Beeckman, one of the Albany Dutch traders, complained of the competition from both Quakers and Jews in the Irish flaxseed trade. In 1760 the French *seigneurs* of Quebec, in their petition supporting Governor Murray, referred to the Jews who "exalt themselves among the king's new subjects" (the French). The seigneurs claimed that unwary Frenchmen had previously not known of "this kind of men and had ruined themselves." Prior to 1760 Jews had been excluded from Canada, but after 1760 many came from other colonies. They included David Lazarus, Uriel Moresco, Samuel Jacobs, Simon Levy, Fernández da Fonseca, Abraham Franks, Andrew Hays, Jacob de Maurera, Joseph Bindona, Levy Solomons, and Uriah Judah. Others commuted between New York and Canada.

The combined pressure of the French and the British army must have had some impact because many Jews left Canada after 1763. Their number diminished from a total of thirty identified in 1760 to only fourteen to nineteen in 1763–74. From 1769 on the Jewish merchants in Montreal obtained licenses for only five canoes a year, a small part of the total, indicating that they had more or less been driven out of the direct trade with the Indians in Canada. However, by 1768 a Jewish congregation was established in Montreal. The congregation was made up of the Portuguese-Dutch-English Jews of the Sephardic community.

The colonial merchants suffered from British regulation and lack of support in the struggle with the French traders more than any other class in America. When the fur trade was monopolized by the French, partially as a result of ineffective British administration, the merchants of New York and Pennsylvania were the major losers. When the merchants turned to land speculation, they were again blocked by the government in London. The transfer of the regiments to the coast in 1768 deprived the merchants of that market. When the Townsend Acts promised to drain sterling from the colonies to pay duties, again it was the merchants who would suffer, as they would no longer be able to pay their suppliers in Britain. Nonimportation, an expression of resistance, cut off the supplies of the frontier merchants and surrendered frontier commerce to the French in Canada and Illinois. There is little wonder that the merchants were among the leaders of the resistance in the 1770s.

## SUGGESTED READINGS

Kenneth R. Andrews, *Trade, Plunder, and Settlement: Maritime Enterprise and the Genesis of the British Empire, 1480–1630* (1984).
Bernard Bailyn, *The New England Merchants in the Seventeenth Century* (1974).
Ralph Davis, *Rise of the Atlantic Economies* (1973).

Richard S. Dunn, *Sugar and Slaves: The Rise of the Planter Class in the English West Indies, 1624–1713* (1972).

Christine Leigh Heyrmman, *Commerce and Culture: The Maritime Communities of Colonial Massachusetts, 1690–1750* (1984).

Stephen Innes, ed., *Work and Labor in Early America* (1988).

Michael Kammen, *Empire and Interest: The American Colonies and the Politics of Mercantilism* (1970).

John F. Martin, *Profits in the Wilderness: Entrepreneurship and the Founding of New England Towns in the Seventeenth Century* (1991).

John J. McCusker and Russell R. Menard, *The Economy of British America, 1607–1715* (1981).

Donna Merwick, *Possessing Albany, 1630-1710: The Dutch and English Experiences* (1990).

Sidney W. Mintz, *Sweetness and Power: The Place of Sugar in Modern History* (1985).

Anthony Pagden, *Lords of All the World: Ideologies of Empire in Spain, Britain and France, c. 1500–c. 1800* (1995).

J. H. Parry, *The Establishment of the European Hegemony: Trade and Expansion in the Age of the Renaissance* (1966).

Oliver Rink, *Holland on the Hudson: An Economic and Social History of Dutch New York* (1986).

# 8

# Illinois:
# Farmers, Traders, Merchants

In the 1760s the term *Illinois* referred to the area east of the Mississippi River roughly corresponding to the modern state of Illinois. This market served by the Ohio, Missouri, and Mississippi Rivers had far greater potential than the other trading areas, Canada and the south. The Illinois climate was more hospitable and the Indian population was larger. North of the Great Lakes in the Hudson Bay area, the density of Native Americans was low. The climate was so severe that mere survival was difficult. South of the Ohio River deerskin was the primary pelt gathered because the warmer climate was not favorable to animals with heavy coats. The more favorable moderate climate of the Great Lakes and the upper Mississippi and Missouri Valleys, including Illinois, offered a bountiful harvest of fur and livable conditions for the Indians, as well as excellent transportation.

Under the French, the commerce of the Mississippi River flowed down to New Orleans from Illinois. Flour, bacon, corn, ham, corned pork, corned beef, beeswax, cotton, tallow, leather, tobacco, lead, copper, buffalo hides, wool, venison, poultry, bear's grease, oil, skins, and hides were all shipped to New Orleans. Indigo, rice, and tobacco went to Europe, and lumber went to the West Indies. The trip downriver from Illinois to New Orleans was easy and could be made in as few as twelve days. However, the trip upstream was extremely difficult; rowing against the current was a seventy- to ninety-day trip. Sails, rope hauling, and rowing were all used to move the boats upstream more than 700 miles, not including the many bends in the river. The French estimated the trip at 400 leagues, or 1,200 miles (the league varied but was usually about 3 miles). The voyage took three months, and the men were weary by the time they reached Illinois. The heat ruined food during the long trip, so the only way that Illinois could be maintained was by increasing the number of farms to make it self-sufficient. Nevertheless, the Mississippi route was easier than other routes. A trader would have to carry his canoe over more than ninety portages between Montreal and the Lake of the Woods at the west end of Lake Superior, whereas he could paddle all the way from New Orleans to the Lake of the Woods on the Mississippi without removing the boat from the water.

One undeniable controlling factor to successful trade was transportation. Moving fur directly back to Philadelphia would have been very costly for colonial merchants, first upstream on the Ohio River and then overland 300 miles to Philadelphia or against the current up the Illinois River to the Great Lakes. Instead, the enterprising colonial merchants sent their furs down the Mississippi River to New Orleans, as the French did; there, some were sold at high prices to French merchants who shipped them to France. A pack of eighty pounds of beaver pelts sold for $67 more in New Orleans than on the East Coast and the transportation cost was less.

The Capitulation of Montreal in 1759 had surrendered the Great Lakes and Vincennes to the British but not Louisiana. In 1763 the Treaty of Paris ceded to Great Britain the minor posts considered part of Louisiana. French posts were located at strategic points along the rivers flowing from the Great Lakes area to the Mississippi River. Before 1764 most of the French habitants in Illinois lived in seven villages: Fort Chartres, Prairie du Rocher, Cahokia, Ste. Genevieve, San Filippe, Massiac, and Peoria. Some of the villages were very small. San Filippe had only 20 inhabitants in 1763 and only 12 to 15 families in 1765. Cahokia had 100 inhabitants in 1763 and 300 French and 80 blacks in 1765. Prairie du Rocher had 100 French inhabitants and 100 slaves in 1765.

Vincennes on the Wabash River, built in 1727, was typical of the villages established by the French. The settlement had 88 landowners in 1733. By 1763 most of the inhabitants were part Indian and part French métis, and many were illiterate. The territory along the Wabash River provided an excellent hunting ground for the Indians, and Vincennes enabled the French to block traffic between Lake Michigan and the Mississippi. The French garrison consisted of 20 married French soldiers and some French inhabitants.

Although the British sent a garrison to Vincennes in 1761 to protect the colonial traders, the French garrison remained. The French traders maintained their friendly contact with the Indians in the neighborhood and continued to trade at the post. In 1763 Aubrey described Vincennes as a fort surrounded by a picket (a wall formed by logs with the larger end driven partly into the ground). The garrison of 20 British troops was captured during Pontiac's Uprising, ending British military occupation of Vincennes.

By 1768 half the inhabitants were newcomers, including French traders from Illinois and British and colonial merchants from Detroit and Fort Pitt. In 1769 the village priest stated that there were 80 farmers in the village and nearly 800 people. Another population estimate in 1769 was much lower—only 50 men able to bear arms, 50 women, and 150 children, including slaves. In 1770 Sir William Johnson called Vincennes a lawless community with vagabond French traders, derelict French soldiers, and hostile Indians, all of whom hated the British and the colonists.

The leading merchant was Nicholas, who in 1768 sold fur worth £6110s. ($7,072) to George Morgan, a partner of Baynton and Wharton. Among the other French traders were Jean-Baptiste Bosseron, Rassicault, Neauveau, Flamboice, Vadrie, and Moros. Baynton and Wharton established a store in the village in the late 1760s in the care of Williamson, who in 1768 rented a house with a cellar to store furs. The merchandise provided by Baynton and Wharton was sold both to the Indians and to the French. The French paid with either cattle or furs. In July 1768 Baynton and Wharton purchased fur, cattle, and tobacco worth more than £2,000 Pennsylvania ($230,000) from the French. In the fall of 1768 Morgan obtained twenty head of cattle for army provisions from Vincennes.

Fort Chartres, founded in 1720, was the major military post in Illinois. This stone fort was built by the French in 1753 and had a garrison of six French companies with 300 soldiers and twenty cannon. The fort included two barracks, a guardhouse, two officers' quarters, a powder magazine, a kitchen, and other buildings around a four-acre parade ground. In 1763 there were still nearly 200 French soldiers in the garrison. The French garrison finally transferred the fort to the British in 1765, and it was renamed Fort Cavendish. The village surrounding the fort had 100 inhabitants in 1763 and about 40 families in 1765. Another estimate in 1765 was 1,000 French and 300 slaves. Various estimates were made of the population between 1764 and 1766, ranging from 1,000 to 2,000 people. By 1767 the estimate was a little more than 1,000, and the same number was used in 1771.

Among the colonial traders at Fort Chartres was Edward Cole, who had moved to Niagara in 1760, then to Detroit in 1761, and to Fort Chartres in 1767, trying to restore his finances as he was not doing well. Another Detroit trader, Winston, had done well in Fort Chartres and planned to pay his debts. He had hidden from the Indians at St. Joseph in 1763 and his goods were stolen by Chevalier.

Kaskaskia, located at the juncture of the Ohio and Mississippi Rivers, was the largest town in Illinois in 1765, with eighty houses, 500 white inhabitants, and 500 blacks. In 1763 Aubrey estimated the population at 400 people. From 1744 to 1756 Kaskaskia was the center of the fur trade for the upper Mississippi, the lower Missouri, the Illinois, and the Wabash Rivers.

Ouiatanon was occupied by the British army in 1761. Lieutenant Edward Jenkins was sent by Captain Campbell from Detroit with twenty men and four months' provisions. However, the garrison was withdrawn during Pontiac's Uprising and the French regained complete control. In 1765, during a peacemaking mission, the Indian agent George Croghan was taken there after he was captured by Indians. The French at Ouiatanon sold goods to the Indians at very high prices.

Alexander Maisonville was the leading merchant. In 1765 Maisonville had traveled up to Detroit and then went to Fort Pitt. In 1765 Baynton and Wharton had £14,000 Pennsylvania ($1,610,000) tied up with Maisonville. Unlike most Frenchmen, Maisonville had a favorable attitude to the British and the colonists. He had bribed the Indians in 1763 not to kill the British soldiers in Ouiatanon. In February 1766 Maisonville and Richard Winston, a British merchant at St. Joseph, ordered a major shipment of Indian goods from John Jennings, Baynton and Wharton's agent at Fort Pitt. The two boats of goods were worth £2,234 Pennsylvania ($257,000). The order included 2,000 French match coats, 2,000 gallons of Philadelphia rum, 30 gross of scalping knives, and 2,000 pounds of gunpowder. This order would have supplied 2,000 adult Indians, a large percentage of all of the Indians living along the Wabash River.

Croghan recommended Maisonville to Samuel Wharton, and negotiations began in early 1766 to send him a shipment worth £1,600 Pennsylvania ($184,000) in May 1766. The arrangement was completed by April 1766, and Baynton and Wharton sent two boatloads of merchandise to Maisonville. He sent the firm 125 packs of pelts valued at £1,542 Pennsylvania ($177,000, an average of £12 7s. Pennsylvania or $1,416 per pack) in payment for the merchandise. The packs were sent down the Mississippi River to New Orleans and carried on the sloop *York* to Philadelphia. The transportation cost was 9s. New York ($57) per pack, for a total of £52 New York ($7,182). The packs from Maisonville likely were mostly deerskin, as a shipment of 62 packs of mixed deerskin and furs to Phyn and Ellice was valued at £1,302 New York ($164,000, or an average of $2,645 per pack, almost twice the value per pack compared with the Illinois average of $1,416). In September 1767 Baynton and Wharton received the shipment.

In July 1767 Edward Cole, the commissary at Fort Chartres, recommended Maisonville to Croghan as a source of provisions. Maisonville was well acquainted with the Wabash Indians and had been working for the Indian Department dispensing presents. He continued to receive goods from Baynton and Wharton and sent the firm pelts by way of New Orleans. In 1768 Maisonville was working with Baynton and Wharton purchasing lead from the French for resale to the Indians and sending out hunting parties for meat for the British army. The only benefit to the colonists of the trade on the Wabash River was supplying merchandise to the French, who effectively had cut off any direct contact between the Indians and the colonists.

St. Louis was established on the west bank of the Mississippi River by Maxent LaClede & Company in 1764 under an exclusive grant from France in 1762 for trade with the Indians. The company built a large storehouse and forty homes for families. When the British occupied Illinois, the French garrison from Fort Chartres moved to St. Louis. Some merchants and traders from Illinois crossed the Mississippi and settled in St. Louis. More than half the men on the St. Louis militia roster listed their occupation as trader, hunter, or rower. A petition signed by the people of St. Louis and the militia roster show that most of the town's population were French from Canada and Illinois; fewer than 5 percent were from New Orleans.

Within a few months after the city was founded, fifteen boats and two pirogues of merchandise left New Orleans destined for St. Louis. Harry Gordon reported that LaClede at St. Louis soon monopolized the trade of the Missouri River, the northern Mississippi, and the Illinois, as well as the business with the Indians near Green Bay, Lake Michigan, and St. Joseph. However, the St. Louis governor, Kerlerec, estimated the value of the Missouri trade at 8,000 French livres ($80,000) in European goods, a relatively small volume.

New Orleans was the link connecting Illinois to Europe and the American colonies. A British officer described it in 1766 as a small town with few houses, but its people were healthy and prosperous. In 1769 New Orleans had 1,902 free people (including 31 blacks and 68 people of mixed blood), 1,225 slaves, and 60 "domesticated" Indians. The main business of the town was trading furs and deerskin from Illinois and sending supplies there.

Although the 1763 Treaty of Paris had given the British navigational rights on the Mississippi, they could not use the port of New Orleans, the only navigable opening of the river entering the Gulf of Mexico. The threat of British smuggling merchandise into Louisiana from West Florida led the Spanish to prohibit British merchant ships from trading in New Orleans. Instead, the British ships loaded with Indian goods went to Mobile and Pensacola. Most of the cargoes were for the large contraband trade with New Orleans that developed after 1763 from West Florida. The trade was illegal because the furs and deerskin from New Orleans were enumerated articles (controlled merchandise) that had been unlawfully taken from British territory in Illinois and the hunting grounds west of Lake Michigan by unlicensed French traders.

Even Baynton and Wharton resorted to purchasing goods in New Orleans in 1767 and 1768. In 1767 MacNamara in New Orleans ordered a cask of wine and cloth for George Morgan. Wine was a major import through New Orleans. In 1768 Morgan ordered four hogsheads and six cases of bottled wine and paid with army bills of exchange. In June 1768 Morgan paid MacNamara for a gross of knives and two hogsheads of wine that were sent up the Mississippi.

Theoretically, the fur trade passed into the hands of the British in 1763 and only a small amount of trade up the western branches of the Mississippi remained in Spanish hands. After 1763 the French government was supposed to turn over Illinois to the British, but the British were unable to move troops into the area, even though merchandise was peacefully sent up the Mississippi River by the French in New Orleans. In practice, the French merchants in Illinois retained two-thirds of the fur from throughout the Mississippi Valley. Therefore, French traders from Illinois continued to influence the Indians despite British regulation until 1765.

The transfer of authority from the French to the British began very slowly. On September 24, 1763, news of the Treaty of Paris, which had been signed March 4, 1763, finally reached Fort Chartres in Illinois. The French commander, Villiers, announced to the inhabitants that he was under orders to surrender the colony to the British but that the people were free to leave and go to new settlements on the western side of the Mississippi that would be under Spanish rule according to the terms of the treaty. By autumn 1763 Florida had been occupied by British troops from Cuba, but no immediate steps had been taken to occupy Illinois.

Despite the ready market for fur in New Orleans, some fur did reach Philadelphia and New York because it could be used to pay debts in England. Baynton and Wharton shipped its fur by way of New Orleans and from there to Philadelphia or New York. In October 1766 Baynton and Wharton hired Captain Dobson to take his ship from New Orleans to New York City, but because Morgan was unable to send the fur from Illinois to New Orleans before Dobson left New Orleans on October 22 shipment was delayed until the following spring. In 1767 Baynton and Wharton needed money and in desperation demanded that its agents in Illinois send as much fur as possible to New Orleans to be placed on the first ship to New York City, Philadelphia, or London.

Some of the fur went to New York City. In September 1767 Peter R. Livingston billed Baynton and Wharton for transporting 217 packs of furs shipped from New Orleans to New York City at a cost of £91 Pennsylvania ($10,465, or $48 per pack). Another shipment arrived on the sloop *York* and was sold to Richard McWilliams in New York for £2,105 New York ($265,230). The shipment included 5,000 raccoon pelts at 2s. 6d. each, 300 otter pelts at 15s., 2,400 pounds of beaver pelts at 6s. 6d., 2,000 pounds of deerskins at 3s. 6d., and 250 bearskins at 10s. A cargo of 125 packs from Maisonville, the French merchant at Ouiatanon who was an associate of Baynton and Wharton, sold for £1,302 Pennsylvania ($149,730).

In November 1768 Morgan in Illinois packed all of his peltry on a boat to New Orleans. He was planning to go to Vincennes to pick up any additional furs to be sent to New Orleans in another boat in time to board a ship for Philadelphia. Baynton and Wharton was in dire need of saleable merchandise at the time, and their furs did reach Philadelphia.

Some peltry reached Philadelphia via the Mississippi route in later years too. For example, in 1771 Baynton and Wharton sent three boatloads of peltry, including 375 packs weighing from 100 to 160 pounds each, down the Mississippi. The price of beaver in London was 5s. sterling per skin, and a skin weighed from 1 to 2 pounds, so an estimate of the value of a pack would be £25 sterling ($5,000). The dressed leather packs were worth only £6 sterling each. Assuming the packs to be half leather and half fur, the Baynton and Wharton shipment was worth £5,800 sterling ($1,160,000), but its sale was a great disappointment to the firm. The shipment was auctioned in small lots in Philadelphia for only about £3,000 sterling ($600,000), and little was exported to Britain for the higher price.

Not all of Baynton and Wharton's fur from Illinois was sent to Philadelphia or New York. In 1767 Morgan sent Young to New Orleans with a few packs of fur to sell or ship and implied that they could be sold to French merchants in New Orleans and presumably sent to France. In 1768 Morgan informed his partners that he wanted to send some furs down to New Orleans but feared that Messrs C. and J., presumably French merchants, would seize the fur when it reached New Orleans as partial payment for bills owed them by Baynton and Wharton.

Trade with the Indians and farming were the main occupations of the Illinois inhabitants. With the end of the Seven Years' War in 1763 French ships were free to enter New Orleans with trade goods for the Indians. The timely arrival of ships from France was crucial to dispatch the convoys of flatboats north on the Mississippi to Illinois. In 1764 the ships arrived late. The ship *Le Missouri* arrived in New Orleans from Bordeaux, France, via Santo Domingo in May, missing the convoy of boats that left on April 19. Severe winter weather in the spring of 1764 also delayed the opening of navigation on the Mississippi and trade with Illinois. The first convoy for

Illinois of four boats and one pirogue, armed and loaded by private merchants, set off up the Mississippi on April 19, 1764. Not only were the French ships late; they did not bring provisions. On April 21, 1764, Dabbadie was forced to ask the British at Mobile for a loan of flour for New Orleans as the supply was exhausted and the troops were on half rations of rice. The loan was refused, but a British merchant sold a small amount of flour to him. On June 4, 1764, Dabbadie purchased flour from Maxent, a St. Louis merchant, who had obtained it from Illinois farmers.

The arrival of merchandise from either New Orleans or Fort Pitt was a major event and a determining factor in the economic welfare of the communities. The timing and the quantity of deliveries determined the availability and price offered to consumers. The arrival of the first convoy from New Orleans was a crucial event for the Illinois merchants as the traders and Indians came early in June. In May 1765 an enormous quantity of goods reached Illinois in April in the first convoy, which had left New Orleans in February. The second convoy arrived on May 19. The cargoes of French merchandise relieved a shortage of goods in Illinois and encouraged the Indians to continue opposing the British. Because of a lack of ammunition, before the convoys arrived the Indians had been on the verge of making peace. Another convoy of fourteen boats and two pirogues arriving in June included two boatloads of British merchandise in French boats. Not daring to travel themselves because of the Indian threat, the British had sold the goods to the French in New Orleans. In 1765 Hugh Crawford reported that on his way downriver he had passed a convoy (probably the one that reached Illinois in June) that included four to five hundred Frenchmen and a large assortment of merchandise.

Much of the farm produce continued to go down the river to New Orleans, but there was some reluctance to send fur because it would rot in the warm climate and there was a greater prevalence of vermin. Even so, the transport downriver was easier, and the price of furs in New Orleans was more than in Canada. Regardless, the colonial merchants who had established themselves in Illinois were willing to ship their fur south rather than send it up the more difficult route via the Ohio River and overland to Philadelphia.

Merchandise from both Fort Pitt and New Orleans was destined for a few settlements clustered in the area where the Missouri and Ohio Rivers joined the Mississippi. There were five groups of consumers in Illinois: Indians, French traders who wintered with the Indians, local French farmers, the British army after it occupied the territory, and the British Indian Department, which made large purchases of presents for the Indians to encourage peace. The total population of Illinois in 1760 was approximately 2,000, including slaves, compared with 3,000 people in New Orleans.

In New Orleans fur was the major business and the most valuable export. The value of the furs that could be obtained in Illinois and the regions served by the French traders was immense, enough to make any firm that was successful in exploiting that market a dominant force in the world fur trade. The Earl of Shelburne, responsible for colonial affairs in London, believed that half of all the Indian trade in North America, including Lake Michigan, Green Bay, St. Joseph, Illinois, the upper Mississippi, the Ohio Valley, and lesser rivers flowing into the Mississippi, was being diverted to France from New Orleans rather than exported to Britain.

Trade in Illinois was relatively inactive until the end of the Seven Years' War in 1763 because French vessels could not reach New Orleans with merchandise from France. However, beginning in 1760, the colonists and the British sent goods to Montreal as soon as the ice melted and the rivers were open. These goods were carried by canoe to trading posts on the Great Lakes, and the French winterers from Illinois obtained supplies at Michilimackinac and continued to trade with the Indians in the Great Lakes area.

The Indians west of the Mississippi were as eager to have European goods as those east of the river who had more experience with French traders. In 1764 Sir William Johnson estimated that the 10,000 Northern Department Indian warriors and their families would be a market for merchandise worth £179,594 sterling ($35,918,000), about £18 sterling ($3,600) per family. Baynton and Wharton estimated £22 sterling per family in Illinois, only slightly more than Johnson's estimate.

The Indians had plenty of fur to trade. The Maumee and Wabash Valleys were rich in fur in 1765 because the Seven Years' War and Pontiac's Uprising had reduced hunting, allowing the animals to multiply. The Indians were in need because of a lull in the trade during the Seven Years' War when the British navy had prevented French vessels from reaching New Orleans with merchandise and exporting furs to France.

The British and colonial merchants had to cope with continued French competition. The French were better than the British at dealing with the Indians and constantly provoked them against the British. The French, actually, could have driven out the British troops with the help of a few Spanish troops and supplies to outfit the Indians. Even so, the French had no wish to continue the fighting.

The French strategy was to use the Indians to block the routes along the Wabash, Ohio, and Miami Rivers and to rob or kill British or colonial traders who ventured south from Detroit or Lake Michigan or west from Fort Pitt. Their knowledge of the Indian languages and customs and their long-standing connections gave the French a distinct advantage over the English. Because of their close ties to the Indians, developed over generations of intermarriage and long experience wintering in the villages, the French were able to sell their merchandise to the tribes for as much as ten times its cost.

Severe winter weather delayed the opening of navigation on the Mississippi and trade with Illinois in the spring of 1764. On April 18, 1764, the ship *Le Missouri* arrived with a cargo of merchandise for New Orleans from Bordeaux. The cargo was transferred to four boats and a pirogue, and on the next day the five vessels armed and loaded by private merchants set off up the Mississippi.

In January 1764 Aubrey reported to Spain that Dabbadie had reconciled the Indians around New Orleans to the treaty between France and England. Aubrey hoped to have the same success with the Indians in the North. The French retained control of the Indians with presents, and friendly connections gave the French a distinct advantage over the colonial traders. As long as the Indians resisted, the British army could not reach Illinois via the Ohio River. Therefore, they tried to go up the Mississippi, but Aubrey believed that the attempt would fail.

Traveling up the Mississippi was impossible if the Indians were not friendly because the Indians could fire continually on the boats as they rowed slowly upstream against the current at only ten miles per day. In contrast, boats going with the current down the Ohio River covered fifty miles per day and could outdistance the Indians on land.

The French could move freely on the Mississippi. For example, at the same time that a British regiment was unable to ascend the Mississippi because of Indian opposition, the French governor of New Orleans sent out in relative safety two convoys of boats, one on April 19, 1764, and the other on May 11, 1764, with goods destined for Illinois. The second convoy included seventy-seven people in three boats.

In 1764 French officials and the French army left Illinois, contrary to British fears. On July 2, 1764, a convoy of twenty-one boats and seven pirogues arrived in New Orleans with six officers, sixty-three soldiers, and others. In June 1764 Louis St. Ange, a French official, told the Miami, Wea, Kickapoo, Mascoutens, and Piankashaw tribes in Illinois (all from the area south and west of Lake Michigan) that they would no longer receive gifts from the French and recommended that they make peace with the British, ending Pontiac's Uprising. Furthermore, he told them that if they surrendered to the British, they would be given just as much help as they had received from the French traders. The Indians refused to surrender, but St. Ange gave them some gunpowder anyway. St. Ange learned from the Indians that they planned to lay siege to Detroit again in the summer of 1764 along with the Shawnees, the Mohicans, and the Ottawas.

On August 24, 1764, Dabbadie sent a third convoy to Illinois under Dernis with seven boats and one pirogue, and another pirogue to Arkansas with 132 people. Explaining his policy to the Spanish government, Dabbadie claimed that the Indians must be given a small quantity of gunpowder and bullets because they relied on their guns for hunting, and through hunting they obtained their food and the furs that contributed to the Louisiana trade.

Contrary to the official stance of the French officials, Alexander McKee, the Indian agent at Fort Pitt, reported that the French had sent five large canoes of merchandise to the Shawnees in Ohio. Thomas Smallman, another agent, reported that the French had sent supplies to the Shawnees twice during 1764. Colonel Henry Bouquet at Fort Pitt also informed Sir William Johnson that Killbuck, a Delaware chief, would tell Johnson privately of intrigue by the French officials who supplied the Indians with gunpowder. Having this information, Johnson was to judge whether the powder was supplied with the connivance of the French commanding officer. Reports that the French had sent large quantities of merchandise up the Mississippi were forwarded to Johnson by Indians who had traveled to Illinois and received presents from the French. Captain William Howard at Michilimackinac received a report in November 1764 that the French had sent an officer to St. Joseph to urge the Pottawatomis to continue the war. Johnson proposed that the British increase their level of giving to compete with the French.

Although St. Ange claimed that he had refused to supply the Shawnees because they continued the war with the English, he did give them a little ammunition to prevent antagonism. St. Ange was embarrassed by the Indian demands that created expenses contrary to Dabbadie's orders, but he had to give them something so that the French would not lose their influence. St. Ange claimed that the Indians would not agree to make peace with the English, and if the Indians did not surrender, the British could not take Illinois, leaving St. Ange to deal with the Indians without the means to provide for them. St. Ange belittled the peace made by Colonel John Bradstreet in 1764 for he knew that the Indians intended to betray the British when the time was right, according to a letter from Pontiac. Pontiac was circulating a belt six feet long and four inches wide to all the nations to request aid in the uprising against the British. The belt was beaded in a pattern that served to remind the carrier of all of the details he needed to convey orally to each group, in the same way that rosary beads are used by Catholics. Each group of beads represented a part of the message, and a belt six feet long carried a long discourse.

After 1763 the French *voyageurs* in Illinois resumed operations, receiving merchandise transported up the Mississippi River and shipping furs down to New Orleans for transport to France, England, the West Florida ports, or other nations. The voyageurs obtained goods in Illinois and traded in the Indian villages, whereas the British army prohibited the colonial traders from leaving the posts. The voyageurs illegally traded in great numbers throughout the area of present-day Illinois, Indiana, Ohio, Michigan, Wisconsin, Minnesota, and west of the Mississippi. The French effectively turned the trade from its natural course to Quebec and competed with colonial traders to within a few miles of Detroit and Fort Pitt.

Illinois provided a haven for renegades, voyageurs who obtained goods on credit from the British, traded them for furs with the Indians, and then paddled their canoes to Illinois to sell the furs to French merchants, keeping the profits for themselves rather than paying their creditors. Occasionally Frenchmen hired by colonial merchants to trade with the Indians murdered their employers, took the goods, and went to Illinois. Illinois was a convenient escape route for any outlaw, as the French ignored the British rules. Later the Illinois French were denied credit by the British and colonial traders because they did not pay their debts. Instead the French took their furs to St. Louis. French vagabond traders were scattered throughout the unoccupied area of the West. In 1765 there were between 400 and 500 French traders illegally in British territory working the older territory east of the Mississippi River and the upper Mississippi River. Using St. Louis as their main base, the French traded in great numbers throughout the area. The Pennsylvania traders, the Canadians from Montreal, and the French from Illinois competed for the Indian trade south of the Great Lakes and in the Mississippi and Ohio Valleys.

The British firmly believed that there would be no peace with the Indians as long as commercial rivalry continued. Colonel Bradstreet, who led the expedition to relieve Detroit, recognized that as long as the French and the Spanish sent traders up the Wabash and the Scioto Rivers from the west, the Detroit and Fort Pitt merchants could not compete there. An Albany trader in Detroit in 1767 complained that even after the British occupation, the French traders from Illinois brought goods to Vincennes, Vermillion, Ouiatanon, and as far north as Miami.

Having failed to move up the Mississippi, the British planned to send an expedition down the Ohio River in 1765 to occupy Illinois but needed Indian permission. General Thomas Gage, commander in chief of British forces in America, was still waiting for news of the treaty with the Delawares and the Shawnees, as Croghan needed their support to persuade some influential Indian chiefs to accompany him down the Ohio. The timing was critical because the 34th Regiment would try to row up the Mississippi from New Orleans in February 1765, and Indian resistance had to be removed for the regiment to succeed.

The troops, led by Captain James Sterling, finally left Fort Pitt on August 22, 1765, and arrived in Illinois on October 9. It was a long forty-seven-day journey on the low waters of the Ohio River during the middle of summer. Forty miles west of the Wabash River they encountered a French trader with two loaded boats and thirty men. The uncooperative French asked that British and colonial traders be kept out for nine months to allow the French to transfer to the western side of the Mississippi. Sterling had traveled without presents because the Indians had taken those bought by Croghan and few goods were left at Fort Pitt. As a result, he was forced to buy goods from the French in Illinois at exorbitant prices. The real problem for Sterling in Illinois could be expected in the spring, when 3,000–4,000 unhappy Indians would arrive expecting presents as they traded their furs.

In Florida the commander of the 34th Regiment, who had been ordered to go up the Mississippi to occupy Illinois, purchased a cargo of deerskin in Mobile with a bill of exchange drawn on General Gage. His intent was to use the deerskin as currency in New Orleans to buy supplies, as British bills of exchange sold at a very poor rate of exchange there. This dealing violated the law prohibiting the export of deerskin to non-British ports, but the governor permitted the transaction on payment of a duty of £178 sterling ($35,600).

Trade goods also went to Florida from New York City and Philadelphia. When Baynton and Wharton learned of the army's proposal to go up the Mississippi in February 1764, the firm joined with Daniel Clark and Jeremiah Warder in a venture, sending goods worth £1,500 Pennsylvania ($172,500) to Mobile for shipment to Illinois. In 1766 Cornelius Mereford left Mobile for New Orleans with a cargo of British or colonial merchandise intending to sell it to French merchants. Bernard Gratz had a quantity of gin and butter in Mobile, which was sold by his agent. Some merchandise went directly to New Orleans. In 1767 Baynton and Wharton sent merchandise worth £384 Pennsylvania ($44,160) to New Orleans on the sloop *Superb* to its agent Bartholomew MacNamara. In 1768 Cornelius Bradford sent a schooner to Philadelphia from New Orleans.

Since 1763 Baynton and Wharton had been making plans to go to Illinois. On May 31, 1763, the partners had sent a huge shipment of goods valued at £13,915 Pennsylvania ($1,600,000) from Philadelphia to Callender & Spear at Carlisle intended for Illinois. The partners in the venture were Callender & Spear (45 percent), Samuel Eldridge (10 percent), and Baynton and Wharton (45 percent). When the Ohio River was blocked by Pontiac's Uprising later in 1763 the large stock of merchandise was stranded in Fort Pitt and was sold to the Indian Department in 1764.

Baynton and Wharton began preparations for another try. Beginning in 1764 the firm zealously assembled merchandise worth more than £19,000

Pennsylvania (almost $2.2 million) to do business in Illinois. It planned to provide for 2,500 Indian families at a rate of £38 Pennsylvania (£22 sterling or $4,370) per family, based on the 5,000 shirts in the stock. The amount of the shipment was based on an estimate of the population provided by Croghan, who was a partner in the venture. Johnson had estimated the total market for the Northern Department—the area north of the Ohio River— at 10,000 adult male Indians. Croghan assumed that the French traders would buy goods from Baynton and Wharton to trade up the Missouri River as well as in the older areas, which would have had at least 2,500 families. In November 1764, Croghan and Baynton and Wharton planned the trading venture to coincide with the official mission to garrison Illinois under the leadership of Croghan. Baynton and Wharton hastened to form a consortium to gain ascendancy in the Indian trade at Fort Pitt and Illinois. John Jennings was hired for twelve months' service on behalf of the partnership at Fort Pitt beginning December 3, 1764. Merchandise was prepared for the expedition. On December 7, five wagonloads (each with one to one and a half tons) were sent to Callender by the three business partners and "etc.," omitting Croghan's name from the transaction. One of the wagons contained five bales of cloth including one bale of blue strouds worth £60 sterling, a bale of twelve scarlet strouds valued at £95 sterling, and a bale of twelve aurora strouds valued at £75 sterling. The value of the five wagonloads must have been more than £2,000 sterling ($400,000). On December 12 five more wagons were sent to Callender from all four partners, with Croghan's name included on this order, and on December 14 three more wagons were sent. The three shipments had a combined value of more than £10,000 Pennsylvania ($1,150,000). On December 24, 1764, Baynton and Wharton received a shipment on the brigantine *Grace* from its primary supplier in London, Richard Neave, for merchandise valued at £2,809 sterling ($562,000). The firm was well prepared to enter the western trade.

In January 1765 Baynton and Wharton made an illegal arrangement with Croghan to acquire a large stock of merchandise to be shipped to Fort Pitt for purchase by Croghan with Indian Department funds and used as gifts to the Indians as part of his peacemaking expedition down the Ohio River. The agreement divided the potential profits, giving Croghan two shares, Robert Field two shares, Baynton and Wharton two shares, Robert Callender one share, and John Baynton one share. The total value of the goods was £19,766 Pennsylvania ($2,273,000), a considerable amount. Field, John Jennings, William Long, William Smallman, and Callender were to move the merchandise by wagon to Carlisle and by packhorse from there to Fort Pitt.

The financial transactions for the trip began in January 1765. Gage provided Croghan with a credit of £2,000 New York ($252,000) to purchase presents for his mission. Croghan, claiming that the goods available in Fort Pitt were old and damaged, purchased new goods in Philadelphia, including wampum and silver for the conferences.

The plan was to send a first shipment of Indian goods worth £2,190 Pennsylvania ($252,000) for sale to the tribes along with additional merchandise of equal value that Croghan would purchase to win their favor. Most of the merchandise was already in the hands of Baynton and Wharton, but large amounts were purchased from other merchants and suppliers in Philadelphia. Croghan's purchases were made from Thomas Smallman (£2,650 Pennsylvania, or $304,750), Field (£1,121 New York, or $141,250), and Baynton and Wharton (£1,900 Pennsylvania, or $218,500), all of whom were involved in the Baynton and Wharton venture. He also purchased goods worth £2,037 Pennsylvania ($234,300) from Simon Levy and Company with Thomas Smallman as cosigner. In March Johnson sent Croghan's first bill to General Gage, for £4,043 New York ($509,500). The amount was more than double the allowance by Gage, who was outraged that Croghan had made such an extravagant purchase without consultation. Croghan's explanation was that silver ornaments were needed to attract and draw in the Wabash Indians.

In 1766 another venture was planned. This time George Morgan, at that time a new partner in the firm of Baynton and Wharton, took charge of the shipment of merchandise that would accompany Croghan's peace mission. The intent, of course, was that Croghan would buy much of the merchandise as presents for the Indians in his public capacity. In contrast to the smaller amount sent in 1765, £20,000 Pennsylvania, Baynton and Wharton sent an incredible amount of goods, worth £50,000 sterling ($10,000,000). The goods were shipped in wagons and on six hundred packhorses to Fort Pitt, where Morgan established a boatyard to build sixty-five boats to carry the goods onward.

Croghan immediately began to purchase large amounts of merchandise to use as presents. Gage authorized the expenditure of £3,445 New York ($434,000), but the exuberant Croghan spent £8,408 New York ($1,060,000), of which £6,480 New York went to Baynton and Wharton for merchandise, including some already at Fort Pitt worth £3,445 Pennsylvania. Francis Wade purchased goods worth £1,670 Pennsylvania ($192,000) for Croghan.

The first step in opening the Illinois market to British goods was taken on March 9, 1766, when John Jennings, William Long, Richard Winston, Thomas Smallman, and others left Fort Pitt for Illinois in five boats loaded with up to seven tons of merchandise from Baynton and Wharton. Because the cargo was too large to be loaded on the boats, forty bundles of dry goods, kegs of knives, and a bundle of saddles were left behind to be sent later.

The second flotilla, which finally set off down the Ohio on June 18, 1766, consisted of thirteen boats, two with Croghan's presents and provisions for Fort Chartres and the remaining eleven with a cargo that Baynton and Wharton intended to sell on the way down the Ohio and in Illinois. Each boat carried up to seven tons of merchandise, a truly large shipment, and these thirteen were only one group of the sixty-five boats being built. The charge to the army for the two boatloads of provisions was £1,577 Pennsylvania (about $180,000). The value of Baynton and Wharton's cargo was £18,832 Pennsylvania (about $2,166,000). Included were guns, brass kettles, match coats, strouds, large knives, vermillion, and wampum, on a list that was twenty-six pages long. Baynton stated that the total venture was the largest shipment ever made down the Ohio and that it would sell at three times its value, still a reasonable price compared with French sales.

Baynton and Wharton continued to buy merchandise and invest more money in the Illinois venture in an attempt to increase revenue. In June 1767 the firm purchased 1,102 pairs of shoes from seven shoemakers in Philadelphia at from 6s. to 9s. a pair, £400 Pennsylvania total—an indication of its attempt to sell to the French in Illinois. Another shipment confirmed the same story. In October 1767 Joseph Hollingshead, one of the best agents working for the firm, set out with three boats from Fort Pitt manned by twenty-five boatmen and twenty riflemen to hunt buffalo for rations to the British army in Illinois. In a third transaction, John Campbell, its agent in Fort Pitt, recommended that the next shipment to Illinois include silverwork for the Indians, 5,000 pounds of coffee, 5,000 pounds of sugar, 1,000 pounds of chocolate, 15 barrels of muscovado (unrefined) sugar, a chest of bohea (Chinese) tea, 100 pounds of green tea, 1,500 pairs of men's stockings, and English cheese. Other than the silver, these goods were for sale to either the garrison or the French. The army had become the major customer for Baynton and Wharton in Illinois.

These three markets—the Indians, the French, and the British army—combined were an impressive potential outlet for British goods imported by colonial merchants. After 1765 the two major mercantile firms competing in Illinois were Baynton and Wharton of Philadelphia and Maxent, LaClede, and Company, the French firm that founded St. Louis. These two companies and their business associates competed for furs from the Indians as well as sterling bills of exchange from the British army, the two most significant assets that could be used to pay for imports to the area. Some farm products found a market in New Orleans to feed the locals, to provision visiting ships, and to export to France and other countries, but farm produce was bulky and difficult to preserve in the warm New Orleans climate.

Baynton and Wharton delivered large amounts of merchandise to Illinois after enormous hardships, but it did not sell quickly. As might be expected, the French refused to buy from the firm. Baynton and Wharton did not have the expertise to deal directly with the Indians in their villages, and any attempts to do so were obstructed by the French. Thus Baynton and Wharton's sales were limited to the few Indians who entered its stores along with the farmers and French traders. Consequently, Baynton and Wharton had a huge inventory of goods purchased on credit in Britain for which it was unable to pay.

The firm's best customers were the French farmers. The French purchased some merchandise from Baynton and Wharton, but on credit, which was difficult to collect because the French sent their furs and deerskins down the Mississippi River to New Orleans. Morgan complained that he was able to get very little fur from the French. The farmers in Illinois had long been deprived of a cheap source of domestic items—first by the war and then by the difficulty of moving the merchandise up the Mississippi. In 1766 Baynton and Wharton purchased fifteen casks of tinware from Benjamin Marshall worth £172 Pennsylvania ($19,780) to be sent to Illinois.

The French merchants controlled the direct trade with the Indians and obtained fur from the Indians in exchange for French merchandise from New Orleans plus some goods that they purchased from Pennsylvania merchants. Baynton and Wharton imported cheaper British dry goods and colonial liquor, but the French were reluctant to exchange an appreciable amount of fur for this colonial merchandise. Instead, Baynton and Wharton was forced to sell its goods to the farmers for farm produce, which was in turn sold to the army for rations. The French farmers would not sell directly to the army because they were reluctant to accept English bills of exchange. French merchants in New Orleans accepted the bills only at steep discounts. But the farmers were eager to exchange the dry goods and liquor from Baynton and Wharton for their produce. Baynton and Wharton, however, was happy to receive bills of exchange because they could be used to pay debts in England. Morgan, Baynton and Wharton's agent in Illinois, used some of the fur he obtained to pay for the merchandise from New Orleans, but most of the fur was sent to Philadelphia.

Colonial merchants purchased provisions from the French farmers with British manufactured goods and then sold the food to the army. Army provisions had to be purchased locally because during the long trip from New Orleans food was ruined by the heat. The army paid in sterling bills of exchange, which the Pennsylvania merchants used to pay debts in England. The army bought some provisions directly from the French with bills of exchange, but the farmers were reluctant to accept them because the French merchants in New Orleans accepted British bills of exchange only at steep discounts.

At the same time, Sir William Johnson promised to favor Baynton and Wharton when purchasing supplies for the Indian Department and also supported the firm's business in Illinois. British troops finally occupied Illinois at the end of 1765, and Johnson sent an Indian Department commissary there in the spring of 1766. His job ostensibly was to supervise trade, but in reality it was to purchase merchandise from Baynton and Wharton to give to the Indians.

To further the business interest of Baynton and Wharton in supplying the troops, Croghan urged Benjamin Franklin to advocate keeping the army in Illinois in 1767 despite the cost. Croghan suggested that if the army were not present there, the French would convince the Indians to make war on the British and the colonists and thereby capture the entire Mississippi Valley fur trade for France. If cost were the major consideration, he said, Gage should accept Baynton and Wharton's offer to supply rations at a much lower price than the competing Franks group. All of these suggestions were to provide Franklin with points in opposing Shelburne. During the late 1760s Franklin represented American interests in London and opposed the attempts of Shelburne and the British government to limit the activities of the colonial fur traders to protect the Indians.

The business in Illinois continued to be active. In November 1768 Robert Callender, a former partner in the Illinois venture, left Carlisle on his way to Fort Chartres in Illinois with 2,000 gallons of rum on one hundred horses and forty horse-loads of dry goods. The dry goods would have weighed 7,200 pounds and the rum 16,000 pounds, for a total of approximately 12 tons, roughly the amount carried by four canoes in the Canadian trade. So this was a major shipment, worth up to £1,600 sterling ($320,000). A week later Joseph Spear, another former partner in the Illinois venture, left Carlisle with sixty horse-loads of rum and Indian goods bound for Fort Pitt. Included in this shipment were ten hogsheads of rum (630 gallons, or thirty horse-loads). The total shipment was more than 5 tons, equal to two canoe-loads in Canada, with a value of £800 sterling ($160,000). The timing of the shipments was significant. The road to Fort Pitt was often closed by snow in December, and the Ohio River was frozen until the following spring. Therefore, these large shipments were made in anticipation of an expansion of trade in Illinois in 1769.

The colonial merchants had hoped, futilely, that the acquisition of Illinois and the right to transport goods down the Mississippi River for export to Europe would be a major benefit of the Treaty of Paris. The persistent French determined otherwise because they—and later the Spaniards— retained control of New Orleans, the only navigable outlet for the trade moving down the Mississippi and entering the Gulf of Mexico.

Consumers in Illinois had two options: to buy from the French merchants in New Orleans or the Pennsylvania merchants who sent their merchandise by way of Fort Pitt. One of the largest mercantile firms in Philadelphia, Baynton and Wharton, began a major effort to monopolize this business in 1764, expecting that its lower prices would overcome French resistance to buying British goods. The partners also assumed that the Illinois French would be eager customers after more than five years without supplies from France during the Seven Years' War. Baynton and Wharton presumed that the major market in Illinois would be the Indians.

As lucrative as the market was, the colonial merchants failed in their attempt to wrest the trade from the French, who remained in control of the Illinois trade throughout the period 1760–74. The merchants had to settle for the French farmers and the British army as their markets. French merchants in New Orleans continued to supply French merchandise to the traders in Illinois. In fact, there were more French-made goods in Illinois than British-made, and continued economic control by French traders deprived the other colonies of the majority of fur and deerskin from the area.

# 9

# Women and Home Life

The part women played on the frontier has been largely ignored, yet they played essential roles in maintaining life in the wilderness. Family life predominated. Widows and unmarried women were seldom found there, where families were the source of sustenance. The new settlers adopted Indian ways. Corn was new to them, and metal pots and guns were new to the Indians. Although the Indians accepted the colonist's material goods, their native culture remained the same.

Indian women were the field workers in the tribes. The Indians in the area north of the Ohio River were dependent on agriculture for most of their food, including corn, beans, and squash. Their diet was primarily corn, supplemented by meat, fish, berries, and vegetables. One estimate was that the Indian diet was 65 percent corn; 13 percent beans; 2 percent squash; and 20 percent meat, fish, and fruit. Each family had a garden plot near the village. Because clearing the land was hard work the gardens were small at first. Every year the family cleared a little more land for the garden until it was as big as needed. Village gardens grew to more than 200 acres as each family added to its garden. Because the family gardens were adjacent to one another, each plot was marked with wood, a mound of earth, or stones at each corner.

Women did most of the work in the garden as well as clearing the land for it. Young men never worked in the gardens. Instead they hunted or went on war parties, including young boys, who guarded the horses. However, old men did help their wives in the garden.

Trees were removed from the gardens because corn did not grow well in the shade. The trees were cut with axes, another welcome tool from the traders. With steel axes, the women could clear land more easily but seldom chopped down large trees, instead choosing open spaces with small trees and bushes. Most of the wood was saved for firewood, but some was burned where it fell, softening the ground and making it loose for planting the next year. Care was taken to rake brush before setting a fire to prevent it from spreading.

The women used wooden digging sticks and bone hoes to plant and cultivate before they got metal hoes from the traders. A digging stick was made of ash three feet long and sharpened to a point on one end. The women opened a field beginning with a small round hole by using a digging stick, knocking off clods and roots of grass, weeds, and small bushes that stuck by hitting the stick. They would then shake the dirt from the roots and place them in small piles to dry. Later they were gathered into a large pile four feet high and burned. To make digging easier, the women worked around the original hole, circling around and around it until a large piece of land was dug up. One fall, for example, five women cleared an area measuring 75 by 100 yards (7,500 square yards, or 1.5 acres). Because the freshly dug soil was too loose they did not plant the area until the following year.

Large tree stumps were allowed to rot while standing, and the corn rows were continued on the other side of the stump. While the corn was growing, the women cleared roots and smaller stumps. The willows and brush were spread around the field. The following year the family burned the willows and the brush over four days. The burn left the soil easy to work, and it was then fertilized with ashes. That spring the women planted eighty-one rows of corn on their 1.5 acres.

Corn needed three months to grow. By staggering planting times, rows of corn would ripen throughout the summer. The women planted the corn in rows of small hills spaced four feet apart. The hills were made from the ashes left from burning the trees the previous year or from soil that had been dug up and the roots removed. The corn was planted in the same hills every year in May when the wild gooseberry bushes sprouted leaves. First the soil was loosened around each hill and all roots of previous corn were removed and burned, leaving a hole nine inches in diameter. The new seeds were planted in the loose soil where the root had been. The women raked the soil with their fingers to make a hole and planted six to eight kernels in each hill, pressing the seed down a half inch and covering it with their hands. The ears would be small if the hills were too close together and if the leaves of the corn touched each other as they grew.

Planting began in the coolness before sunrise. By 10 a.m. 250 hills could be planted, and the women returned to their lodges during the heat of the day. At this pace the crop took nearly a month to plant. The women of a family usually did her family's planting, although neighbors would help when women could not work because of sickness. As many as thirty women might come and plant an entire crop in one day.

No land was wasted. Beans were planted later, between the rows of corn. One family garden was 180 yards by 90 yards (16,200 square yards, more than 3 acres). The size was determined by how well the woman worked and by the number of persons in the family. One family had ten people—a father, his two wives, three sisters of the wives, and four children.

The garden was cultivated with hoes, usually when the corn was three inches high, to remove the weeds. A bone hoe had a handle three feet long to which the eight-inch-long shoulder bone of a large animal was tied at a right angle with strips of leather or sinew. Usually the weeds did not grow again. The field was cultivated a second time when the corn was higher, to remove any weeds and to mound the hills to secure the plants against wind damage. Even though crows, magpies, and blackbirds plucked young corn plants, each was replaced. To replace seed that was eaten by crows to match the size of the other plants, the women soaked kernels in warm water for four or five days until the seeds sprouted a third of inch before planting them. Scarecrows were made from sticks covered with an old buffalo robe to look like a man.

In most of the tribes around Detroit, the women cultivated Indian corn, beans, peas, squash, and melons. Girls were posted to watch the cornfields to scare away crows and other predators. They sat on platforms and sang to scare away the birds. Girls began watching when they were ten and continued their entire life. While watching and singing the women did embroidery using porcupine needles. These guards also watched for boys who would steal ripe corn to roast and to feed their horses. Boys visited the watchers and flirted with the girls, not speaking but smiling. If they were related, the girls would feed the boys. The girls did not speak either but merely smiled at the other boys to encourage them. If the girls did not smile, the boys went away. Young girls on watch, supervised by older women, sang songs that ridiculed the boys. The boys used bows to hunt birds, and the girls' songs would tease them, saying that their bows were like basket hoops and their arrows were worthless. The girls also sang songs accusing the boys of running away instead of fighting when they went on war parties to prove their bravery.

While watching, the girls and women also cooked in round booths made of willow branches placed near the garden. A booth could be ten feet in diameter and six feet high, with a fire in the center. Fresh or dried buffalo meat was brought from the village. Fresh meat was broiled, and dried meat was toasted on the end of a stick. Squash was boiled in pots. Green corn and beans was a common dish. The corn was shelled from the cob and boiled with the green beans, which had been either shelled or boiled in the pod. The corn and beans were eaten from wooden bowls with spoons made of squash leaves. Some corn was shelled, ground in a mortar, and then boiled. Shelled hard corn was often boiled with beans and fat. At dusk the women carried the leftover food back to the lodge.

A second batch of corn was planted in June to be ready for eating in the fall. By June the first planting was ripe enough to be boiled and eaten. Green, or unripe, corn was boiled on the cob. If not harvested within ten days it became too hard to boil. Green corn was also roasted as a delicacy but never used as the main course. After the husk was removed the corn was placed on a bed of coals and rolled to cook evenly.

Green corn was also dried and stored for the winter. The ears were placed in a pile in the field and left overnight. The next morning the women brought the corn back to the lodge and husked it by a fire. The ears were then boiled in water until half cooked and dried overnight. Later placed on an animal skin, the green corn was shelled using a pointed stick. The corn could also be roasted, instead of boiled, then shelled and dried. It was dried for four days and then winnowed to remove the chaff and placed in sacks.

Because corn was such an essential part of the Indians' diet, harvesting was a ceremonial event that might continue as long as three days for a small family. The women and girls often danced at night wearing a white shift beaded with wampum, greasing their hair, and painting their cheeks with vermillion. They danced to the sound of drums and the rattle of gourds filled with shot. Four or five young men beat the drums and sang while the women, girls, and old men danced the night away.

After the corn was picked and piled, the whole family began husking the ears. Young men might come to help and be fed. For young men and women the work was a party. Attractive girls were delighted to have several young men ready to help them husk. The corn husks were braided into strings and the ears were hung on poles to dry. The husk was bent back and used to tie one ear to another. Fifty ears in a string was the weight a woman could carry.

Some kernels were saved for use as seed the following year. Seed was carefully selected; only the medium kernels from the center of the ear were chosen rather than the large and small kernels at the two ends. The seed was usable for one or two years but not longer. If the harvest was good, enough seed was stored for two years to ensure against a bad harvest when no seed would be left over for the following year. Frost could destroy most of the crop, so a year's reserve of seed corn was essential. This reserve rule was followed for all of the crops—squash, beans, sunflower, and tobacco. Some families did not save enough for two years and were forced to buy from others. A string of braided seed corn sold for one tanned buffalo skin. Over the years saving seed corn could be very profitable.

The remainder of the crop was used immediately. The kernels of mature corn were removed from the cobs by beating the dried ears with flails. Most of the kernels came off and the few remaining were removed by hand. The cobs were burned and the ashes, called "spring salt," were saved for seasoning the boiled dried corn.

The kernels were dried overnight. If they broke with a snap, they were properly dried; if still soft, they dried another night. The next day the corn was winnowed by pouring the contents of a half basket of kernels slowly into another basket, allowing the wind to remove the dust or chaff.

Some Indian tribes grew more than enough corn to last the year and sold some of it to other tribes in exchange for meat and buffalo skins. The Indians grew a variety of corn: hard white, soft white, hard yellow, soft yellow, gummy, blue, dark red, light red, and pink top. Hard white corn was the most common, often cooked in boiling water with dried squash and some beans.

To parch corn, sand was often used. Clean sand from the river was placed in a pot and heated until the sand was red hot. Then the pot was removed from the fire and two handfuls of corn were thrown in and stirred with the sand. When the corn was hot, the pot was again placed on the fire and stirred. Soon the kernels cracked with a noise like popcorn. The corn was separated from the sand and used for various dishes such as mush. To make mush, the parched corn and animal fat were pounded in a pestle and then added to boiling squash and beans. When cooked, the mush was ready to be eaten. A second recipe was dried corn, not parched, pounded into meal and boiled with beans without adding fat or meat. A pot of cornmeal was always on the fire in the lodge.

Beans, another source of nourishment, were planted between the rows of corn in small hills. The seeds were first sprouted by wetting and placing them in moist grass leaves for three days near the fire. Then two women would do the planting. The first would loosen an area fifteen inches in diameter with a hoe and make a small hill, preferably in the same place as the year before. The second woman planted the sprouted bean seeds, four seeds to a hill, in pairs twelve inches apart on the sides of the little hills to protect the seeds from the rain.

Squash was planted in late May or early June and harvested in the fall. It grew very fast and was picked off the vine every four days. Each hill would grow two or three squash in four pickings. Some was eaten fresh and the rest was sliced and dried for winter. Women sliced the squash with a knife made from the shoulder bone of a buffalo, later replaced by steel butcher knives. The slices were spitted on three-foot-long sticks. The slices of squash were placed a half inch apart on the sticks, which were then placed on a rack to dry. After three days the dry squash was strung on strings of dried grass forty feet long. Fresh squash was sliced and boiled with sunflower leaves. Very little water was used to allow steam to cook the squash. When done, the sunflower leaves were discarded. Ripe squash was also roasted by burying it in the ashes of the fire.

The Indians moved each spring to a summer village by a river and in the fall back to the winter village. Food was stored over the winter in caches and pits in the summer village. When the Indians returned in the spring, the cached food was available while new crops were growing. The cache had an entrance two feet in diameter at the top and became larger at the bottom, up to six feet in diameter. The cache was eight feet deep, lined with corn on the cob and then filled with shelled corn and squash. The opening was covered with a hide, a layer of grass, some planks, another hide, and then ashes and dirt.

In times of bad harvest, the Indians relied on the Indian Department and the army for food. Prior to contact with the Europeans, the Indians went hungry after a poor harvest, but fortunately the British offered the Indians an alternate source of food. In 1760 Sir William Johnson fed many Indians as a result of the bad harvest. At a conference at Fort Pitt in April 1760 the hungry Indians demanded food. The practice of feeding the Indians became widespread. After complaining in 1769 of military rations being used to feed the Indians, General Thomas Gage ordered that in the future the Indians be fed only in an emergency. In 1773, when a hard winter interfered with hunting deer, the starving Indians at Michilimackinac were supplied with food by the British army.

Because the Indian villages were small, seldom exceeding a few hundred people, obtaining a suitable husband for daughters was not easy. The Indians were well aware of the likelihood of birth defects if a man and wife were closely related. Finding a husband not related to his daughters was a common difficulty for fathers in the villages. When an Indian girl became old enough to marry, her father gave her to a young man, along with all of her younger sisters. Because of the lack of medical care, death in childbirth was not uncommon. When this occurred, the younger sisters, also not closely related to the husband, could take the place of the departed sister. They were also able to care for her children.

There was a high mortality rate among Indian males because of the dangers of life in the forest and conflict with other tribes. The desired quality in a prospective husband was being a brave warrior and a good hunter because he would often have a household of eight persons to care for.

Because of the kinship problem, Indian women were not expected to remain faithful to their husbands and cohabitation with visitors was accepted. (An extreme example of this problem was found among the Inuit, who lived isolated lives and expected any visitor to sleep with their wife.)

Prostitution was not common on the frontier. The practice in the eighteenth century required a large market of unmarried males and was usually confined to cities and seaports. Venereal disease was not easily cured. George Croghan, the Indian agent, had such a serious case that at one point he was forced to wear a kilt to avoid discomfort. A few Indian women were used as prostitutes by the white traders and soldiers. In May 1762 Captain James Sterling, who was trading in Detroit, had a serious problem with the delivery of a cargo because of a drunken orgy. The canoe had arrived from Fort Niagara with its goods in poor condition because of inadequate management by Colbeck, who represented Sterling's business interests at Fort Niagara. Sterling discovered that Colbeck had been drunk for fourteen days with the army sergeants while his men spent the time in a brothel with Indian women at Fort Niagara.

One Pennsylvania trader had a string of twenty horses to carry his goods and hired two Indians to manage them. In addition he had a young Pawnee girl slave whom he had purchased from the Indians who had captured her in one of their raids west of the Mississippi River.

Indian women were not passive or submissive to their treatment. In July 1762 General Jeffrey Amherst, commander of the British forces in North America that year, approved the hanging of the Indian women who were convicted of murdering a trader, John Clapham, on his way to Detroit, which caused relations between the British army and the Indians to deteriorate further.

There were many white women on the frontier as well. Along with the wives of settlers, women were attached to the British army. In 1763 Fort Pitt had a garrison of 330 soldiers, 104 women, and 106 children, plus some traders. The 34th Regiment in Illinois also had a large contingent of women and children. The women were part of the regiment and received army rations along with their children. Many were wives of the soldiers and did laundry and other tasks in return for their rations. The women and children maintained communal vegetable gardens to improve the rations and did most of the cooking for the regiment. The women also cared for the sick and the officer's children. Officers' wives maintained households complete with servants.

Most of the women on the frontier were wives, and a few were indentured servants working for settlers. Wives worked not only in their homes but also in the fields. They did not do as much field work as their Indian counterparts but had somewhat different chores. The white women were responsible for the livestock. Every farm had horses and oxen to pull its wagon and its plow and cows to provide milk and meat. Pigs were an essential source of meat, and most pioneer recipes call for bacon or fat. Many farms had sheep and goats as well. Milking the cows was a daily chore that could not be neglected, although older children assumed this duty in some families. Feeding the livestock was an arduous task that included pushing the hay down from a loft in the barn and emptying heavy bags of grain into the troughs.

Life was exhausting for the women and older girls. Preparing foodstuff for the table occupied wives most of the day along with caring for the children. They cured meat, pickled vegetables, and preserved fruit. The menu included beef, pork, wild birds, venison and other wild animals, fish, milk, butter, and eggs. The hogs rooted in the woods for acorns and roots. The busy wives of hardworking, patient farmers who wrested a meager living from flinty soil had the industry, initiative, and imagination to transform spartan basic foods into delicious dishes that otherwise could have been monotonous, though nourishing.

One of the major tasks of the pioneer housewife was baking bread, the staple food. One pound of flour produced a one-pound loaf of bread. A family of four needed three pounds of bread a day. (The daily ration for a soldier was a full pound of bread.) The family recipe was 6 cups of flour, 2 1/2 cups of warm water, yeast, 1 1/2 teaspoons of salt, and 1 teaspoon of sugar (a luxury item that was not always available). The homegrown yeast was stored in a jar in a dark place. The salt was purchased in the nearest store, often many miles away. The flour was ground from the settlers' wheat at the nearest gristmill. All the ingredients had to be on hand at all times, with the exception of the sugar, which was a luxury item.

The preparation took two days. The yeast, salt, and sugar were combined with the water, and 2 cups of the flour was stirred in gradually and beaten with a wooden spoon. The mixture was allowed to stand for at least 12 hours. On the second day an additional 4 cups of flour were added and the mixture was stirred until thick. On a flat surface powdered with flour the dough was spread and kneaded by hand for 10 minutes until it was smooth. The dough was placed in a bowl, covered, and allowed to rise for an hour. It was ready when touched and the indention remained. The dough was flattened, divided, rolled into two balls and allowed to rise for 10 minutes, placed in two greased pans to rise for 45 minutes, and then baked for 45 minutes. This daily routine was in addition to the wife's many other chores.

Colonial wives were hard pressed by food scarcities and inadequate cooking equipment. The early settlers had a difficult time because they needed so much, had so little, and could acquire hardly anything. The essential cast-iron cooking utensils were scarce. Families fortunate enough to own iron pots lived on one-dish meals.

Staple foods were beans and rice, which could be stored indefinitely. Fat was heated in a pan and a cup of rice was stirred and cooked for 2 minutes. A cup and a half of water was added, along with salt and pepper. The pan was covered and the rice cooked until the water was absorbed. Beans were soaked overnight and heated. Flavoring ingredients were added and the mixture was heated until warm.

Venison was readily available. To cook it, fat was heated in a large pan. Two pounds of venison were cut into one-inch chunks and browned in the pan. Four cups of water were added, along with salt and pepper, and the meat cooked slowly for 40 minutes. Carrots or other vegetables were sliced and added to the mixture, which cooked for another hour. A cup of flour and water was added to thicken the stew to provide an ample dinner for as many as eight people.

For a more balanced diet, ten cups of any kind of greens such as spinach and mustard greens were washed and torn into pieces. Five slices of bacon were cut into strips and fried. The greens were cooked in a pan with two tablespoons of bacon fat until tender and then sprinkled with small pieces of bacon and vinegar.

A common dish was the one-pot boiled dinner. Three pounds of salted meat and a pound of the leanest salt pork from brine were soaked in cold water overnight. The meat was placed in cold fresh water and cooked slowly until midday. Then the pork was removed, trimmed, and cut into squares. It was returned to the pot and cooked with the rest of the meat until sunset. As the meats cooked, turnips, onions, and cabbage were washed and quartered. When the turnips were almost done, whole carrots and potatoes in their skins were added. If beets were available, they were boiled separately and put on the table with dinner.

Roasting any kind of flesh or fowl was a primitive affair, but the settlers' simple methods worked. Before roasting, the meat was rubbed with fat and sprinkled with flour or cornmeal. One basic principle had to be followed: when roasting over an open fire, meat must be turned constantly to be cooked through. Turning the roast could be accomplished using a peg, a string, and a stone. A peg was driven into the mantel directly above the center of the fire, and one end of a stout worsted string was tied onto the peg. Meat weighing up to six pounds was trussed in the middle of the string. A stone was tied to the other end of the string to hold it down. Depending on the fire the roast was hung near to or away from the blaze. The string was twisted taut, and the meat turned slowly as the string unwound and rewound under its own momentum. The string had to be twisted again when it ran down after five minutes. Any child could do the work and have fun at the same time.

The roast had to be turned upside down when it was half cooked so that the juice did not all gather in one end. A dripping pan was placed under the roast, which was basted with the drippings. Birds and other small game and meat were roasted in this way. The method amused guests and provided a subject for conversation.

When winter set in and snow piled the countryside settlers had to rely on salted meat, usually pork because hogs were easier to raise and more prolific than other meat animals. There were many methods of curing. To make salt pork, the fresh meat was placed in the bottom of a barrel and covered with coarse salt one inch deep. Another layer of pork was added and covered with another inch of salt, and this layering continued until all of the pork was packed. The whole batch was then covered with strong brine. The pork was packed as tightly as possible, with the rind down or next to the barrel. The pork was held under the brine by an inner cover and well-scrubbed weighing stones. If scum rose it was skimmed off the brine, scalded to purify it, and more salt was added. Old brine was boiled down, skimmed, and used for another salting down. The thickly salted water brine had to be heavy enough to float an uncooked chicken's egg.

Early settlers soon discovered that the long stretch between early winter and the end of the chilly spring meant long abstinence from fresh field and garden greens. In the springtime these industrious women gathered leaves and flowers of various kinds of greens for medicines, wines, and vinegar. The dandelion was most prized for its medicinal properties. The pioneer women had to know a thing or two about home cures.

Concoctions were made of dandelion roots and leaves, but extracts were the best. Dandelion extract was made from the roots, which were gathered in September, cleaned, and bruised in a mortar. The juice was pressed out, strained, and placed on a plate in a warm room to evaporate, rendering a thick and solid paste. Dandelion beer was made from dandelion roots and water. It was boiled with maple sugar, vinegar, and yeast.

Wives of early settlers learned about new foods from the Indians, particularly corn. Corn was easy to grow and could be planted in the garden several times in the summer and ready to eat in sixty days. By staggering the planting time, some ripe corn would be continually available. Corn was ground into a coarse meal and boiled as mush or baked as cornbread. It was used whole with other vegetables, such as beans; boiled into porridge; or pounded to meal in a mortar. One of the oldest maize dishes is hulled maize porridge. To remove the hard hulls of corn to cook the soft kernels, ash lye was added to the water in which the stripped corn was soaked. The corn was then rinsed several times and boiled until it became a porridge.

Baking soda was used to hull corn by stirring one teaspoon into two pints of yellow corn covered by cold water. In an hour the hulls began to separate from the kernels. The water was drained, washing away the hulls. The corn was boiled for 2 to 4 hours in slightly salted water, drained, and boiled again in fresh water for another 45 minutes. By then the porridge was ready to eat, delicious hot or cold with molasses or maple syrup. Cornmeal, the staff of life for the settlers in North America, lent itself easily to fill the human need for sustenance. It made wonderful breads and puddings and was easy to handle.

Hearth hot bread, or ash cakes, was made with 1 pint each of boiling salted water and yellow cornmeal and 1 tablespoon of maple sugar, syrup, or molasses. A dough was made of the water, sweetening, and cornmeal. It was placed in a warm place while the embers and ashes were cleared from a spot on the hearthstone that would remain hot overnight. The stone was rubbed with a rind of fat salt pork. The dough was formed into tiny loaves 3 inches long, 2 inches wide, and 1 inch thick. The loaves were buried under live ashes on the stone. When the cakes were ready, baked brown, they were removed, the ashes brushed off, and after a quick dip in boiling water were served at once.

Stir-about pot pudding, or hasty pudding, was easy and quick to make, good to eat, and cheap. One pint and 1 gill of water (about 3 cups in all) was boiled. When the water rolled to a boil, 1/2 cup of cornmeal was slowly slipped in from the palm of the left hand while the right hand stirred the mixture with a wooden spoon. A small teaspoon of salt was added, and the pudding bubbled slowly and constantly for 30 minutes. Greasing the pot did not prevent sticking. Scorching or sticking was prevented by using a good, heavy cast-iron pot and stirring constantly.

Johnnycake, or journey cake, was made with 1 cup of boiling water stirred with a melted piece of shortening as big as a hazelnut (1 rounded teaspoon) and a heaping 1/4 teaspoon of salt. The liquid was poured on 1 cup of cornmeal and whipped smooth. This fairly thick batter was spread on a board or pan in a slanting position before the fire and baked 3/4 hour. This bread was called journey cake because it was easily made by travelers near campfires.

Because of their all-day duties, especially food preparation, and the sparse population, there was little social life among the frontier settlers. Visitors were a major event. Sometimes families would gather together to cook, spin, dip candles, or make quilts. Helping new neighbors build a house was a social event. At harvest time neighbors gathered to shuck corn all day and then danced in the evening.

Women wore calico dresses, aprons, caps, white linen shifts, and petticoats. Most women married before they were twenty. Marriage at sixteen was usual and at fourteen was accepted. There were no ministers to perform a marriage ceremony.

Indentured women performed most of the household chores—cooking, laundry, mending, cleaning, and caring for children. Their help was essential for bachelors and for families with a large number of children. They also worked in the fields and at harvest time. The indentured women were a problem as they were a constant temptation to the men and often ran away from their masters, who had purchased their service for a number of years. Destitute women in Britain would often sell their services—indenture themselves—for the cost of the sea voyage to America. At the end of their service they were free to seek other employment or marry. Many married their master if his wife had died, a common occurrence as a result of poor care at childbirth.

A lot of hard work was necessary on the farms, and children had to help out. They did many jobs such as carrying wood, husking corn, gathering berries, leading oxen, carding wool, gathering eggs, and churning butter.

When children had time to play, they enjoyed games that children still play today, like tag, hide-and-seek, and hopscotch. These games taught children skills needed later in life as farmers and parents. Games taught children how to aim and throw, how to do things with their hands, how to follow directions, and how to be fair. Colonial children also learned to make do with whatever they had. There were no factories to make toys. Toys were found in nature or around the house, or adults and the children themselves made them. They made dolls from corn husks and rags. Scraps of wood and string were used to make spinning tops. A piece of wood and some chicken feathers were transformed into shuttlecocks for a game played with "battledores," which were used to bat the shuttlecocks back and forth. Since many families had five or six children, brothers and sisters always had playmates who helped them learn to socialize.

On winter days many colonial families gathered around the kitchen fireplace to stay warm. Fathers repaired tools, mothers spun yarn, and children played board games or did tongue twisters when they did not have to card wool or churn butter. On warm days children played outside with marbles, hoops, and battledores.

Even though it was filled with work, life was not always hard or boring. Early Americans turned work into fun by singing or telling stories, and by having spinning or quilting bees. They also liked to dance to fiddle and fife music.

Some women spun and wove a rough cloth called homespun, but most cloth was purchased. Unlike housewives in Great Britain, very little spinning and weaving was done by women in the frontier homes. Better-quality cloth from Britain was relatively inexpensive compared with cloth produced at home, where other duties were more pressing.

Cloth was sold by the "piece," which was approximately 20 yards in length and 1 yard wide. The length varied from 12 to 50 yards and the width, or "ell," varied from 27 inches for Flemish cloth to 45 inches for some English cloth. The cost of the piece was equal to two to three weeks' wages of a mason, but it represented the weekly output of a family including the weaver, his wife, and his children.

England had long been the world center for wool manufacture and wool was its leading export. Before 1750 wool was the dominant cloth made in England, offering more employment than any industry other than agriculture. There are two general categories of wool, short staple and long staple. Short-staple wool (two and a half inches long) from merino sheep is finer than long-staple wool. It is curly and felts well. Felting is the process of taking rough woven wool and teaseling it to raise short fibers called the nap. The wool fibers have scaly surfaces and naturally cling together, so when the cloth is ironed the fibers mat together. Originally the sheep came from Spain but they were later raised most successfully in Saxony. Merino wool was used for fine cloth by the Flemish and the French. The English developed a crossbred merino sheep that produced short-staple wool, but the quality was inferior to the original. Long-staple wool is like hair, with fibers as long as ten and a half inches, making it difficult to felt. It comes from alpaca, mohair, and Lincolnshire sheep.

Woolen fabrics were made from short-staple wool shrunk and felted until the weave pattern was lost. Then the nap was raised to produce a soft, velvety surface. Because woolens with short fibers and a fuzzy surface do not hold a crease, they are used for blankets and coats. Worsted wool made with long-staple wool that has long fibers and requires more processing. Worsted (such as gabardine, serge, and crepe) is smoother, lighter, and less bulky. It holds a crease, does not sag, and wears longer.

The woolens used on the frontier came mostly from Britain: stroud, kersey, half-thick, matchcoating, penistone, walsh cotton, ratteen, serge, drugget, and camlet. Duffle and callimanco came from Flanders. The coarse woolens (stroud, duffle, ratteen, kersey, half-thick, and matchcoating) were used to make blankets and loose overcoats called match coats. Serge and penistone were used for trousers, stockings, and other outer garments. Drugget, which had a pattern printed on one side, was used for covers for carpets, beds, and other items. The finer cloths (walsh cotton, callimanco, and camlet) were used for stockings, garments, and decoration.

Stroud, a coarse woolen made from rags and used for both clothing and blankets, was produced in a variety of colors including black, red, and blue.

The word also referred to a blanket made from stroud material. A blue stroud in 1755 cost £9 sterling ($1,800); in 1768 a stroud cost £4.5; and a piece ordered by Sir William Johnson for his household was priced at 76s. The sharp drop in price reflects the impact of the Industrial Revolution and the introduction of machines in the textile industry that took place during the Seven Years' War. Ratteen was much like stroud, a thick woolen twill with either a frieze or a curled nap that was used for coats and blankets.

Kersey worsted made of long-staple wool was made primarily for export to the Continent and America. It was a coarse material used to make heavy coats and blankets that sold for 4s. 6d. each in the colonies. The kersey did not wear well and after two or three years a coat would became threadbare. Three yards of cloth were needed to make a coat plus one and a half yards for the lining, which was usually a flannel.

Half-thick, a coarse woolen, was used for cheap blankets; a piece of white half-thick sold for 72s. in 1755. Warm half-thick was in demand by the Indians. In 1765 Baynton and Wharton purchased two pieces from Thomas Clifford and two pieces from Stephen Carmick.

Matchcoating or match cloth was a coarse woolen used in making match coats, which were copied from loose coats made of sewn-together skins worn by the Indians. A blue stripe one and a half inches wide was printed across one end of a piece of matchcoating on the inside. In 1762 John Strettel of London sold five bales of match coats to the Pennsylvania Indian Commission for £162 sterling ($32,400). Strettel made a similar sale three months later.

Duffle was a coarse woolen with a thick nap or frieze used for making blankets and coats. A twelve-yard piece cost £7 in 1755 and 70s. in 1768, a sharp drop in price due to the Industrial Revolution.

Penistone, or forest whites, was a coarse woolen used for stockings and linings that came in white, blue, Saxon green, and red. Penistone pieces fifty yards long cost 50s. in 1768. Walsh cotton, or Welsh flannel, a very fine woolen flannel with a nap, was also used for stockings. It was a mixture of wool and coarse cotton.

Callimancoe (also callimanco and calamanco), from the Latin word for "headdress," *calamancus*, was a coarse woolen twill with a fine gloss and checks in the warp visible on one side only. It was woven in bright colors of crimson, black, and blue. Daniel Clark shipped some to Quebec in 1760 priced at £5 per piece for crimson and 72s. to 75s. for other colors.

Serge was a fine woven worsted twill of combed long-staple wool with very little pile. It came in many colors: pink, cream, tawny, light and golden brown, yellow, white, and black. In the early eighteenth century, the standard piece of serge was 22 yards long and sold for 26s. to 37s. depending on its quality. Large pieces were from 30 to 40 yards long and 1/2 to 3/4 yard wide and sold from 54s. to 80s. per piece. Johnson purchased pieces 37 yards long at 152d. per yard, or 48s. per piece. Women in the coastal cities played a major role in sewing products from the many types of fabric available for the frontier traders.

Despite the great differences in their cultures, the women of the Indian tribes, the army regiments, and the pioneer settlements performed similar tasks. All were very concerned with caring for their children. The food they ate and the ways they prepared it were very similar. Laundry and sewing were ongoing activities. The Indian women played a more significant role in agriculture, but tending gardens was also part of the life of army and settler wives.

It is ironic that women who did so much of the difficult and boring work necessary for survival on the frontier are ignored in most accounts. Without them life would have been almost impossible there. Although men could survive for long periods without women and enough free white men could be found to work the fields, history records that these settlements seldom lasted many years. Even though women are seldom mentioned by name in the financial records and correspondence of the time, they were active in many areas in the settled areas of the colonies. However their role was more limited on the frontier because the need for safety required inclusion in a family or an organization such as a regiment. They did make the clothing sold to the Indians on a large scale in Philadelphia. Women were essential ingredients to the development of a profitable economy on the frontier.

## SUGGESTED READINGS

Joy Day Buel and Richard Buel Jr., *The Way of Duty: A Woman and Her Family in Revolutionary America* (1984).

Ronald Hoffman and Peter J. Albert, eds., *Women in the Age of the American Revolution* (1989).

Linda K. Kerber, *Women of the Republic: Intellect and Ideology in Revolutionary America* (1980).

Mary Beth Norton, *Founding Mothers and Fathers: Gendered Power and the Forming of American Society* (1996).

———, *Liberty's Daughters: The Revolutionary Experience of American Women, 1750–1800* (1980).

Marylynn Salmon, *Women and the Law of Property in Early America* (1986).

Laurel Thatcher Ulrich, *The Age of Homespun: Objects and Stories in the Creation of an American Myth* (2001).

———, *Good Wives: Image and Reality in the Lives of Women in Northern New England, 1650–1750* (1982).

# 10

# Slaves and Indentured Servants

The three common types of slaves on the frontier in the eighteenth century were Pawnee captives, blacks, and indentured servants. Many individuals and groups needed some form of help to support their business goals and lifestyles. The Shawnee tribe north of the Ohio River crossed the Mississippi River and took captives from the Pawnees in raids on villages on the west side of the river. The Shawnees either adopted the captives into their villages or sold them to other tribes and to the colonists and the French at Detroit and in Illinois.

The blacks were imported from Africa and would remain in servitude until the nineteenth century. The indentured servants at least had the prospect of serving their limited time period or purchasing their freedom.

Slaves from Africa supplied farm labor for the West Indies sugarcane fields and the tobacco farms in Virginia in the southern colonies, Detroit, and Illinois. In the northern colonies, slaves were often employed as household servants and as unskilled labor in distilleries, flour mills, and other workshops. To supply the huge quantities of rum being sold to the army and the Indians, some Philadelphia merchants began to distill rum locally using slave labor rather than importing the rum from New England and elsewhere.

The African slaves were a major commodity in the British imperial economy. The West Indian trade in cotton, slaves, and sugar created the fortunes that financed the industrial expansion in England. Liverpool was the center of the trade with Africa, exporting wool, cotton, guns, and metalware, some of which had been imported from Holland. In 1750 the leading slave merchants included Aspinall, Cunliffe, Leyland, and Fildart.

The West Indies was Great Britain's major trading party. About a fourth of all British imports came from the West Indies, which was also the leading destination of colonial ships. Imports to Britain from the West Indies in 1770 were valued at over £3 million ($600 million). In 1761, while it was occupied by the British army, Guadeloupe alone exported goods valued at £603,269 to Britain, two-thirds sugar and one-third cotton. In comparison, Canada sent furs worth only £14,015 to Britain that year. Canada shipped less than £100,000 sterling in fur per year from 1764 to 1774, far less than the value of the sugar trade. Most of the sugar came from Jamaica, where 1,000 to 2,000 ships departed for Britain each year. Antigua, St. Christopher, Barbados, and the Virgin Islands cleared fewer than a thousand ships a year. In 1763, when the British controlled Cuba, the port of Havana cleared a thousand ships.

About half of the West Indies exports, including sugar and small amounts of coffee, indigo, and dye woods, went to Britain. In 1773 the British West Indies exported nearly 2.8 million gallons of rum to Britain and 3.5 million gallons to North America including Canada.

The islands also provided Britain with large amounts of gold bullion and gold coins. Before 1766 Spanish ships went to the British West Indies to purchase slaves and British goods with gold and silver coins, even though this trade was illegal under both Spanish and British law. Both sides of the transaction were illegal since the Spanish prohibited the export of gold or silver other than to Spain and the British prohibited the sale of slaves to the Spaniards. Until 1763 enforcement of the laws was lax, but that year the Royal Navy increased the level of enforcement of all Navigation Laws and the trade with Spain declined.

Supplying Spanish colonies in America with slaves and other products provided Spanish specie (silver and gold coins). The Spanish coins were used by the British in India to purchase cotton and calico cloth suitable for the warm weather in the West Indies and Africa. The cloth was sent to England and then onward to Africa to purchase slaves or to the West Indies to clothe the slaves on the plantations. The cloth from India, rum from the West Indies, and Spanish gold were used in turn to buy slaves in Africa along with British manufactured goods.

The British merchants constructed small forts, or slave stations, along the west coast of Africa at the river mouths. The stations were used as depots for slaves purchased from the local African kings in return for guns, cotton, and metalware. The slaves were held in compounds until a ship arrived and were then sold in large lots to slave-ship captains for merchandise. The captains preferred to buy from the British slave stations because they could fill their ships faster and did not have the problem of negotiating with the African kings. The British merchants had ample supplies of slaves and sold to any ship that arrived. The slave ships also purchased gold dust and ivory with liquor and other goods. The gold dust and ivory were sent to England as profits from the trade.

Most slaves were shipped to the West Indies. In the 1730s a British slave ship took on 524 slaves, including 224 men, 139 women, 113 boys, and 48 girls. The merchants paid about £10 sterling ($2,000) in trade goods for prime men and as little as £3 10s. for the least valuable girls. The adult male slaves were sold in the West Indies for £20, double their cost. The profit on a voyage was usually 100 percent.

By 1760 the British no longer relied on the Dutch for goods for the slave trade. British production increased in quality and quantity and American rum became available. The importation of slaves in the West Indies doubled from 1758 to 1762 because the slaves did not reproduce under the harsh conditions on the plantations. No attempt was made to breed slaves, as would be common in Virginia in later years. The loss of work time for the pregnant women and the cost of raising the children was not cost effective considering the low cost of new slaves from Africa.

Slave mortality was very high. Because of the poor conditions, the average slave lived only seven years after reaching the Americas and had a life expectancy of twenty-five to twenty-seven years, causing a turnover of 15 percent per year. The life expectancy of white males in Europe in the eighteenth century was thirty-five. Most slaves were imported when they were around eighteen to twenty years old. Very few black children were born. The shorter life expectancy of slaves is attributable to many factors, including poor food and hard forced labor. As a result, there was a steady demand to replace slaves who had died from overwork and to open new plantations to satisfy the growing demand for sugar in Britain and America.

A minimum turnover in the slave population of 100 percent within twenty years was assumed in the eighteenth century although in reality it could take only seven years. There were 70,000 slaves in Barbados in 1763 and 35,000 more were imported in the next eight years. But in 1771 there were only 74,000 slaves there. In only eight years 31,000 slaves, nearly one-half, of the 1763 number either died or were exported.

The British supplied an average of 12,000 slaves a year from their slave stations in Africa, and the French sent about 7,000 each year to the West Indies. Britain had 150 slave ships importing slaves to the West Indies. The French illegally purchased slaves from the British slave traders in Africa because they were cheaper than those offered by French slave traders. The French paid for the slaves with goods that the British merchants used to buy more slaves. During the Seven Years' War, when Britain occupied Guadeloupe and Cuba, the British sent 19,000 slaves to Guadeloupe from 1759 to 1763 and 11,000 to Cuba from August 1762 to January 1763. The British planters who had taken over the French and Spanish plantations developed them assuming that Britain would retain the islands after the war.

The life of the British planters in the West Indies was not pleasant. The climate was very hot and the potential of slave revolts was a constant threat. Because eighteen slave revolts erupted in the West Indies in the eighteenth century, the planters were heavily armed. Each plantation consisted of about two or three hundred acres planted in sugarcane (the minimum size of a Midwestern U.S. farm in the year 2000), some acres to grow food for the slaves, and, possibly, a pasture for cattle. Woods provided lumber for shelter and firewood to boil the cane to convert it to sugar. Each plantation had a wind-driven mill that crushed the cane and a boiling house to reduce the cane juice to sugar and molasses. The most profitable use of the land was growing sugarcane, so food and lumber usually were purchased rather than produced on the plantation.

There was an average of one slave for each acre of land cultivated. Sugarcane required more care compared with the ten acres of corn or wheat cultivated by farmers on the frontier. Feeding the slaves was a profitable business for Pennsylvania and New York, which exported food to the West Indies. New England rum was used in purchasing slaves. The slave traders in Africa paid for the rum with sterling bills that were used to pay for British imports to the colonies. In 1770 the American colonies sent 316,000 gallons of rum to Africa on twenty-nine ships, each carrying almost 11,000 gallons.

The middle colonies sent grain and flour to feed the slaves in the British West Indies while New England sent lumber to build shelter for them. In 1766 James Eddy ordered Joseph Bullock (a ship's captain who later took a harness shipment to the West Indies) to take twenty-four barrels of herring from Philadelphia to the West Indies and bring back "good" sugar, or, if sugar was not available, Spanish dollars. Eddy cautioned Bullock to sell the fish quickly and not wait for a high price, as the hot weather would spoil it. In 1765 Daniel Roberdeau, a Philadelphia merchant, sold five tierces of sugar (each 42 gallons) for a total of 4,000 pounds of sugar to Michael Gross of Lancaster. In 1766 George Alsopp reported to Baynton and Wharton, Philadelphia merchants, that a venture to buy Canadian wheat at Quebec for shipment to the West Indies had fallen through because the French wanted cash in advance, and Alsopp could not pay cash because Baynton and Wharton normally did business on credit.

The high value of exporting food from the colonies to feed the slaves was an argument used to promote the British acquisition of Guadeloupe in 1763 rather than Canada. In addition, the thirteen colonies could obtain cash by selling provisions and lumber to the Spanish islands. However, exports by the mid-Atlantic states to British West Indian colonies could not pay for all their imports of British goods, according to Lieutenant Governor Cadwallader Colden of New York, because the British sugar islands required only a fraction of the products raised in America. He advised that acquiring Canada would be far more advantageous because the American Indians consumed far more British goods per capita than the slaves in the British West Indies.

Slavery was common in Louisiana, which included all the French possessions west of the Mississippi as well as Illinois. The slaves were used in Louisiana's rice fields. The plantation system, with large fields and the necessary supply of labor, was better adapted to raising rice than small farms. Rice was the primary crop in Louisiana and was exported to southern Europe.

Gangs of black men and women first cultivated the rich soil with hoes. The upturned soil was formed into trenches for planting and the slaves hurried up and down the rows dropping in the seed. "Sprout water" was let in to stand for eight or nine days in the trenches. The rice was then left to dry until it put out leaves. The floodgates were then reopened and the "stretch water" covered the fields to draw the young plants to the desired height. To prevent the stalks from falling without the supporting stretch water, the water was drawn off slowly. In about a week the ground was dry enough for the first hoeing, immediately followed by the second. The fields were flooded and drained intermittently until the "harvest water" stood on the fields while the grain matured. The water was then drawn off for the last time. As soon as the ground dried, the slaves hurried into the fields to thresh the grain at once, before the sky darkened with flocks of hungry bobolinks flying southward to escape the northern winter. The kernels were whipped from the straw in primitive rice mills.

To supplement their business the British merchants in New Orleans imported large numbers of slaves to provide labor for the rice plantations. After the area east of the Mississippi was ceded to Britain in 1763, free transit was granted to British ships through New Orleans. The British dealers sold three hundred slaves to French plantation owners in 1767. The slaves were also sent north to Illinois. In 1768 slaves were selling in Illinois for £360 Pennsylvania ($41,400). The lower New Orleans price was £200 Pennsylvania. Slaves were a valuable commodity needed to work the plantations around New Orleans and the farms in Illinois. A single shipment of three hundred slaves was worth £34,500 sterling ($12.3 million) in New Orleans, while the total value of the Canadian fur trade was less than £100,000 sterling.

Slaves were in such demand that the French farmers in Illinois were eager to sell flour, cattle, and salt beef to both colonial and French merchants for them. The provisions received for the slaves were in turn sold to the British army.

Slavery was also prevalent in the North. The Schenectady merchant partnership Phyn & Ellice was active in the slave trade in the eighteenth century. The partners sent William and Alex Forsyth of Aberdeen, Scotland, a bill of exchange for £600 sterling ($120,000) in 1767, which they ordered the Forsyths to pay to William and Norman Durward in London. Among the items Durward had provided were one young black male slave and two female slaves. Durward was the contact with the slave traders as well as the suppliers of glass, white lead, black cloth, pewter inkstands, and stockings. Later, Phyn & Ellice again ordered a young black male slave and two female slaves from Durward.

In 1769 Phyn & Ellice were trying to buy a black boy and two girls for James Sterling in Detroit but could not at the price set by Sterling. The going price was £80 to £90 sterling ($18,000) for a boy and £60 to £70 for girls. Sterling did not want "green" Negroes (recent arrivals from Africa who had not yet become resigned to their condition), who sold at a lower price, about £20. Few green slaves were imported to New York in the 1760s. If Sterling were willing to pay a higher price, Phyn & Ellice promised to provide the boy and two girls. In 1770 Phyn and Ellis received nine Negro boys from the New York Jewish merchant Hayman Levy and quickly sold all but one. The following year Sterling and his partner John Porteus sent a slave to New Orleans from Detroit for sale and the proceeds were forwarded to Phyn & Ellice by Hayman Levy and credited to Sterling's account. The price less commission was £41 sterling ($8,200), double the price of a slave imported into the West Indies. In 1769 Sir William Johnson sold two slaves to Robert Adams, who was active in the fur trade in the Mohawk Valley and acted as Johnson's agent at the Fort Stanwix conference in 1768.

Slaves were used as unskilled labor in Pennsylvania. The Chevalier family, in December 1761 and in partnership with Baynton and Wharton, operated a still house and invested nearly £1,000 to buy Negro slaves, bricks, nails, and molasses. On December 21, 1761, they sold five sixty-three-gallon hogsheads of rum to John Mitchell for £78 Pennsylvania ($8,970) and within the next few weeks sold twelve hogsheads to Townsend White for more than £200 Pennsylvania. William McKee ordered six hogsheads of molasses, earthenware, and a thirty-two gallon still, obviously intending to set up the still for the manufacture of rum to compete with the stills of Philadelphia and the importing business.

Slaves were also imported into the southern colonies (the Carolinas, Virginia, and Maryland) for work on the tobacco and rice plantations. Slaves did not play as significant a role in the economy of the northern colonies as they did elsewhere, evidenced in the fact that not as many were needed. Imports of 4,400 slaves into the thirteen colonies were recorded, only 4 percent of the total number of slaves sent to America by all European nations and only 7.4 percent of the slaves purchased by the British. Most of the slaves went to the West Indies to work in the labor-intensive sugar-cane plantations.

Slavery was common in Detroit, based on the right to sell captives. Many French families had Indian and black slaves employed as house servants or working for the fur traders. At Michilimackinac both Indian and black slaves were present as early as 1743, when the birth of Veronique was recorded, the daughter of a fur trader and his black slave girl. In 1770 John Askin had three black slaves working in his stores in Michilimackinac.

In the Detroit 1750 census 33 slaves are recorded. In 1773 there were 83 slaves. By 1782 there were 179 slaves, indicating that Indian raids during the Revolution had led to the capture of some black slaves from southern plantations.

Some of the Indian slaves in Detroit were Pawnees from the Missouri River taken captive by war parties. Records of the period refer to the Indians as "panis." White captives were also sold as slaves to the French. In a raid on a settlement near present-day McConnellsburg, Pennsylvania, in 1755, Charles Stuart, his wife, and two children were captured by some Delawares, Mingos, and Shawnees. They were taken to Kittanning by the Wyandots and then to Sandusky and Detroit. In 1756 Stuart and his wife were compassionately ransomed by Father Potier in Detroit for £24 Pennsylvania's worth of goods. In return for the favor Stuart and his wife worked for eight months at the Huron Mission. By March 1757 they had worked off the ransom and then worked an additional month for thirty livres. In the spring of 1757 they were sent as prisoners to Quebec along with Captain Smith, Richard Joyce, Thomas Millaken, William Brattin, and John Gill. Later they went to England and then back to New York. There is no mention of the fate of the children.

The farmers in Illinois made widespread use of slaves in the eighteenth century. There were over a thousand slaves in Illinois before the British occupation, primarily working as agricultural laborers. When the British occupied Illinois they cut off the supply of slaves from New Orleans for the French farmers. Despite the contrary tenets of their Quaker religion, Baynton and Wharton were deeply involved in the slave business in Illinois. In their wide-ranging assortment of goods for sale to the French, the partners added slaves in 1767. In January 1767 they were offering slaves in lots of four to Nicholas Chapau of Vincennes for 12 cattle, 200 otter, 450 beaver, or 1,700 raccoons. When purchased in quantity, the slaves were offered at discounts.

Beaver pelts sold in Illinois in 1768 for £2 sterling ($400) per pound and the average skin weighed 1.5 pounds, so the price demanded for four slaves was about £1,350 or £390 ($78,000) each, a very high price. Otter sold for £4 each, so the price for four slaves was £1,600. The price demanded was incredibly high considering that the price of a slave in New Orleans was only £200. Baynton and Wharton paid Bean and Cuthbert £35 ($7,000) each (a total of £5,355 Pennsylvania) for ninety slaves delivered to Philadelphia on the sloop *Polly* September 10, 1767. The slaves were intended for sale in Illinois. In December 1767 George Morgan was selling the slaves in Illinois in exchange for furs, Spanish silver dollars, bills of exchange, and farm produce. His terms were 10 percent down and the remainder payable on May 1, 1768.

The French, who had formerly traveled downriver to New Orleans to buy slaves, could not compete with Baynton and Wharton, who preempted the business. Morgan hoped to gain a monopoly by paying for flour with slaves and then selling the flour to the British garrison.

By February 1768 Morgan was having trouble selling his remaining slaves either because the price was too high or the French farmers did not want to buy from a colonial merchant. Boloin (possibly Daniel Blouin), a French merchant, was planning to go to New Orleans to purchase sixty slaves in the spring. The price there was only £200. Anticipating lower prices from Boloin, the Illinois French farmers delayed purchasing slaves from Morgan, who was offering them at £360 each. Unable to sell the slaves, Morgan used them himself to farm 60 acres of a 1,500 acre parcel of land that he had acquired in payment of a debt growing tobacco and corn. He also fattened cattle on the land and raised hogs to supply the army with pork.

In March 1768 John Baynton wrote to James Rumsey thanking him for handling the movement of Jamaican slaves to Illinois. Rumsey had been an ensign in the British 42nd Regiment in 1764 and became a trader in Illinois from 1767 to 1773. He was associated with William Murray, Bernard Gratz, Alexander Ross, and David Franks. Murray was also planning to enter the slave trade in Illinois using slaves to purchase flour, cattle, and salt beef to compete with Baynton and Wharton in supplying rations to the British army garrison.

Indians were also used as slaves and were considered a commodity in New York, just as black slaves were in the South. Indian women became common-law wives of even the wealthy. Some owners had compassion for their long-time servants to the extent of including them in their will. An example is Sir William Johnson, who fathered eight children by his Indian housekeeper, Mary Brant. Johnson left one-fourth of his slaves and cattle to his son, Sir John Johnson, in his will in 1774. He left Brant and their children varying amounts of money ranging from £1,000 sterling ($200,000) to £100 sterling ($20,000) each. He also left sums to Brant's other children, Brant and William, who were both half Mohawk. He left a "negro wench" named Jenny to Mary Brant.

Another form of servitude common in the colonies was the indentured servant. Indentured servants were a form of quasi-slaves in the colonies. An Englishman could sign a contract to work for a number of years for a colonial farmer in return for his transportation to America. Children were commonly indentured to tradesmen by their parents, providing the tradesman cheap labor and the parents a sum of money plus relieving them of the burden of caring for their children. The children would learn a trade in the process.

In June 1768 William Murray was closing up his affairs in Carlisle in preparation for his move to Illinois. He left all of his land deals in the hands of Michael Gratz. One of the personal items was Murray's instruction to Gratz to provide for "the little ones down the river," whom Murray wished to be bound to a tradesman in town. The "little ones" were illegitimate children of an Indian woman whom Murray wished to have indentured to ensure their well-being. George Croghan purchased two indentured servants for £40 sterling in October 1769 and charged the expense to the Indian Department.

The Indians practiced another form of slavery on the frontier. As part of the process of maturity, young men formed war parties that attacked rival tribes; for example, the Shawnees sent war parties west to attack the Pawnees, and the Iroquois sent war parties to attack the Cherokees. The war parties would often return with Cherokee women and children captured in the raid who became members of the Iroquois families. The Indians also captured white women and children in the same fashion. A brave might have a wife from his own tribe and another captured from a different tribe. The captive children would become part of an Indian family. However, the captives were considered property and could be sold. Some were sold to colonial merchants and fur traders. William Maxwell purchased a Pawnee slave in 1768 in Detroit, perhaps to work with a baker that Maxwell was setting up. Maxwell was an established merchant there in the late 1760s. In Detroit in 1778 there were 127 slaves, 39 female indentured servants, and 172 male indentured servants for a total of 338, along with 858 free adults and 968 children. One fur trader from Pennsylvania had a Pawnee girl as his companion.

Although there were comparatively few slaves and indentured servants on the frontier, they played a significant role in specific areas. In Detroit and Illinois the French farmers were completely dependent on slaves to cultivate the fields. Although they were not treated as slaves, the captured Cherokee and

Pawnee women with their children were an essential part of the Indian families north of the Ohio River, bringing new bloodlines that eliminated the danger of intermarriage. Young black men and women were employed as household servants by the wealthy while the older adult males worked the fields and provided unskilled labor to the new industries in Pennsylvania and New York.

The unsettled frontier was not suitable for forced labor as escape was easier than in the more developed areas, and thus slavery and indenture were not widely practiced there. Indentured servants were more common on the seaboard than on the frontier, but some were employed by the pioneer farmers in clearing the land and cultivating the crops. And ransom was paid to the Indians for white captives in return for a period of indentured service in Detroit.

# 11

# The Army

Only a few British regiments were sent to America prior to 1754, and they were withdrawn after each war because each colony had been responsible for policing its own frontier. After the cessation of hostilities in 1760 during the Seven Years' War, a sizable force of British regular troops remained to occupy frontier forts. The colonists believed that they had no need for this protection before the war and even less after the war. The only need for garrisons was in Canada and Florida. The army found itself with the impossible task of trying to protect the colonial traders—impossible because most of the transactions were outside of the forts where the soldiers did well to survive themselves.

The British army in the 1760s was organized in regiments that usually had one battalion. However some regiments, for example, the 60th Royal Americans and the 42nd Black Watch, had two or more battalions. In 1766 the authorized strength of a peacetime British battalion was 1 colonel, 1 lieutenant colonel, 1 major, 7 captains, 9 lieutenants, 8 ensigns, 1 chaplain, 1 adjutant, 1 quartermaster, 1 surgeon, 1 surgeon's mate, 18 sergeants, 9 drummers, and 441 men for a total of 500.

The British organization was designed for warfare in Europe and ill suited to America. The weight of the equipment each soldier was supposed to carry on the march was 64 pounds, too much on rough forest trails. The British troops were not trained to fight in the forest. Later, the British formed ranger companies and light infantry trained to fight the Indians, but the bulk of the regiments were still cumbersome and unsuited for Indian warfare.

Duty in America apparently was not considered a hardship by the British troops. In 1767 the 14th, 46th, and 28th Regiments and two battalions of the 42nd Regiment were rotated back to Great Britain. From these five battalions 450 men volunteered to remain in America and were transferred to the 21st and the 31st Regiments in Florida. In 1769, about half of the 9th and the 34th Regiments, 266 men, volunteered to remain in America when their regiments were sent back to Great Britain. The desire to remain in America can be explained by the slack discipline in the American garrisons. Back in England the returning soldiers would face the rigid discipline of the army barracks. Some soldiers had families in America and did not wish to leave them.

Sickness was a major problem of the British army in America. In 1762 after capturing Cuba many regiments returned to Canada and the thirteen colonies badly depleted by sickness. The regiments had suffered from an epidemic of yellow fever. That August, four battalions were returned from Cuba, including two battalions of the 42nd Royal Highlanders, Montgomery's Highlanders, and the 17th Regiment, all of which had many men so seriously ill that they were not fit for duty. When troops were needed to reinforce Detroit in 1763, only small detachments could be sent from these regiments. Scurvy was also a problem. In 1759 more than half the troops at Quebec had scurvy, caused by the lack of vitamin C in their rations.

Sickness continued to be a problem in the South. In November 1765 the 21st and the 31st Regiments in Mobile and Pensacola were suffering and the commander, Colonel Henry Bouquet, died of illness. In 1767 reinforcements for those Florida regiments were held in New York City until the sick season had passed to save them from the same fate of the men already there.

Discipline and drinking were major problems. A trader's agent, Colbeck, was drunk at Fort Niagara with the sergeants of the garrison for fourteen days while his men stayed in the storehouse, drunk as well, with a "seraglio" of Indian women. The formal relations between officers and men and the rigid patterns of barracks life, which were necessary to sustain order in the army, were almost impossible to maintain in the one- or two-company garrisons. Splitting the regiments into small garrisons destroyed the discipline of the troops.

One obvious indication of the problems of the army was the high rate of desertion. General Thomas Gage sent returning deserters to Grenada rather than back to their old regiments for fear that they would desert again. Men were needed constantly to fill the ranks of the regiments reduced by sickness and desertion. In October 1762 the First and Second Battalions of the 42nd Royal Highlanders were combined, and a cadre was sent back to Scotland to recruit new men. In January 1767 Lieutenant Colonel James Prevost brought 188 recruits from Hamburg, Germany, to New York City to fill the 60th Regiment, which originally had consisted mainly of Germans. Despite official policy to the contrary, many regiments recruited Americans to replace their losses.

American recruits were also prone to desert, however. In 1764 the Province of Pennsylvania promised to raise troops for the Bouquet expedition to combat Pontiac's Uprising, but not replacements for the regular regiments; the Pennsylvanians preferred to serve with provincial regiments because of the higher pay. Of the more than 900 men from Pennsylvania who were recruited for the campaign, 200 had deserted before the army marched and more deserted later. Bouquet was rather disgusted with the Pennsylvanians, writing in July 1764 that after all the talk, the frontiersmen preferred to be wagoners and drivers rather than soldiers. Although many Virginians had volunteered to serve in his expedition, not a single Pennsylvanian volunteered. Bouquet suggested to Gage that because many regular army deserters were in the countryside, a pardon might be offered to old soldiers who returned. Each of the old soldiers was worth three recruits in Bouquet's mind.

In 1761 General Jeffrey Amherst issued orders to garrison the territory acquired from the French. He sent the 80th Regiment with 300 men to Detroit in 1761 under Major Henry Gladwin, who sent small detachments to Michilimackinac, St. Joseph, Green Bay, Miami, and Ouiatanon. One hundred men of the 80th remained at Fort William Augustus on Lake Erie. Gladwin was also instructed to explore the Great Lakes, and then to return to Fort William Augustus, leaving as much of the 80th Regiment with Captain Donald Campbell as needed to garrison the various posts. In addition, 100 New York troops were to go from Oswego to Fort William Augustus to help with repairs. This widespread scattering of troops indicated that Amherst had no fear of an Indian uprising.

In 1762, the tempo of the war tapered off in North America to an even slower pace than in 1761. Although some of the British regiments had returned from the West Indies to New York City, they came back in a depleted state with many of the soldiers sick. Some regiments were disbanded and the officers returned to England. Others were recruited to full strength with American recruits because there were few potential soldiers remaining in England after six years of war.

The signing of the preliminaries of peace in November 1762 decelerated the war in North America, and more British regiments returned to North America from the West Indies by the end of 1763. Injury and death in battle combined with illness had thinned the ranks of all the regiments that had fought in the tropics. Some of the regiments that had 700 to 1,000 men when they left Canada and the American colonies returned with only 200. By the end of 1764, there were twenty regiments in North America including seven in Canada, four in the Province of New York, two in Pennsylvania, five in Florida, and two in other areas of North America. The major movement of troops from the West Indies was to Pennsylvania, New York, and Florida. Florida had been given to Britain as compensation for the return of Cuba to Spain. The expenditures to maintain the regiments from the West Indies boosted only slightly the colonial economy, which was sagging after the war boom years. The return of the British regiments, however, with their need for rations and other supplies, provided some sterling bills of exchange.

The peacetime existence of the regiments in America that created the unique environment began in 1762. The regiments in America were scattered in small garrisons in Canada, on the frontier, in South Carolina, and in Georgia. In December 1762 the army of 8,000 men was distributed as follows:

| | |
|---|---|
| Canada | 3,650 |
| Nova Scotia, Cape Breton Island, Newfoundland | 1,700 |
| Upper New York Posts | 1,250 |
| Western Pennsylvania | 400 |
| Michigan | 350 |
| South Carolina and Georgia | 450 |
| New York City area | 200 |

Pontiac's Uprising created a major crisis in 1763. The French encouraged the Indians to oppose the British and supplied them with weapons. French intrigue inspired Pontiac's Uprising, which initially was successful. Many smaller posts were taken by the Indians and numerous colonial traders were killed in the wilderness. As reports of Indian victories were received, Amherst, who previously wrote bravely of punishing wrongdoers, had only a few military reserves to counter the attacks.

The British were slow to react. Many of the regiments were still in the Caribbean after the conquest of Cuba. The regiments that had returned were reduced by sickness from their wartime strength of 1,000 men to a few hundred. Of the eleven regiments in Canada, New York and Pennsylvania, the 47th, the 17th, the First Battalion of the 42nd, and the 77th were sickly from service in the West Indies, and the remainder had been scattered in small units on occupation duty, which seriously reduced their effectiveness. On June 12, 1763, Amherst ordered the 42nd Regiment and the

77th Regiment, both recently returned from Cuba, to send their light infantry companies to Philadelphia to begin the reinforcement of western Pennsylvania. The remaining nine companies of the 77th Regiment had 80 men left of the authorized 900. The light infantry company of the 17th Regiment went to Albany immediately, and the remainder of the regiment was to follow when ready. Amherst had probably ordered the three regimental commanders to transfer whatever healthy men were in their regiments to the light infantry companies and to dispatch those companies while he searched for more men to fill the remainder of the companies in the regiments. Nevertheless, these weak forces, after suffering numerous defeats in 1763, were able to hold Detroit, Niagara, and Fort Pitt, and in the following year regain control.

In July 1763 Amherst received more military reinforcements from the West Indies. Five regiments arrived in New York, but the men were in poor condition and had to be placed on garrison duty. Men gathered from three regiments were sent to Detroit and were badly defeated by the Indians in an attempt to sally out of the fort and capture Indian supplies. The British received a further setback with the defeat of another force in Niagara on July 31, 1763. Amherst was desperately trying to send as many men forward as possible to halt the Indians' attack.

The British continued to send more and more troops to the West, as the weakened regiments from the West Indies replaced the healthy regiments as garrisons in Montreal, Quebec, and elsewhere. Amherst even had plans for launching an attack from Fort Pitt toward Presque Isle with the objective of relieving Detroit, while General Gage sent troops of the 80th Regiment from Fort William Augustus via Niagara to Detroit.

Even though the Indian trade was halted in May 1763 by Pontiac's Uprising, commerce with the West was not at a standstill in 1764. Because of the military activity, there was a vigorous market selling provisions and sundries to the army. Bargaining with the Indians required a large supply of presents both on the Pennsylvania frontier and through new connections, with Johnson providing presents for the Great Lakes area.

In February 1763 the army in America was authorized to include fourteen battalions plus the 55th Regiment, which was to be sent to Ireland in 1765. The total strength including ten companies of artillery was 8,050 officers and men.

The peace was signed in Paris on February 10, 1763, but even before that, on February 1, King George III and Lord Ligonier, the British commander in chief, had agreed to ask Parliament for an overall peacetime army of eighty-five regiments. However, because of parliamentary objections this number was reduced to seventy-five. Initial discussion took place in February, and the intent of Parliament was that the colonies assist in financing the army in America. On February 24, 1763, a meeting of the king's ministers called for an army in Britain of about the same size as before the war, but an increase of the North American army to 7,500 men. On February 25 Parliament authorized seventy-five regiments and stipulated that England would support the battalions in America for the first year but after that the cost would be borne by the colonists. The plan called for twenty regiments consisting of 7,500 men to be maintained in North America, including the continental colonies and the West Indies. In March 1763 the House of Commons approved the measure for the maintenance of twenty regiments in America with the understanding that American taxation would supply £50,000 sterling ($10 million) of the estimated cost of £250,000 ($50 million). The colonists welcomed the profits from supplying the army but did not wish to be taxed to pay for it.

On June 8, 1763, the Board of Trade reported to the Earl of Egremont, a foreign secretary in the British cabinet, that part of the overall plan for North America should be a sizable military force to defend against possible French or Indian uprisings and also to provide military government for the Indian territory and protect the Indians from abuse. On July 14, 1763, Egremont informed the board that the king had approved this plan.

A probable unstated reason for having these troops in America was the practical matter of maintaining a reserve of regiments for the general defense of the empire. By stationing the units in America, the traditional aversion of the British people to a standing army could be avoided. Furthermore, the American deployment promised American revenue to support fifteen of the regiments. To reduce the army in America to fifteen regiments, some were disbanded in 1763, including the Third and the Fourth Battalions of the 60th Royal American Regiment and the 77th, the 78th, and the 80th Scottish Regiments.

On February 12, 1763, the secretary at war ordered General Amherst to submit a plan for the distribution of the troops that would be cost-effective and at the same time accomplish their mission. Not until April did Amherst reply that the Mississippi River and Canada would require the most troops, to guard against a Spanish invasion and to control the Indians. Other soldiers would be needed in Florida but none were to be assigned to the seaboard communities.

Of the fifteen battalions (350 to 500 men each) in North America, seven were stationed along the St. Lawrence Valley and four were in Florida. Four regiments were assigned to the frontier in 1763; two were in northern and western New York, one was scattered along the Great Lakes, and one was in Fort Pitt. By August 1763 no battalions were stationed in the densely settled parts of the original thirteen colonies.

The official explanation for the large peacetime army in America was to manage the Indians and to control the newly acquired territory. The British government expected that the troops in strategically located posts could protect traders from robbery and murder by the Indians. At first the colonial merchants did not see the frontier posts as symbols of oppression but, rather, as a means to aid them in their economic struggle to wrest the trade from the French and also as potential customers for colonial products. Although the army could protect the traders and prevent unscrupulous traders from using excessive amounts of rum in the posts, it could not safeguard colonial traders in the Indian villages.

The overall military establishment in America decreased in size from twenty regiments to eighteen. The greatest reduction was in New York, where the 44th Regiment was withdrawn to Canada and the 55th and the 80th Regiments were disbanded. Business with inhabitants in the West was reduced by the limitations imposed by the military on shipments to Detroit and Fort Pitt and the great danger from the Indians. The result of this sharp imbalance was a lack of specie and bills of exchange to send to England in payment for goods received. This shortage was felt throughout the colonies, in New York, Philadelphia, Boston, and Virginia. The New York newspaper the *Mercury* estimated the debt payable to England by the merchants at £4 million sterling ($800 million) in 1764.

On September 17, 1764, Bouquet started down the Ohio Valley with a battalion of the 60th Regiment, the 42nd Highlanders, and a detachment of the 77th Highlanders. The army soon met with the Senecas living along the Ohio River (the Delawares and the Shawnees) and held a conference in Muskingum in October 1764. Edward Moran, an Indian trader, thought that the Indians were "damnably scared" at seeing such a large army in their country.

Only a minimal number of troops were needed to garrison the few forts that were reestablished in 1764. An army of fewer than 1,000 under Colonel Bouquet was adequate to bring order to the Ohio Valley, and a similar force under Colonel John Bradstreet brought peace to the Great Lakes in 1764. An occupation force of perhaps four battalions distributed on the Great Lakes, the Ohio River, and the Mississippi would have been sufficient, plus at least two additional regiments in reserve, the number normally assigned this responsibility until 1768. The other nine regiments assigned occupation duties in Canada and Florida were excessive and not related to the fur trade.

Many of the British merchants in Canada were Scots who had originally come to Canada as soldiers, as did some of the other British merchants. The preponderance of Scots was discharged from the Scottish regiments that fought in North America because of British ministerial policy dating back to 1756. After the Jacobite Uprising was overcome in 1745, the Highlanders who had spent their lives training to be soldiers were without an occupation. Many of them turned to service in the British army beginning in 1749 with the 42nd Regiment (the Black Watch), originally formed in 1743 from Scottish militia companies.

In 1756 the Black Watch was sent to America, and in 1757 William Pitt, Britain's wartime leader, ordered the creation of two additional Scottish regiments, the 77th and the 78th, each to consist of 1,000 men. Fearing the Scots would not be loyal, the Duke of Argyle, the leading political figure of Scotland, was asked to recommend reliable officers to recruit these regiments. The 77th was raised by the Honorable Archibald Montgomerie, who recruited thirteen companies for a total of some 1,400 men, well over the number requested. Most of the men enrolled were from the Fraser, MacDonald, Cameron, and Maclean clans, although some were brought in from other areas. The 78th was raised by the Honorable Simon Fraser, son of Simon, Lord Lovat, a prominent Jacobite rebel executed in 1745. The Fraser, McTavish, and McGillivray clans from Lovat's estate provided many recruits. By July 1757 both regiments had been sent to America. An additional 1,000 men were recruited later to provide replacements for the three Highland regiments in America, the 42nd, the 77th and the 78th. In two years 4,000–5,000 Scottish fighting men had been recruited into the three regiments. Despite official rules to the contrary, many English regiments stationed in Scotland or in the northern counties of England recruited Highlanders to fill their ranks during the early years of the Seven Years' War. Scots made up more than one-sixth of the 30,000 British troops in America.

The Scottish regiments had outstanding military records during the Seven Years' War, and all three regiments suffered heavy casualties during the campaigns in the West Indies. After 1763 the British disbanded these regiments in America, the 77th in Pennsylvania in 1764, and the 78th in Canada in 1763. The 42nd Regiment had two battalions, each with an authorized strength of 1,000 men. The Second Battalion of the 42nd was disbanded in Canada in 1763, whereas many soldiers of the First Battalion of the 42nd were released in America at the end of their enlistment although the regiment continued to exist.

The men discharged from the three regiments were given three alternatives: accept land and remain in America, reenlist in the 42nd Regiment, or return home. Many soldiers of the 77th Regiment and the First Battalion of the 42nd remained in Pennsylvania, whereas many from the 78th Regiment and the Second Battalion of the 42nd elected to remain in Canada. These discharged soldiers and their relatives, whom they encouraged to come to Canada in later years, formed the nucleus of the band of Scots in the fur trade, as well as in land development.

Many of the "British Canadians" in the period from 1760 to 1774 had clan names linking them to the 42nd, the 77th, and the 78th Regiments. Sir William Johnson wrote to Lieutenant Governor Cadwallader Colden of New York in 1765 concerning Hugh Fraser, formerly a lieutenant in Colonel Simon Fraser's regiment (78th), who had been discharged in Canada. Hugh Fraser had brought some industrious people from Scotland in 1764 and asked for one hundred acres for each of his people plus an additional grant for himself. If Colden were to grant this land, Fraser promised to bring more Scots, a move that Johnson supported.

Regardless of the deep-seated prejudice of the English against the Scots, which distorted some of the documents, evidence indicates that the Scots did have some weaknesses. Guy Carleton, the governor of Canada, wrote to the Earl of Shelburne, on the one hand, that most of the British inhabitants in Canada were either disbanded officers and soldiers who had settled there when they were discharged, or "adventurers" in trade who could not remain in England and came to Canada to make their fortunes. On the other hand, many accounts describe the hardy character of the Scots who gained their fortunes not by political connections but by hard work.

Supporting the British regiments on the frontier was expensive. Most of the money was used for pay and rations. The British Treasury engaged money contractors who provided cash in America for army pay through agents at a commission of 2 percent of the total. The Spanish dollars or colonial currency used to pay the troops and buy other items was purchased in New York City from bankers and merchants with sterling bills of exchange. The contract to deliver rations included a fixed cost per ration that was paid to the contractor in sterling bills of exchange. These were used by colonial merchants to pay for imports from Britain.

The British rations and money contractors engaged colonial merchants to transact the business in America. In 1755 Gerard Beekman was engaged to provide pay, rations, and clothing for the army in America, receiving a 5 percent commission for purchases of food and merchandise and 2.5 percent for providing cash. Beekman was paid in sterling bills, Spanish dollars, and Jamaican rum. In 1761 Ward Apthorpe, a New York merchant, purchased 2,000 Spanish dollars ($86,000) from John Collins, an agent of Baynton and Wharton in Quebec, with a sterling bill of exchange. The dollars were used to pay the soldiers then in Quebec. Collins also sold Spanish dollars worth £400 sterling ($80,000) to Alexander Campbell, the paymaster of the 74th Regiment, for a bill drawn on George Ross of London, presumably an agent for the money contractor in London.

Selling rations to the British army was a major source of profit. Before 1760 the rations contract had been held by Sir William Baker, a member of Parliament, and Christopher Kilby, a Connecticut merchant. The next contractors were Sir Samuel Fludyer and Adam Drummond. In 1762 a new contract was let to Sir James Colebrooke, his brother George Colebrooke, Arnold Nesbitt, and Moses Frank at 4³/4d. sterling ($3.94) per ration with transportation charges in America to be paid for by the government. Oliver DeLancey and John Watts continued as agents in New York while David Franks and his associates became the agents in Philadelphia. In 1764 the contractors appointed David Franks, John Inglis, and David Barclay of Philadelphia as agents to provide rations at a rate of 4³/4d. per day per man. Sir Samuel Fludyer and John Drummond (both members of Parliament) and Moses Frank (the patriarch of a family that had many relatives in business in America) replaced the Colebrookes, Nesbitt, and John Thomlinson as money contractors in 1766.

The agents for the contractors also made money selling luxury items to the army: tea, coffee, chocolate, wine, rum, sugar, molasses, tobacco, cloth, and other dry goods. The army officers were free to purchase these items from other merchants. Collins sold miscellaneous products including rum to the army. Lieutenant Colonel Prevost purchased clothing for his regiment, the 60th Royal Americans, from Duncan Phyn in 1764.

The major task was providing food for the troops. In 1766 the contracted cost was 6d. sterling per ration, food for one soldier for one day. In 1766, a deduction of 2¹/2d. ($2.08) per day was made from the pay of each soldier for his rations, which were supposed to cost £22,242 sterling (about $4,448,000) for fifteen battalions then in America. The actual cost for rations in 1766 was £72,729 ($14,546,000). Estimating each battalion at a peacetime strength of 500 men, there were 7,500 soldiers in America. The daily amount of the estimated £22,242 sterling would have been £61 sterling, or 2¹/2d. per man per day. Instead, the actual daily amount in 1766 was £199 sterling or 7¹/2d. ($6.24) per man per day, three times the estimated amount and more than the 4³/4d. provided by the contract. Much of the difference resulted from transportation costs not included in the contract price. Because of those costs, feeding the regiments on the frontier was much more expensive than feeding those on the coast. The cost of the rations alone in 1766 demonstrated clearly the value of the military market to the colonial economy.

Feeding a regiment of 300 men could be a profitable enterprise. The standard ration was 1 pound of flour and 1 pound of beef per day, or 9,000 pounds of each per month for a regiment. In 1762 flour sold at Fort Pitt for £2 Pennsylvania ($230) per hundredweight ($2.30 per pound) and beef at 7d. Pennsylvania ($3.36) per pound. Venison sold for only 2d. Pennsylvania per pound. The cost of a ration at Fort Pitt therefore was approximately

7d. sterling ($5.66). The cost of feeding a regiment of 300 men for a month at Fort Pitt prices was £103 10s. sterling ($20,700) for the flour and £150 ($30,240) for the beef, for a total of £253 10s. ($50,940). The London contractors bid the ration at 4³/₄d. sterling a day and were obviously looking for a better price than the 7d. sterling ($5.66) possible with Fort Pitt prices, even though the army paid more than the contract price to cover the cost of transportation.

The cost of a similar ration in New York City was less than 6d. sterling. In New York City in 1762 beef sold at £4 New York ($504) per barrel (220 pounds) and wheat at £1 New York ($126) per bushel. The 60 pounds of wheat in a bushel could be ground into 60 pounds flour and sold for 3d. sterling ($2.10) per pound plus an allowance for grinding the wheat. The cost of beef was less than 3d. sterling ($2.29) per pound, for a total of a little more than 5d. sterling ($4.39) for a ration. The price of a ration in New York City was significantly lower than the 7d. at Fort Pitt and only slightly higher than the contract price of 4³/₄d. sterling. The New York prices quoted here were considered high because of poor crops for the past two years caused by drought.

The crushing blow that would finally destroy the merchant firm Baynton and Wharton was the award of the army rations contract to David Franks. William Murray was on his way in July with a cargo of merchandise including silver ornaments, linen, twenty rifles, rum, sugar, and other Indian goods worth £1,200 Pennsylvania ($138,000), a comparatively small amount. As a private venture he was taking shoes and stockings worth £400 Pennsylvania to sell to the soldiers. George Morgan, who became a partner in Baynton and Wharton and was placed in charge of the Illinois business, did not believe Murray would do well unless he spoke French fluently, and Morgan intended to try to buy the entire cargo from Murray when he arrived. Because of the award of the rations contract Morgan had previously abandoned the idea of sending hunters out to shoot buffalo for meat, but now he wanted to subcontract the meat ration from Murray and send out hunters again.

In April 1768 John Campbell, the Baynton and Wharton agent at Fort Pitt, sent a hunting expedition down the Ohio River to obtain meat for sale to the army in Illinois. Campbell had difficulty finding men and finally recruited eighteen white men and three black men to serve under the direction of Captain Robertson. Campbell hired a butcher, Frederick Dunfield, who knew how to cure and pack meat.

Another rich source of profit was selling luxuries such as fine wine to the officers. Army officers were good customers and paid with bills of exchange. By September 1761 business in Detroit was going well and James Sterling was complaining about the quality of merchandise sent by his suppliers. He reported that silver and chintz were the best items and wampum and ribbons the poorest. He complained that the shirts were badly made of poor-quality linen. In October Sterling ordered Madeira wine, shrub (a beverage with some alcoholic content), loaf sugar, fine salt, and gunpowder from James Syme, a London supplier who later formed a partnership with Christopher Kilby, a former provisions contractor for the British army in America.

In Detroit Sterling acted as the banker for the garrison in 1762. He purchased army vouchers used to buy supplies from other traders at a 25 percent discount because there was no army deputy quartermaster general in Detroit to reimburse the merchants with cash or bills of exchange. The local merchants (especially the French) would not wait for the vouchers to be paid, so Sterling provided them with bills of exchange drawn on his New York City partners in return for the merchants' vouchers. The local merchants could use these bills to pay their debts in Montreal and elsewhere. Sterling sent to his partners in New York for payment of the vouchers that he had purchased and bills of exchange from the paymaster of the 80th Regiment, Mr. Hall, and two other officers, Captain Balfour and Lieutenant Williams. In January 1762 Sterling sent to Syme in London £150 New York ($19,000). Sterling apportioned £60 New York of the bill to pay Gerrard Banker for a small keg of merchandise that Sterling had sold for him in return for acting as Sterling's agent in New York City. Sterling sent Syme another bill of exchange for £90 Pennsylvania ($10,350) drawn by Captain Thomas Barnsley, the paymaster of the First Battalion of the 60th Regiment (the Rangers). The cash provided by Sterling was used to pay the troops.

In April 1762 a warrant (an authorization to spend) for £3,000 New York ($378,000) arrived from Fort Pitt to pay for military expenses in Detroit until September 14, 1762. Joseph Spear, an associate of Baynton & Wharton, purchased the warrant from Campbell for £3,601 Pennsylvania ($414,000) in bills of exchange drawn on Baynton and Wharton that Campbell then used to pay the army's debts to the other merchants. Sterling's share was £900 New York, almost one-third. Spear sent the army warrant with a list of bills he had drawn to Baynton and Wharton.

By June 1762 Sterling was in the banking business in earnest. He sent his partners a bill of exchange for £1,477 Pennsylvania ($170,000) from Callender and Spear drawn on Baynton and Wharton, which Sterling had purchased with billets (French paper money) obtained from the French in return for his merchandise. The troops in Detroit were paid in billets. In addition Sterling sent three other bills including Lieutenant McDonald's bill on Captain Barnsley, the paymaster of the 60th Regiment, for £200

Pennsylvania; another bill by Lieutenant McDonald on Lieutenant Hall, the paymaster of the 80th Regiment; and a bill for £85 from Sir Charles Davers on William McAdam of New York City. The billets paid by the French to Sterling for merchandise were sold to Campbell to pay the troops.

Meanwhile the British were trying to send the 22nd Regiment up the Mississippi to occupy Illinois. The 22nd Regiment had 351 men, having been reinforced by drafting all the men from the Third Battalion of the 60th Royal American Regiment not entitled to discharge when the battalion was disbanded at Pensacola, Florida. In addition, many of the men who were discharged from the Royal American regiment were persuaded to reenlist in the 22nd.

The expedition began with an attempt to find a passage at Iberville, but the waterway was clogged with trees. The regiment then went to New Orleans on February 12, 1764, to prepare for the trip up the Mississippi, and while they were there 30 troops deserted. Finally, on February 27, 1764, the regiment set out with 320 soldiers, 30 women, and 17 children in ten flat-bottomed boats that could be rowed and two pirogues (dugout canoes made from large tree trunks). By March 15, 1764, 50 more men had deserted and 7 had died. On March 19 and 20 Indians attacked the expedition 200 miles north of New Orleans, so the regiment returned to New Orleans on March 26.

While the British were unable to move troops up the Mississippi because of Indian opposition, the French had no difficulty. The French governor safely sent two convoys of bateaux, one on April 19, 1764, and another on May 11. The convoys carried goods for both the Illinois and the Arkansas trade. The second convoy included 77 people in three bateaux under the command of Berard with supplies for the French garrison in Illinois.

Once the 34th Regiment reached Illinois, providing it with rations was a struggle because of the difficulty of either transporting food there or purchasing it locally. By 1766, the 34th Regiment was established in Illinois, and its enormous cost was reflected in the bills of exchange and accounts sent to General Gage. The rations alone cost as much as £15,000 sterling ($3 million) per year. The average cost of rations for a regiment elsewhere in America was only £4,849 ($970,000). The transportation to Illinois further increased the burden. To supply the regiment required that forty-five boats be sent down the Ohio River each year at a cost of about £5,200 sterling ($1 million).

The magnitude of the rations problem in Illinois can be seen in the details. In 1765 the 34th Regiment was issued 6,178 rations, enough for 140 men for 44 days, for its trip up from Mobile to New Orleans. However, given the consumption of 48,121 rations during the 155 days it took to reach Illinois, the rations strength including women and other attached personnel was probably about 300 people. The rations issued in Mobile included:

---

4,014 pounds of flour
3,260 pounds of bread
420 pounds of beef
4,558 pounds of pork
63 pounds of butter
180 gallons of peas
304 gallons of rum (9,728 gills)

---

The ration for 1 day was 1 pound of bread, 1 pound of meat and 1 gill of rum. The expedition therefore had rations for about 25 days to reach New Orleans. The regiment was resupplied at New Orleans with 24,484 rations (82 days for 300 people). It probably stopped for some days at the Yassov River to wait for supply boats from New Orleans. A supply convoy evidently did catch up with the regiment there and issued the regiment 17,459 rations (58 days for 300 persons).

The 34th Regiment consumed a total of 48,121 rations on its journey from Mobile to Illinois: 6,178 from Mobile to New Orleans, 24,484 from New Orleans to the Yassov River, and 17,459 from the Yassov to Illinois. The customary charge to the regiment of the rations was £501 sterling ($100,200) or $2^{1}/_{2}$d. sterling per ration. The actual cost was probably four times that amount. In New York, flour sold at 10s. New York per hundred-weight ($.63, a little less than 1d. sterling per pound) and beef at 10d. New York per pound ($5.23, a little more than 6d. sterling) in 1768. The cost of the pound of beef and the pound of flour in New York would have been 7d. sterling ($5.86). Rum sold at about 4s. New York ($25.20) per quart, or less than 4d. sterling ($3.15) per gill, increasing the cost of the ration to about 11d. sterling more than four times the allotted price. A total purchase of colonial food and rum of £2,000 sterling ($400,000) was a considerable amount and did nothing more than feed a regiment on its way to Illinois.

When the regiment arrived in Illinois it was very short of provisions. The commander, Colonel Robert Farmar, was able to purchase 50,000 pounds of flour in Illinois, which was sufficient for 221 days, so he was feeding about 226 people, including the women who normally accompanied a regiment in the eighteenth century. The flour would last until July 1766 and meat could be obtained by hunting buffalo. However, many Indians were expected in the spring and the French custom was to feed them a double ration (two pounds of bread and two pounds of meat). More flour was needed, and

Farmar pressed Gage to ensure that a supply came from Fort Pitt early in the spring of 1766.

A major task confronted Gage—how was he to continue feeding the 34th Regiment at any cost? The route from Philadelphia was 1,400 miles long and lasted many weeks. Gage's plan to buy food locally faced difficulty because many French farmers were reluctant to sell to the British. The substitution of cornmeal for flour and buffalo for beef was a temporary solution. There were large herds of buffalo along the Ohio River only a hundred miles from Fort Pitt in 1766. In March 1766 the regiment was very short of food and had lived on bread and Indian corn for four days. They hoped that hunters would bring in three boatloads of buffalo meat within a few days.

The commandant at Fort Pitt was ordered to use Indians in canoes to supply the provisions while waiting for boats to be built at Fort Pitt to transport provisions and the new men who had been recruited in Pennsylvania to fill the depleted ranks of the 34th Regiment. The regiment was still short of food in July 1766. Even though Indian cornmeal was substituted for wheat flour, there was not enough to provide the full daily ration. Gage suggested that a semi-military colony be created in Illinois to raise the food needed by the garrison.

The commanding officer in Illinois was free to purchase his supplies from whomever he wished until the contractor was able to provide the ration. Most of the ration business was enjoyed by Baynton and Wharton, who maintained good relations with the commander. When Morgan established a store at Vincennes under the management of Alexander Williamson, he described the manner in which rations were gathered for the army. Williamson had past experience as a guide, which was of great benefit in dealing with the Indians. He was warned to tell his friends in Detroit that business was very bad; otherwise they might come down and compete with him. The local French farmers paid for merchandise with flour, tobacco, Indian corn, and hogs. Flour was accepted only at a price approved by Morgan and in quantities that could be sold to the army. All tobacco of good quality was to be taken at 20 sols ($4.20) per pound, made into "carrots" and sent to Kaskaskia. Indian corn was to be taken only in quantities that could be fed to hogs and cattle that had been purchased. Hogs were to be purchased at 18 sols ($3.78) per pound. When a hundred pigs had been purchased, Williamson was to hire two people to drive them to Kaskaskia, preferably in October or November. Cattle were purchased at 10 sols ($2.10) per pound, or 200 livres ($1,600) for a three-year-old ox, and delivered to Kaskaskia. Cows sold at 150 livres ($1,200) in Kaskaskia, so they were purchased for less.

A potential source of profit for Baynton and Wharton was the sale of rations to the army in Illinois. Providing a reliable source of rations for the

British army at Fort Chartres at the lowest cost had been a major problem for General Gage. In January 1767, George Croghan advised Gage that the best way to supply the garrison was to obtain flour, peas, Indian corn, buffalo, and beef at Vincennes. However, the Illinois French farmers would not sell their produce for bills of exchange drawn on the army, the usual way provisions were purchased, because New Orleans merchants would accept British bills of exchange only at a 50–60 percent discount, to discourage the French from selling to the British. The French had no faith in the local paper money left over from the French regime because it fluctuated in value. The farmers would accept only hard cash (Spanish silver dollars and other gold and silver specie) or merchandise.

Therefore, the best way to obtain provisions was either to send specie (usually Spanish silver dollars) to the commanding officer of the garrison (a risky undertaking, and hard cash was always in short supply in the colonies) or to have a merchant exchange goods for produce, which would then be sold to the army for bills of exchange. Croghan estimated the plan could be accomplished at a cost of 12d. Pennsylvania ($5.75) per ration. It was not coincidental that Baynton and Wharton was the only colonial firm in Illinois that had the merchandise to exchange.

The plan would have many benefits: giving the garrison a secure source of provisions, eliminating the burden of transporting the provisions down the Ohio River, giving the French farmers a good market for their grain and beef as an incentive to produce more, breaking the reliance of the French on the French merchants in New Orleans, and encouraging the French who had moved east of the Mississippi to return to Illinois from St. Louis and resume farming. The plan was implemented, and Baynton and Wharton began to receive large payments for rations.

Baynton and Wharton attempted to obtain the rations contract in 1767 on a permanent basis. In January they sent proposals to Gage and to Lauchlin MacCleane in London with the offer of a bribe to MacCleane to use his personal influence in presenting their proposal to the British Treasury. Baynton and Wharton proposed to feed a regiment of 500 men in Illinois for a period of five, six, or seven years using buffalo meat, flour, cornmeal, and peas at a cost of 1s. sterling ($10) delivered to Fort Chartres. Given the price of beef and flour at Fort Pitt and the cost of transportation, this offer was reasonable. With the buffalo and cornmeal available in Illinois, Baynton and Wharton expected to make a substantial profit—about £3,000 sterling ($600,000) on a gross of £10,000 sterling ($2 million). The partners asked for an advance of £3,000 sterling ($600,000) to deposit a stock of provisions for 500 men. They also asked that no stills be set up in Illinois that would compete with their sale of rum to the troops.

The advantage of the Baynton and Wharton offer was that it would be a more reliable source of food for the army in Illinois. The Ohio River was navigable only two months in the spring and two months in the fall when the water level was higher. During the summer and winter the troops were often short of food. In September 1766 the 34th Regiment had rations for only two months on hand, a slim margin. Adding danger to the complexity of finding food, the Indians could block movement on the Ohio River any time they wished.

In 1767 the rations contract for the American seaboard colonies was held by Sir Samuel Fludyer, a member of Parliament; Adam Drummond, also a member of Parliament; and Moses Franks, a Jewish merchant in London. The latter's brother, David Franks, was their Philadelphia agent and also the competitor of Baynton and Wharton in frontier trade. David Franks offered to provide rations to Illinois for 9$^1$/2p. sterling ($7.90) per ration deposited at Fort Pitt, which required the army to build boats and transport the food down the Ohio River. Baynton and Wharton estimated that transportation down the Ohio River cost the army over £5,000 sterling ($1 million) per year. The proposal of Baynton and Wharton would have reduced the cost of feeding the troops in Illinois by about £5,000 sterling by providing a daily ration at 12d. sterling delivered to Fort Chartres.

Baynton and Wharton estimated their offer would save the army 50 percent and guarantee that the food would be available, whereas currently the troops were not being fed. In addition, buying grain from the French farmers would make them friendlier to the British. The farmers would not accept army bills of exchange or paper money in payment for their produce, but Baynton and Wharton would barter merchandise that the farmers needed. The partners claimed to have £30,000 sterling ($6 million) in merchandise in Illinois that could be used for this purpose.

The partners' proposal was forwarded to the Earl of Shelburne, in charge of colonial affairs in the British government, with the comment that Baynton and Wharton were the most extensive traders in North America and that the proposal proved that the Illinois garrison could be supplied at a reasonable cost. Morgan very much wanted the contract, believing that if it were awarded to his firm, it would get the entire trade in Illinois. If not, he felt that the firm should withdraw from Illinois as it would be better to lose £10,000 than to send more goods and lose £20,000. His hopes grew dim as Robert Leake, the commissary-general in New York City, advised Gage to reject Morgan's proposal on the grounds that buffalo meat would not remain edible for six months and could not be stored for emergencies. Leake warned that a more permanent supply was necessary in the event of an Indian siege. Because of the danger of an Indian uprising in Illinois, the garrison must have a one-year supply on hand, and the buffalo would spoil. Leake suggested that each spring the rations contractor be required to send salt pork, which would not spoil in barrels sufficient to feed 300 men for nine months.

In April 1767 the 34th Regiment had enough provisions but no reserve stocks. Gage expected Lieutenant Colonel John Reed, commander of the 34th Regiment, to have a year's supply of rations in Fort Chartres at all times in the event of an Indian attack. The Indians could take the fort only by a surprise attack or by starving the garrison out. In July 1767 Gage sent Reed £1,000 sterling ($200,000) in Spanish dollars to buy food locally. In July 1767 Baynton and Wharton hoped to supply the 34th Regiment with provisions until the contract was awarded.

Baynton and Wharton was also concerned with supplying the troops at Fort Pitt. Joseph Spear at Carlisle tried to sell all of his goods to the army when the plan was announced to send troops down the Ohio to Illinois. At Fort Pitt he sold some goods and received a bill of exchange from the 42nd Regiment for £200 Pennsylvania ($23,000) that he forwarded to Baynton and Wharton to credit his account.

Other merchants were making profits from sales to the army, however. John Hughes, who had been trading with the Indians since 1756, was supplying the army in Pennsylvania in 1764, with Joseph Spear acting as his agent. In July 1764 Spear reported that all of the goods and liquor belonging to Spear & Hughes was being sent forward but that prospects were poor, as too many people were permitted to trade with the army. However, Spear did well and in August 1764 he reported that sixty horse-loads of goods had been loaded as part of Colonel Bouquet's expedition to punish the Indians for Pontiac's Uprising. Hughes was having difficulty with Neave over the matter of payment, although the problem in that case was the British government's delay in paying bills.

Spear was very active in many business affairs in 1764. He not only acted as Baynton and Wharton's major contact at Carlisle and had entered partnership with Callender for a large shipment of goods, but on May 11, 1764, he made a purchase of £745 Pennsylvania ($85,675) on behalf of the partnership of John Hughes, Theodorus Swaine Drage, and himself. At the same time he purchased £278 Pennsylvania ($31,970) on his own behalf from Baynton and Wharton. He also acted on behalf of Edmund Moran, who left his goods with Spear's clerk at Fort Pitt when Moran went off with Bouquet's expedition.

At Carlisle, Callender was supplying the army contractors, Plumsted & Franks of Philadelphia, and receiving in return drafts from the army pay-master, John Nelson. On August 18, 1764, Callender turned over to Baynton & Wharton in payment of his debts a draft from Nelson for £2,000 sterling ($400,000), a major boost to the firm's financial position at that time. Robert

Leake, the army commissary-general in New York, had nearly £1,000 sterling ($200,000) in outstanding bills to Callender in August 1764. On October 1, 1764, Callender's account with Baynton and Wharton was credited with £908 Pennsylvania ($104,420) for cash received from Nelson.

A major change in the trade occurred when the contract of Plumsted & Franks to supply rations to the army expired on June 7, 1764. In July 1764 the men of the 60th and the 77th Regiments at Fort Pitt mutinied because of bad flour provided by the contractors. General Gage had little confidence in Plumstead & Franks and believed that the partners would use every chicanery to profit. Franks, with new partners John Inglis of Philadelphia and his son-in-law, David Barclay, received the new contract. Franks was a Jewish merchant in Philadelphia with ties to Croghan, Johnson, the Gratz family, and Baynton and Wharton. Inglis previously had been buying and selling in the West Indies and shipping slaves.

Business with the army was a major part of the colonial economy. The payments from the army were made in sterling that was then used to pay for the colonial imports from Britain—manufactured goods, cloth, and other luxuries. When the British attempted to reduce the cost of the army by obtaining the necessary funds from taxation in America, it created widespread resistance. The objection was not so much the amount of the taxes but that they had to be paid in sterling, which would replace the sterling bills that previously had flowed into the hands of colonial merchants supplying the army. Even if the taxes had been paid in local currency, this currency would have replaced the sterling from England that previously had been used to buy colonial provisions and to pay the soldiers. Removing the army from the frontier and reducing the cost of the rations and transportation had an adverse reaction as well, cutting the revenue obtained by the merchants.

The colonial merchants wanted the British army on the frontier both as a tool to restrain the French fur traders and as a customer. The army failed in the first task and in 1768 purchased fewer goods and services when the regiments were transferred to the coast. The British regiments were no longer useful to the merchants and instead were used against the colonists. It was no coincidence that resistance to London increased dramatically after 1768.

## SUGGESTED READINGS

Stephen Brumwell, *Redcoats: The British Soldier and War in the Americas, 1755–1763* (2002).

Guy Chet, *Conquering the American Wilderness: The Triumph of European Warfare in the Colonial Northeast* (2003).

# 12

# Conclusion

People immigrated to America for many reasons. Some fled starvation, disease, the ravages of war, or political or religious persecution in Europe. Others came to further their fortunes, first in the fur trade and later in farming and business. In England population growth and industrial reform led to large-scale social change. In the age of waterpower, rivers and streams were the main highways. Waterpowered mills made flour, sawed wood, and operated the early machines used in many industries, including making cloth and forging iron.

The effects of the Industrial Revolution in England in 1750 were far-reaching worldwide. With the advent of the Seven Years' War, suddenly there was an enormous demand for equipment, clothing, and guns in Europe. Manufacturers realized that they needed better ways to make consumer products as well as war supplies. The demand for cloth led to various machines to increase worker productivity. Increased need for food led to development of fertilizers and better breeding of livestock. The new industries not only increased the demand for raw materials and food from America, but also the prosperity resulting from the war created a vast new market for luxury items, especially sugar.

There were few large urban centers in Europe and farming was still the primary industry. The money circulated during the war made it possible for people to leave Europe for America so that they could own their land. In

Europe the aristocracy owned most of the land, and peasant farmers were tired of giving half of their crop to their landlords.

The rulers in Europe saw the new world as a vital source of raw materials to make products for Old World consumers. In the seventeenth century the French established Canada in the north and Louisiana in the south. As the loser in the Seven Years' War, also known as the French and Indian War, France ceded Canada to England and Louisiana west of the Mississippi River to Spain. Great Britain chartered the thirteen American colonies and favored certain entrepreneurs with large land grants that were sold in small parcels to the immigrants. Virginia and Pennsylvania granted land to the ex-soldiers from the Seven Years' War in appreciation for their services.

As the population grew in America, pressure increased to expand beyond the western boundary of the Appalachian Mountains. After the Seven Years' War, however, the French fur traders and the Indians effectively resisted the encroachment of the colonists. England maintained an army purportedly to keep order but instead used it to restrain the colonial farmers and protect the Indians.

There were remarkably few people on the American colonial frontier in the mid-eighteenth century. In the area north of the Ohio River there were some 10,000 Indian families. The white population centers were Canada, New York, Pennsylvania, and Illinois.

People on the frontier in Canada included those living and working in the Detroit area and Michilimackinac. In Detroit there were 2,500 people on sixty farms, an average of 100 soldiers in the fort, 500 French in the town, and 20 colonial traders, for a total of more than 3,000 people. Several hundred traders and French farmers lived at Michilimackinac. Small numbers of French winterers lived in Indian villages all across the area. In addition, 1,000 canoe men visited the area each summer. Roughly 5,000 French and colonials in all lived and worked on the Canadian frontier.

In New York there were at least 1,000 settlers on the frontier and 200 traders at Oswego, Fort Niagara, and Schenectady. In Pennsylvania there were 400 people at Fort Pitt, 200 settlers in the immediate neighborhood, and 1,000 more on farms close to the frontier. Illinois had at least 4,000 white inhabitants plus 1,500 slaves.

Population of the American
Frontier in 1760

| | |
|---|---|
| Canada | 5,000 |
| New York | 1,600 |
| Pennsylvania | 1,600 |
| Illinois | 5,500 |
| Total | 13,700 |

Included in the total were nearly 2,000 slaves, mostly in Illinois and Detroit. Among the French and colonial farmers in Canada, Illinois, New York, and Pennsylvania were 2,000 men, 2,000 women, and 4,000 children. More than 2,000 men were employed in the fur trade in Canada, Illinois, New York, and Pennsylvania.

Others related to the frontier business were 10,000 people in Montreal, 18,000 in Albany, several thousand in the towns along the Forbes Road in Pennsylvania, and more than 3,000 in New Orleans.

These few people formed a complex economy that was somewhat self-sufficient and produced furs and agricultural products in exchange for manufactured goods. Roughly £100,000 sterling ($20 million) in furs were exported from Canada and a similar amount from New Orleans each year. Perhaps £20,000 sterling in fur was exported from New York and Pennsylvania legally, and a much larger amount was paid illegally to smugglers. The value of the agricultural products exported was much less, as most were consumed locally.

The value of the products imported by the Great Lakes area was estimated at £82,600 sterling, including £30,600 in merchandise plus army rations, which included a substantial amount of rum and manufactured goods from Britain worth about £20,000 sterling. The value of goods sent to the various posts in the lower lakes was determined by the number of canoes that traded at a post each year. The frontier commerce of New York required £40,000 sterling in merchandise carried in 180 canoes that set out from Schenectady annually. Eighty stopped at Oswego with merchandise worth £13,600, which was traded for furs and deerskin worth £20,400. The remaining 100 canoes contained £17,000 in merchandise and paddled out to Niagara, Toronto, Detroit, Michilimackinac, and Illinois. Detroit received £1,000 in rum and other heavy items. Merchandise worth about £2,000 was sent south to Ouiatanon, Miami, and Vincennes and traded for furs that were then sent to Illinois.

As much as £40,000 sterling in goods and provisions was sent up the Mississippi River from New Orleans and a much smaller amount went down the Ohio River. The total value of merchandise and produce sold in the area north of the Ohio River was £150,000 sterling. The area exported well over £220,000 sterling in furs and £70,000 in sterling bills of exchange.

The Indians profited from the new situation in 1760 after the surrender of Canada to the British. Competition developed between the French and the newly arrived British and colonial merchants. After Pontiac's Uprising the French formed connections with British merchants and through them ordered goods directly from Britain at lower prices than the colonials offered. The close cooperation of the French and British merchants also worked to the disadvantage of the colonial traders, who were all but eliminated from the fur trade by 1768 although they continued to supply the French traders with rum. Because of the timeless friendly relationship between the French and the Indians, the tribes to all intents had little contact with the Pennsylvania traders by 1768. The New York traders dealt mostly with the Iroquois at Fort Niagara and Oswego.

Both the French and the Indians prospered after 1763. With the assistance of French fur traders, the Indians prevented any large-scale incursion into their land. The British government prevented the advance of the settlers and did little to assist the colonial efforts either in obtaining land or in acquiring a share of the fur trade.

The French farmers profited from the sale of their surplus produce to supply the substantial market created by the British regiments north of the Ohio River. Previously there had been only 1,000 French fur traders needing meager provisions. After 1760, as many as 10,000 British soldiers needed a pound of bread and a pound of meat every day. Although most of the soldiers received rations from Britain and the American colonies, at least 1,000 troops looked to the French farmers in the St. Lawrence Valley, Detroit, and Illinois for their daily ration. The French domination of the fur trade after 1763 provided employment for young farm boys and ready cash to their families.

The French fur traders in Canada were severely handicapped immediately after 1760 as they were cut off from France and the usual source of trading goods. However, British merchants came to their rescue in Quebec and Montreal, providing merchandise at lower prices than France. The furs were sold to English hatmakers and to buyers from Holland and Portugal. An ever-increasing number of canoes left Montreal each year, an indication that the fur trade was prospering.

The colonial settlers with different goals were frustrated in their search for new land to farm. The British government prohibited settlement west of the mountains by the Proclamation of 1763, which was enforced by the British army. Any attempt to settle illegally was endangered by Indian attacks, and so new farms were limited to the unsettled areas east of the mountains. During Pontiac's Uprising some settlers were killed or captured on the frontier. The 1760s was a dangerous time for the settlers, who saw the British government as their enemy on the one hand when it supplied the Indians with guns and scalping knives as gifts from the Indian Department. On the other hand, the army did provide a market for the colonial farmers who sold surplus produce, making farming profitable but only at the expense of very hard labor.

The New York fur traders were also frustrated by the new conditions after 1760. Rather than enjoying free access to an enormous new market in the

West, they were driven out of Michilimackinac and the area northwest of Lake Superior by the Indians with French encouragement. The British government tried to limit trade to the posts to protect the Indians, which would have favored the New Yorkers, but it was unable to enforce the rule. The result was that the New York traders obeyed the restrictive rule and lost the trade to the French who ignored it. To further obstruct the New York traders, the British rules limited the amount of rum that could be sold, effectively destroying the New Yorker's strong suit.

The Pennsylvania traders moved swiftly into present-day Ohio after 1760, but many were killed during Pontiac's Uprising. Nevertheless, a number returned after peace was restored. But the French traders from Illinois were in competition with them almost to the gates of Fort Pitt. By the end of the 1760s the French had practically regained their monopoly of the trade in Ohio, for the most part as a result of the British rules restricting trade to the posts and limiting the amount of rum. The traders saw British regulations as destructive, and the colonial merchants suffered the most from British rule.

Conversely, the merchants in Britain and America profited from the frontier trade. They were bound together by ties based on family, religion, prior military service, and prior commercial dealings. The merchant communities in Britain and America had many overlapping connections in a dense web of transactions as assets in the form of bills of exchange and cargoes of fur, flour, lumber, slaves, sugar, and other products crossed the Atlantic. The fur was exchanged for the major commodities imported to the frontier— metal goods, cloth, and liquor. However, it was far from a simple exchange, and fur was only one of the many assets of frontier commerce. Other assets were bills of exchange for feeding the British army and farm products sent down to New Orleans from Illinois. The demand for goods in the West provided a market for British manufacturers and was a stimulus to the colonial economy. Although the major source of metal and cloth was Europe, items such as rum, metal tools, and clothing were made in America. All merchandise increased in value after processing and transportation, permitting a livelihood for thousands of colonial merchants and tradesmen.

The people on the frontier were all interdependent. Some were satisfied with the status quo, while others wanted radical change. Some profited at first from the new situation created by the acquisition of Canada by Britain, while others were forced to struggle to regain their position. All were subject to the environment, which determined what they ate and what they wore. In the long run, however, the whims of the government in London destroyed the balance. When the British army was withdrawn from the frontier the British government eliminated a valuable market for the merchants and gave free rein to the French to regain absolute control of the fur trade. The vast majority of furs left directly for England via Quebec or for France via New Orleans, leaving very little profit for the colonial merchants. Deprived of this profit the merchants joined the opposition to Britain, and the turmoil that followed created chaos on the frontier. Everyone suffered, and decades would pass before peace returned to the frontier people.

## SUGGESTED READINGS

David Ammerman, *In the Common Cause: American Response to the Coercive Acts of 1774* (1974).

Bernard Bailyn, *The Ideological Origins of the American Revolution* (1967).

Richard D. Brown, *Revolutionary Politics in Massachusetts: The Boston Committees of Correspondence and the Towns, 1772–1774* (1970).

Jon Butler, *Becoming America: The Revolution before 1776* (2000).

Robert A. Gross, *The Minutemen and Their World* (1976).

Nathan O. Hatch, *The Sacred Cause of Liberty: Republican Thought and the Millennium in Revolutionary New England* (1977).

Pauline Maier, *American Scripture: Making the Declaration of Independence* (1997).

———, *The Old Revolutionaries: Political Lives in the Age of Samuel Adams* (1980).

———, *From Resistance to Revolution: Colonial Radicals and the Development of American Opposition to Britain, 1765–1776* (1972).

Robert Middlekauff, *The Glorious Cause: The American Revolution, 1763–1789* (1982).

Edmund S. Morgan and Helen M. Morgan, *The Stamp Act Crisis: Prologue to Revolution* (1963).

Peter Shaw, *American Patriots and the Rituals of Revolution* (1981).

John W. Tyler, *Smugglers and Patriots: Boston Merchants and the Advent of the American Revolution* (1986).

Gordon S. Wood, *The American Revolution: A History* (2002).

———, *The Radicalism of the American Revolution* (1991).

Alfred F. Young, *The Shoemaker and the Revolution: Memory and the American Revolution* (1999).

# Select Bibliography

Adam, Frank. *The Clans, Septs and Regiments of the Scottish Highlands.* Edinburgh: W. & A. K. Johnston & G. W. Bacon, 1965.

Alvord, Clarence W., and Clarence E. Carter, eds. *The Critical Period, 1763–1765.* Illinois Historical Collections. Vol. 10. Springfield: Illinois State Historical Library, 1915.

———. *The Illinois Country, 1673–1818.* Springfield: Illinois Centennial Commission, 1920.

———. *The Mississippi Valley in British Politics.* 2 vols. Cleveland: Arthur H. Clark Co., 1917.

Askin Papers. Burton Historical Collections of the Detroit Public Library.

Baby Manuscripts. Burton Historical Collections of the Detroit Public Library.

Baynton, Wharton & Morgan Papers. Microfilm. 10 rolls. Original in Pennsylvania Historical Commission, Harrisburg.

Beer, George L. *British Colonial Policy, 1754–1765.* New York: Peter Smith, 1933.

Byars, William V., ed. *B[ernard] and M. Gratz.* Jefferson City, MO: Hugh Stevens Printing Co., 1916.

Chevalier, John, and Peter Chevalier. Daybook, Pennsylvania Historical Society, Philadelphia.

Colden Papers, *New York Historical Society Collections,* 1876.

Dorn, Walter L. *Competition for Empire, 1740–1763.* New York: Harper Torchbooks, 1940.

Dunham, Douglas. "The French Element in the American Fur Trade." PhD diss., University of Michigan, 1950. (Microfilm in State Historical Society of Wisconsin, Madison.)

Dunn, Walter S. Jr. *Frontier Profit and Loss.* Westport, CT: Greenwood Press, 1998.

———. *The New Imperial Economy.* New York: Praeger, 2001.

———. "Western Commerce, 1760–1774." PhD diss. University of Wisconsin, 1971.

Edgar, William. Manuscripts, 1760–1769. Vol. 15 in the Burton Historical Collections of the Detroit Public Library.

Egnal, Marc. *A Mighty Empire: The Origins of the American Revolution.* Ithaca, NY: Cornell University Press, 1988.

Eyck, Erick. *Pitt versus Fox: Father and Son.* London: G. Bell and Sons, 1950.

Fleming, R. H. "Phyn, Ellice and Co. of Schenectady." *Contributions to Canadian Economics* 4 (1932): 7–41.

Gipson, Lawrence H. *The Coming of the Revolution, 1759–1766.* New York: Harper, 1954.

Gratz, Michael. Letter Book. Etting Collection, Pennsylvania Historical Society.

Gunderson, Mary. *Oregon Trail Cooking,* Mankato, MN: Capstone Press, 2000.

———. *Pioneer Farm Cooking,* Mankato, MN: Capstone Press, 2000.

Hamilton, Edward P. *The French and Indian War.* Garden City, NY: Doubleday, 1962.

Harrington, Virginia D. *The New York Merchant on the Eve of the Revolution.* New York: Columbia University Press, 1935.

Hazard, Samuel, ed. *Pennsylvania Archives,* 1st series. 12 vols. Philadelphia: Joseph Severns & Co., 1851–1856.

Henderson, W. O. *Britain and Industrial Europe, 1750–1870.* Leicester: Leicester University Press, 1972.

Hough, Franklin B. *Diary of the Siege of Detroit. . . .* Albany, NY: J. Munsell, 1860.

Hutchins, Thomas. *A Topographical Description of Virginia, Pennsylvania, Maryland, and North Carolina Reprinted from the Original Edition of 1778.* Cleveland: Burrows Bros.

Innis, Harold A. *The Fur Trade in Canada.* New Haven, CT: Yale University Press, 1930.

Jenness, Diamond. *The Indians of Canada.* Toronto: University of Toronto Press, 1977.

Jensen, Arthur L. *The Maritime Commerce of Colonial Philadelphia.* Madison: State Historical Society of Wisconsin, 1963.

Jensen, Merrill. *The Founding of a Nation.* New York: Oxford University Press, 1968.

Johnson, Sir William. *The Papers of Sir Williams Johnson.* 14 vols. Albany: State University of New York Press, 1921–1965.

Kellogg, Louise P. *The British Regime in Wisconsin and the Northwest.* Madison: State Historical Society, 1935.

Kenny, James. "Journal of James Kenny, 1761–1763." *The Pennsylvania Magazine of History and Biography,* vol. 37 (1913).

Knollenberg, Bernhard. *Origin of the American Revolution: 1759–1766.* New York: Free Press, 1965.

Lajeunesse, Ernest J. *The Windsor Border Region: Canada's Southernmost Frontier.* Toronto: University of Toronto Press, 1960.

Lanctot, Gustave. *Les Canadiens Français et Leurs Voisins du Sud.* Montreal: Bernard Valiquettes, 1941.

Lawson, Murray G. *Fur: A Study in English Mercantilism, 1700–1775.* Toronto: University of Toronto Press, 1943.

Lees, John. *Journal of [John Lees] a Quebec Merchant.* Detroit: Society of the Colonial Wars of the State of Michigan, 1911.

Martin, Calvin. *Keepers of the Game.* Berkley: University of California Press, 1978.

McClusker, John J. *Rum and the American Revolution: The Rum Trade and the Balance of Payments of the Thirteen Colonies.* 2 vols. New York: Garland Publishing, 1889.

McMillan, Alan D. *Native Peoples and Culture in Canada.* Vancouver: Douglas & McIntyre, 1988.

*Michigan Pioneer and Historical Collections.* 40 vols. Lansing: Wynkoop, Hallenbeck, Crawford Co., 1874–1929.

O'Callaghan, Edmund B., ed. *Documentary History of the State of New York.* 4 vols. Albany: Weed, Parsons, & Co., 1849–1851.

O'Callaghan, Edmund B., and Fernold Berthold, eds. *Documents Relating to the Colonial History of the State of New York.* 15 vols. Albany: Weed, Parsons, & Co., 1853–1887.

Parkman, Francis. *A History of the Conspiracy of Pontiac and the Indian War after the Conquest of Canada.* New York: Macmillan Co., 1929.

Pease, Theodore C., and Marguerite J. Pease. *George Rogers Clark and Revolution in Illinois, 1763–1787.* Springfield: Illinois State Historical Society, 1929.

Peckham, Howard H. *Pontiac and the Indian Uprising.* Princeton, NJ: Princeton University Press, 1947.

*Pennsylvania Colonial Records.* 10 vols. Philadelphia: J. Severns & Co., 1851–1852.

Phillips, Paul C. *The Fur Trade.* 2 vols. Norman: University of Oklahoma Press, 1961.

Ray, Arthur J. *Indians in the Fur Trade: Their Role as Trappers, Hunters, and Middlemen in the Lands Southwest of Hudson Bay, 1660–1870.* Toronto: University of Toronto Press, 1974.

Robinson, Percy J. *Toronto during the French Regime, 1615–1793.* Toronto: University of Toronto Press, 1965.

Russell, Nelson V. *The British Regime in Michigan and the Northwest, 1760–1796.* Northfield, MN: Carleton College, 1939.

Sellers, Linda. *Charleston Business on the Eve of the Revolution.* Chapel Hill, NC: University of North Carolina Press, 1934.

Short, Adam, and Arthur G. Doughty. *Documents Relating to the Constitutional History of Canada 1759–1791.* 2 vols. Ottawa: J de L. Tache, 1918.

Shy, John. *Toward Lexington: The Role of the British Army in the Coming of the American Revolution.* Princeton, NJ: Princeton University Press, 1965.

Slick, Sewell E. *William Trent and the West.* Harrisburg: Archives Publishing Company of Pennsylvania, 1947.

Sosin, Jack M. *Whitehall and the Wilderness: The Middle West in British Colonial Policy, 1760–1775.* Lincoln: University of Nebraska Press, 1961.

Spruill, Julia C. *Women's Life and Work in the Southern Colonies.* New York: W. W. Norton & Company, 1972.

Stevens, Wayne E. *The Northwest Fur Trade, 1763–1800*. Urbana: University of Illinois, 1928.

Wade, Mason. *The French Canadians, 1760–1945*. Toronto: Macmillan Co. of Canada, 1955.

Wainwright, Nicholas B. *George Croghan, Wilderness Diplomat*. Chapel Hill: University of North Carolina Press, 1959.

Wilson, Charles H. *Anglo-Dutch Commerce and Finance in the Eighteenth Century*. Cambridge: Cambridge University Press, 1966.

Wilson, Gilbert L. *Buffalo Bird Woman's Garden: Agriculture of the Hidatsa Indians*. St. Paul: Minnesota Historical Society Press, 1987.

# Index

# About the Author

WALTER S. DUNN JR. is an independent writer and researcher. He received his PhD from the University of Wisconsin, Madison. His recent publications include *Opening New Markets: The British Army and the American Frontier, 1764–1768* (2002).